60 0304517 8

KU-529-288

6 00 304517 8

PRE-PLÉIADE POETRY

FRENCH FORUM MONOGRAPHS

57

Editors R.C. LA CHARITÉ and V.A. LA CHARITÉ

For complete listing, see page 154

PRE-PLÉIADE POETRY

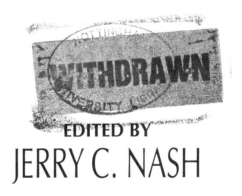

WITHDRAWN

EDITED BY

JERRY C. NASH

FRENCH FORUM, PUBLISHERS
LEXINGTON, KENTUCKY

304517

Copyright © 1985 by French Forum, Publishers, Incorporated, P.O. Box 5108, Lexington, Kentucky 40505.

All rights reserved, including the right to reproduce this book, or parts thereof, in any form, except for the inclusion of brief quotations in reviews.

Library of Congress Catalog Card Number 84-81851

ISBN 0-917058-57-7

Printed in the United States of America

FOREWORD

With the exception of my introductory survey of the critical literature on pre-Pléiade poetry, the other ten essays in this book were first presented at the "Symposium on Pre-Pléiade Poetry" sponsored by the Modern Language Association of America and the University of New Orleans and held in New Orleans on March 24-25, 1983. As director of the Symposium, I did not wish to limit the speakers to a single topic, but preferred a more diverse presentation of themes, chosen by the participants themselves, which would more closely reflect the range and scope of pre-Pléiade poetry studies today. These published results offer the reader a balanced collection of different critical approaches to pre-Pléiade poetry, with newer critically oriented readings alongside more traditional historically oriented essays.

I wish to thank the French Sixteenth-Century Literature Division of the MLA for its sponsorship of the Symposium. The University of New Orleans has been extremely generous in its strong institutional support of the Symposium and in its financial assistance that has made this publication possible. I am especially grateful to Dr. Cooper R. Mackin, Acting Chancellor, and to Dr. Edward M. Sócola, Dean of the College of Liberal Arts, for their genuine interest and support. I am also grateful to Editors Raymond C. La Charité and Virginia A. La Charité of French Forum, Publishers, for their assistance in publishing this collection. Finally, the splendid spirit of cooperation of the ten critics themselves helped greatly in my work as editor of this volume.

J.C.N.

CONTENTS

The Literary Legacy of Pre-Pléiade Poetry

Jerry C. Nash

It is not difficult to understand why the pre-Pléiade poets like Jean Lemaire de Belges, Mellin de Saint-Gelais, Clément Marot, Louise Labé, Pernette du Guillet, and Maurice Scève have had a rather dubious secondary standing in French literary history. In a way, their literary legacy was written during or shortly after their own lifetimes. In the vast amount of Pléiade propaganda authored primarily by Ronsard and Du Bellay, the pre-Pléiade poets comprising the "vieille garde poëtique françoyse" are already indicted for "ignorance" and "obscurité." In his "Ode à Madame Marguerite, sœur du Roy" of 1550, Ronsard helps to set the negative tone for future assessments of pre-Pléiade poetic productions:

> Ainsi tu allas trouver
> Le vilain monstre Ignorance,
> Qui souloit toute la France
> Dessous son ventre couver.
> L'Ire qui la beste eslance,
> En vain irrita son cœur,
> Poussant son mufle en defence
> Encontre ton bras veinqueur.[1]

Du Bellay, of course, played his part in castigating the early Renaissance poets. In Book II, Chapter II, entitled "Des poëtes françoys," of his *Deffence et illustration de la langue françoyse,* Du Bellay severely criticizes, among other early poets, Lemaire, Marot, and Scève for not having properly used and poetically perfected the French language. He places blame not on the inadequacy of "le vulgaire," of the language of French as a vehicle for poetic expression, but squarely on their lack of poetic ability and skill: ". . . je ne le ["le vulgaire"] puis mieux defendre, qu'atribuant la pauvreté d'iceluy, non à son propre & naturel, *mais à la negligence de ceux qui en ont pris le gouvernement.*"[2] Thus, according to the Pléiade poets, their predecessors in poetry are justly doomed for posterity. Here is Ronsard's

final evaluation, in itself a quite severe condemnation, as well as his pre-
diction of what the future will hold critically for the pre-Pléiade poets:

Mais que doit on esperer d'eus? lesquels, étans parvenus plus par opinion, peut-estre,
que par raison, ne font trouver bon aus princes sinon ce qu'il leur plaist, et ne pou-
vants souffrir que la clarté brusle leur ignorance, en medisant des labeurs d'autrui
deçoivent le naturel jugement des hommes abusés par leurs mines? . . . Bien que telles
gens foisonnent en honneurs, et qu'ordinerement on les bonnette, pour avoir quelque
titre de faveur, si mourront ils sans renom et reputation, et les doctes folies de poëtes
survivront les innombrables siecles avenir.³

It is inevitable that such negative views on the pre-Pléiade poets by Du
Bellay and Ronsard would have a negative impact on the subsequent
literary criticism of the period. There can be little doubt that the assessment of the early Renaissance poets by the principal modern literary histories was conditioned by the Pléiade pronouncements. Until very recent
times, the student who consulted the standard histories of French Renaissance literature encountered either no mention at all of the pre-Pléiade
poets and their poetry or else laconic and usually critically biased, negative
treatment of them. In what is considered the first monumental survey of
French literature in modern criticism, Gustave Lanson serves as a good
example.⁴ Pernette du Guillet does not appear anywhere in Lanson's
detailed presentation. Scève and Labé are accorded a cursory glance, with
Scève receiving the old familiar Pléiade criticism of obscurity: "Maurice
Scève, compliqué, savant, singulier, obscur . . . Louise Labé, la fameuse
cordière, qui fit le sonnet mignard aussi brûlant qu'une ode de Sapho"
(p. 276). Lemaire and Saint-Gelais bear the worst brunt of Lanson's criticism. In a word, they both lack poetic ability or genius, once again, a re-
hearsal and echoing of the same negative views that were formulated in the
Renaissance by Ronsard and Du Bellay. Lanson says of Lemaire and the
rhétoriqueurs: "Les plus supportables sont ceux qui ont moins de génie:
leur platitude les condamne à être intelligibles, ou à peu près. Tels sont
Jean Marot, ou Jean Lemaire de Belges" (p. 186). About Mellin de Saint-
Gelais, Lanson writes: "Il est entortillé, pincé . . . La forme est sèche, la
pensée est aussi frivole, et moins sincère" (p. 245).

Henri Guy⁵ and Henri Chamard⁶ do little to rescue the early poets
from the Pléiade bias and propaganda of the 16th century. Though the
pre-Pléiade poets are presented in less disparaging terms, the sole basis
nonetheless, according to both Guy and Chamard, for which they should
be read and studied is simply because they are the precursors of Pléiade
poetic greatness. In particular, according to Guy, they are precursors in
name and in time only; for this critic, the early Renaissance poets had
virtually no formative influence on the Pléiade poets, nor did the poetry

of the two groups have much in common. Guy is fond of pointing out that the latter indeed rejected the former in favor of classical, non-native sources and models (cf. his discussion in I, 174-206). Furthermore, both Guy and Chamard share the critical opinion that the pre-Pléiade poets were simply occasional poets composing curiosity pieces and working without any French context and without any relationship to each other, in sum, merely producing on demand "poèmes de circonstance." And finally, by the time we come to Joseph Vianey at mid-century,[7] the critical assessment problem of how to present the pre-Pléiade poets has taken care of itself by Vianey's deleting them from consideration. Marot is the *only* pre-Pléiade poet given any prominence in this anthology-reference work purporting to cover 16th-century poetry.

More modern scholarship and criticism are just beginning to propose some positive reasons for a needed critical reassessment or at least a more serious and objective reconsideration of the pre-Pléiade poets. The current, ongoing critical revision of early Renaissance poetry has come about only in the past decade or so. With it there promises to be a healthy reassessment of the entire period. The old notion of Pléiade as distinctly unrelated to pre-Pléiade poetry is being corrected; so too is the old view of the pre-Pléiade poets working alone in a contextual and poetic vacuum. Though without a manifesto or any clearly delineated poetic program, the pre-Pléiade poets do indeed have a common intellectual background and similar literary interests and aspirations, as more modern criticism is recognizing today. The biases built into past evaluation and scholarship are also receding; increasingly, the pre-Pléiade poets are acquiring a critically long-overdue, new identity. Instrumental in bringing about this change in critical thinking has been the recent appearance of important studies in textual criticism as well as literary criticism of certain pre-Pléiade poets.[8]

Equally helpful in the shift toward a more positive view of the early poets are other recent studies which approach the early Renaissance period in general. One of the most important and critically influential features of I.D. McFarlane's *Renaissance France 1470-1589*[9] is this scholar's insistence that we in French Renaissance studies have far too long neglected the "minor" poets of the period. For McFarlane, they deserve to be studied in their own right; as a corollary, this research will shed light on the "major" poets as well and the whole period. Rather than accepting and continuing the old critical attitudes of the past, McFarlane rejects any notion of antagonism and unrelatedness of pre-Pléiade and Pléiade poetry and, instead, stresses the view of poetic continuity and similarity, in short, the critical notion of poetic evolution rather than revolution. As a result of McFarlane's book and others, we are coming ever closer to realizing that pre-Pléiade poetry does not simply die out in order to give rise to the new Pléiade poetic greatness (Guy, Chamard). On the contrary, the former actually paves the way for the latter and makes this success possible by announcing and developing what will become Pléiade poetic concerns. With a sense of literary justice that distinguishes McFarlane's *Renaissance France* as a whole, what this scholar has to say in his chapter on "Early Humanism and the Rhétoriqueurs" is true and applicable to the pre-Pléiade poets in general:

It is, however, essential not to lose sight of this serious purpose [i.e., the dignified way the rhétoriqueurs conceived of poetry] and not to contrast too favourably the later sixteenth century with the literature of Louis XII's reign . . . The rhétoriqueurs maintained their position and prestige for a long while yet; their works were regularly reprinted during the first half of the sixteenth century, and indeed beyond, and Du Bellay's attack on the old French school hardly implies a defunct tradition . . . The rhétoriqueurs set a respectable example. Their concept of poetry, as we have seen, was a dignified, indeed an aristocratic, one, very similar to the Pléiade's in certain respects . . . The fact that the Pléiade could innovate so much depends in part on *the continuum already provided by the national tradition.* (pp. 37-38)

These same corrective arguments will be found in the cogent rethinking of the pre-Pléiade *versus* Pléiade question proposed by Pierre Jodogne in his seminal essay, "Les 'Rhétoriqueurs' et l'humanisme. Problème d'histoire littéraire."[10] Here is the conclusion Jodogne offers us:

Ils ["les écrivains de la Pléiade"] furent incapables de reconnaître ceux qui les avaient conduits là où ils étaient arrivés. Au lieu de savoir gré à leurs prédécesseurs d'avoir, en même temps que les humanistes, cultivé la rhétorique, ils leur lancèrent l'insulte de "rhétoriqueurs" que reprendront les historiens modernes. Séduits par les proclamations des poètes de la Pléiade, ces historiens seront impuissants à revaloriser la période antérieure. Ainsi s'explique le grand mépris dans lequel sont restés tant d'écrivains que depuis une époque récente seulement on commence à étudier sérieusement et avec sympathie. (p. 168)

Even a first reading of the pre-Pléiade poets will suffice to demonstrate the fundamental accuracy of these admonitory observations by McFarlane and Jodogne. Early Renaissance poetry abounds in fascinating and fruitful material awaiting textual and literary interpretation.

Very similar observations and further refinement of the pre-Pléiade/Pléiade critical assessment picture are being made in even more recent publications. In a chapter devoted to "French Literature" in *The Present State of Scholarship in Sixteenth-Century Literature*,[11] Donald Stone, Jr. agrees that "there has been a disproportionate amount of attention paid to a small number of writers" (p. 64). As a result, as Stone demonstrates, not only literary unfamiliarity with the period but even distortion and misconception of its poets and poetry have been allowed to develop. A case in point is to be found in yet another recently published, helpful critical corrective. In a very informative essay by François Rigolot, "'Rhétorique' et 'Poësie' à l'aube du XVIe siècle: la double postulation de l'*Amant Vert*,"[12] the apparently original and much paraded Pléiade concern with "noble poësie" is shown actually to have been formulated and implemented textually much earlier by Jean Lemaire de Belges: "Dès 1505, dans les *Epîtres*, puis en 1511, dans la *Concorde*, nous trouvons une célébration de 'noble poësie' dans les termes mêmes qui seront ceux de la Pléiade" (p. 533).

In an effort to contribute further to the work of rethinking critically pre-Pléiade poetry, the essays presented in this volume represent the first-ever attempt at one time by ten French Renaissance critics to focus squarely on the early poetry. This collective undertaking to revalue pre-Pléiade poets is, in itself, enough to indicate how far pre-Pléiade poetry studies have progressed since the publication almost a hundred years ago of Lanson's *Histoire*. During that time, new critical insights, attitudes, and approaches have been made available. In light of these developments, the scholars represented in this volume propose to reconsider pre-Pléiade poets and texts and to offer additional new perspectives on them. Let me mention just a few of their conclusions which await the reader. The old familiar critical notion of poetic antagonism of pre-Pléiade and Pléiade becomes even further undermined and debunked. Donald Stone, Jr. shows that the epigrammatic mode as defined and practiced by Saint-Gelais and other early poets binds not only these early poets to each other but also to the later poets of the Pléiade. The gains in epigrammatic poetry achieved by the Pléiade were determined in no small part by the earlier efforts to examine and perfect the same medium. Secondly, Doranne Fenoaltea, in using the poetry of Marot and Scève as a case in point, increases our awareness that the pre-Pléiade poets, far from working totally independently and in isolation of each other, were consciously cultivating some of the very same linguistic and poetic habits and tendencies. In her intertextual study which concludes this volume, Fenoaltea demonstrates in very specific ways how the French poetic idiom and style as perfected by Marot also find their way into the dizains of the *Délie*.

Other essays in this collection on Marot, Lemaire, Labé, Pernette, and Scève will, I believe, convince the reader that these pre-Pléiade poets quite often met and even surpassed the demands placed on a first-rate poet by Du Bellay, even though the latter could not or would not recognize such an achievement by the early Renaissance poets: ". . . celuy sera veritablement le poëte que je cherche en nostre Langue, qui me fera indigner, apayser, ejouyr, douloir, aymer, hayr, admirer, etonner, bref, qui tiendra la bride de mes affections, me tournant ça & la à son plaisir" (Chamard, p. 179). Finally, these essays serve to remind us that pre-Pléiade poetry studies have at last come of age and that there remains much to be done in rewriting the legacy of this important and rewarding early Renaissance literary period.

NOTES

1. *Le Premier Livre des Odes*, Ode IV, in *Oeuvres complètes de Ronsard*, ed. Gustave Cohen (Paris: Gallimard, 1950), I, 373.

2. Henri Chamard, ed. (Paris: Marcel Didier, 1966), pp. 101-02. All italics in this essay are mine.

3. "Au lecteur," *Les Quatre Premiers Livres des Odes*, Cohen, II, 974.

4. *Histoire de la littérature française* (Paris: Hachette, 1894).

5. *Histoire de la poésie française au XVIe siècle* (Paris: H. Champion, 1910).

6. *Les Origines de la poésie française de la Renaissance* (Paris: E. de Boccard, 1920).

7. *Les Poètes du XVIe siècle* (Paris: Hatier, 1948).

8. At the risk of not listing all the recent titles which deserve to be, I wish to mention, nonetheless, these significant studies of the past decade or so which have and which are continuing to reshape our critical thinking on the early Renaissance poets: for Jean Lemaire de Belges, Pierre Jodogne (*Jean Lemaire de Belges, écrivain franco-bourguignon* [Brussels: Palais des Académies, 1972]) and Paul Zumthor (*Le Masque et la lumière* [Paris: Editions du Seuil, 1978]and *Anthologie des grands rhétoriqueurs* [Paris: Union Générale d'Editions, 1978]); for Clément Marot, Robert Griffin (*Clément Marot and the Inflections of Poetic Voice* [Berkeley: Univ. of California Press, 1973]) and P.M. Smith (*Clément Marot, Poet of the French Renaissance* [London: The Athlone Press, 1970]); for Mellin de Saint-Gelais, Donald Stone, Jr. (*Mellin de Saint-Gelais and Literary History* [Lexington, KY: French Forum, Publishers, 1983]); for Louise Labé, Enzo Giudici (*Oeuvres complètes de Louise Labé* [Geneva: Droz, 1981]and *Louise Labé: essai* [Paris: Nizet, 1981]); for Pernette du Guillet, Victor Graham (critical edition of the *Rymes* [Geneva: Droz, 1968]); for Maurice Scève, I.D. McFarlane (critical edition of the *Délie* [Cambridge: Cambridge Univ. Press, 1966]) and Dorothy Gabe Coleman (*Maurice Scève, Poet of Love. Tradition and Originality* [Cambridge: Cambridge Univ. Press, 1975]) and Doranne Fenoaltea (*"Si haulte Architecture." The Design of Scève's* Délie [Lexington, KY: French Forum, Publishers, 1982]).

9. London: Ernest Benn Limited, 1974.

10. In *Humanism in France*, ed. A.H.T. Levi (Manchester: Manchester Univ. Press, 1970).

11. William M. Jones, ed. (Columbia: Univ. of Missouri Press, 1978), pp. 45-69.

12. *Romance Philology*, 33 (1980), 522-34.

Cosmic Metaphor in La Concorde des deux langages

Robert Griffin

In order to approximate what I have in mind, the title of this essay should also point to the syllogistic proposition of: the universe as metaphor, the poem as metaphor and, therefore, the poem as universe. All of these equations apply to *La Concorde des deux langages* and their complex associations provide a framework for exploring basic features of the narrative poem at the beginning of the 16th century. My thesis is that by ignoring these features one risks missing not fine points so much as *the* point of a text. Recent efforts, led by the books of Paul Zumthor and the work of various other scholars, have done much to displace the occasionally aberrant views about the rhétoriqueurs that have held ground since Henry Guy's *Histoire de la poésie française au XVIe siècle*; and these recent efforts have succeeded largely by avoiding generalizations about the "school" of the grands rhétoriqueurs, preferring instead to extract poetics from close and patient exegesis. Guy was especially incensed by the rigidity and abuses of allegory, which his volumes end up taking for granted. Following him, W.F. Patterson further vaporized "the bloodless abstractions of allegory" by depicting them "without flesh and bone."[1] By thus detaching imagery from a solid context of prevailing esthetic, philosophical, political and moral values, and labeling the isolated icon as "merely decorative," this generation of earlier readers committed the cardinal sin —Anachronism—in evaluating any archaic text. Their example reminds us that allegorical reading is a technique slowly acquired and easily lost. Whatever else it may be, it is always an exercise in recognizing and unfolding significant details, words and images with unapparent and highly associative values. Details will naturally strike us as random if we fail to grasp their purpose, and no Renaissance manual of rhetoric that I have ever seen allows for embellishments that do not enhance the argument. The most valuable arm of the modern reader who would reconstruct the lost arguments of the Renaissance, then, would be a Socratic humility in recognition that our lack of understanding and taste for allegory should not be confused with a lack of intrinsic interest, that more will likely remain unknown than be known about any vibrant text, and that one must explain more about a text and about a poet's ontology and epistemology than the author himself had to know. Due to their staggering length, many allegories of the late 15th and early 16th centuries would make such commentary endless. But the relative familiarity of *La Concorde des deux langages*, its important position in the canon of a major poet, and its modest length all make it ideal for selective commentary on the use of allegorical imagery in the early Renaissance.

Definition of allegory as sustained metaphor—an axiom in manuals on rhetoric for the two millennia preceding Lemaire's poem—is at least precise. It has the further advantage of suggesting that allegory reflects not so much the dominant values of a period as the culture's assumptions about the ability of language to dramatize values—values, as the term's etymology suggests, beyond (*allos*) the reach of sight and of the marketplace (*agora*). But if simple definitions are not accompanied by demonstration of textual complexity they will only confirm one-to-one relationships of vehicle and tenor. In the process, they will reduce the dynamism of allegory to the status of cookbook recipes, and lead even the sharpest critical eye to partial views. Edwin Honig and others since have shown that "allegory as an extended trope may include the functions of all other tropes—metaphor, irony, metonymy, and synecdoche."[2] But in the vastness of the *Illustrations de Gaule* Lemaire's succinct invitation to "cueillir assez de fruit allegorique et moral souz couleurs poëtiques"[3] becomes irresistibly quotable. In the same way, Erasmus's definition of allegory as "nothing but" (*neque aliud*) a continuous metaphor is more easily digestible than his cryptic notion that allegory is a universal occurrence.[4]

Yet, from the earliest Church Fathers and through diverse occult traditions, the idea of the universe as allegory, of the world as a book, received powerful sanction from Genesis I through the gospel according to John and from commentators who solicited dozens of passages in between. Since the concept of allegory assumed sacred and revered subjects, notably the extension of divine thought from the abstract to the concrete, it furnished the best means of apprehending the grand design of creation, if only through a glass darkly, by conceiving the world or any part of it as a text in which to decipher the metaphor of God's device. The poet reinvests the external world with the kind of lost internal spiritual dimension that primitive myth instinctively assumed in order to gain access to and participate in the acquisition of important spiritual truths.

The common sense of Franco Simone and Pierre Jodogne have laid to rest the scholar's reflex of citing Florentine models as implied sources for northern European views on the status of poetry at the turn of the century. Still, the question of Florentine contact continues to pose itself in the case of *La Concorde*, seduced as we are by Lemaire's travels through Italy (1504-08). I think the question is provocative but idle. The realities of self-effacing court patronage in France and Burgundy surely removed Lemaire from the unfettered boldness of Florentine *theologia poetica* and from its bent for deeply enigmatic and introspective allegory. But even more to the point, poets and theoreticians of all stripes drew similar ideas from a larger fund of common culture.[5] It is a commonplace in art history to read the panel distribution of the Sistine Chapel ceiling as a graduated reconciliation of opposites where order (Cosmos) mediates between ambiguity (Paradise) and disorder (World) in a controlled complex of pyramids: God creates with his right hand; Eve is corrupted by reaching with her left hand; the Virgin mediates in the atonement [at-onement] for Adam's sin of concupiscence, and so on.[6] An Italian connection is not needed, however, to establish the prevalence of the role of God as artisan and mediator of the universe. In a chant-royal that is roughly contemporaneous with *La Concorde*, Cretin presents the builder of paradise as a "chef en l'art d'architecture" whose *œuvre* prefigures both antique sculpture and perspectivist painting, and includes the three theological and four cardinal virtues; following the Fall, divided opposites are brought into coincidence in the Virgin Birth.[7] The same general theme, language and "Dieu, qui tout moyenne," recur in Lemaire's *Concorde du genre humain* (vv. 305 ff.). So the question of French or Italian primacy in influencing his thought should be broadened and flattened out. From the fountainheads both of French and Italian culture cited by Lemaire in the prologue of *La Concorde des deux langages* many examples can be culled that differ in degree and emphasis, but not in kind, on this concept of creation-through-mediation, just as *natura naturata* is the verso of *natura naturans*. Boccaccio praises the "mediations" of the allegorist graced with inspiration whose "interweaving of words, and thoughts" in a fixed order (*Genealogia deorum*, XIV, 7) is echoed at the beginning of *La Concorde* (vv. 397-99), whereas the speech given by Alanus de Insulis to embodied Natura is so close to the final scene of Lemaire's allegory that it deserves to be cited at some length:

I am she who have [sic] fashioned the form and eminence of man into the likeness of the original earthly mechanism, that in him, as in a mirror of the world itself, combined nature may appear. For just as, of the four elements, the concordant discord, the single plurality, the dissonant consonance, the dissenting agreement, produce the structures of the palace of earth . . . .[8]

The analogy of deity and poet mediating creation in a common universe of calibrated values has an obvious importance in ennobling the status of the court laureate, in assuring a more uniform reading of *La Concorde*, and in assessing the range of pre-Socratic and neo-Platonic ideas which echo through the "Couronne Margueritique" and the *Illustrations de Gaule*. One advantage of attending to the Pythagorean model is that the Greek philosopher makes entirely specific what the Judeo-Christian tradition only implies about the efficacy of metaphor in bearing God's own truth. The implications of this model are so consequential for an appreciation of the ways allegorical metaphor translates meaning from the conceptual level to the physical and back, and thus mediates the entire hierarchy of creation, that we must delay our discussion of *La Concorde* for a few more pages.

In incorporating ideas of Pythagorean universal harmony into Renaissance poetics, the poet was seen as creating in the likeness of the creating godhead through the use of metaphor. The sustained and sustaining metaphor of allegory holds the same connection to God's universal metaphor as the two creators hold to each other. While the complete universe subsumes the poem farther down in the scale of created things, the poet reenacts the role of creating deity by recapturing and shaping the common pattern and rhythms of life that obtain at all the horizontal levels in the cosmic paradigm, commonly known as the Great Chain of Being. Thus, Plato's often cited criticism at the end of the *Republic* that poets merely chase shadows of reflections does not seem nearly so devastating; Ficino's assertion that the thinker who is possessed of divine enthusiasm can become "as if" a god, does not seem nearly so heretical. Whether vatic or didactic, whether the poet's preeminence stems from his creative powers to fashion an analogous cosmos by his word made flesh or whether his claim to rank derives from a command of full human experience, he stands high in the taxonomy of the species. Even though the sense-perceptible qualities of his metaphor are but an image of essential reality, just as the sensient world is but an imperfect replica of cosmic order, the poet can avoid flights of irresponsible fantasy, that "mistress of falsity and error," and ensure the truth of his creation by adhering to the divinely ordained connections between the physical and conceptual worlds. As in the case of Cretin above, the poet's imagination can reshape the architectural splendor of the world edifice as it was before Eden, or he can hold his eye on the world of time and history as a means of gauging its imperfections, or else he can follow in the speculum tradition of Alanus by adumbrating a reconciliation of all opposites.

Such a reconciliation allows us to understand that allegory and the metaphor, synecdoche and metonymy that comprise it were categories of thought before they were ever codified in any *corpus juris* of rhetoric. Judgment of a segment (of time, life, history or, theoretically, even of the smallest detail of poetic imagery) should be made only in the context of the greater category from which it is drawn and to which it contributes in a rationalized yet intuitive reflex seen in too many facets of Renaissance culture to be effectively catalogued here. In the *chiaroscuro* of romance from Ariosto to Spenser, the temptress (Alcina, Melissa, Duesa and other lodestars of desire) is most alluring at the moment of seduction for it is then that her beauty is most necessary in order to call forth her opposite persona who is blessed with grace. The Christian prototype for this needed redemption and reconciliation of the part with the whole, for the definition of reality through opposites that illuminate one another, was of course the original Fall from grace. Going back past Augustine to Pythagoras, the universe is conceived of as a metaphor for God, expressing the view that the infinite variety of creation is paradoxically yet exquisitely ordered; that the vertical scale of values is intersected by horizontal scales of seemingly random words, events and actions that derive their meaning and inherent qualities from the value system; and that each separate segment is subject to further and ordered subdivisions, and in its internal organization is analogous to each of the other parts in the cosmic scheme.

As a little world, separate from the elemental, celestial and angelic worlds yet contingent upon them, the human microcosm is endowed with the capacity to discover partial metaphors throughout the continuum of existence, to project and extrapolate them into the inclusive metaphor of the "universal world," and thus to apprehend more sharply the similarities among all four realms.[9] An image drawn from the categories, let us say, of the elements, humors or the seasons is a miniature of the whole, a metaphor for any other category, and thus points to an integrated understanding of life as a whole.

The system has important implications for generating reception theories for Renaissance poetry or, to put it more modestly, for avoiding reading blunders. A reader must be alert to the deduction of a whole from its part, to the implied activation of the whole scheme of universal correspondences by a solitary metaphor. The poet creates a network of analogies ranging from the highest levels of creation to the lowest, just as God fashioned a continuum of graduated meanings in his universal metaphor. In turn, the reader assumes a role analogous to that of the poet and Creator because, like them, he perceives the work as an integrated whole, *sub specie aeternitatis*. Since meaning in a poem's web of active correspondences is conveyed through structure, metaphor—as in all schemes of rhetoric—is taken as the prime mode of discourse. Structure is itself a metaphor, revealing the divine plan in action, as we can see in that microcosm of time, Pe-trarch's 366 *Rime sparse*, in Du Bellay's integral and supposedly autobio-graphical experience of separation-initiation-return, in suggestive juxtapo-sition among Montaigne's essays, or, as I hope to show, in *La Concorde des deux langages*.

Since the allegory is a literary microcosm in which temporal succession and place of action have no meaning apart from the collective scheme of meaning—and disappear altogether when the poetic metaphor is reduced to pure form—perhaps it is high time to stop caring for such gossipy con-jecture as whether *La Concorde* portrays a young Lemaire who, like Pe-trarch, actually had a passionate attachment or whether in the passage from Venus to Minerva the historical Jean Lemaire de Belges has somehow mended his ways.[10] In allegory, in a sonnet sequence or, again in Montai-gne's *Essais*, the reader is not confronted with a Cartesian accretion of consecutive statements where an effect is linked to and generated by an immediately preceding cause. In allegory the action, characters and setting that constitute the narrative are only trappings that are needed to "clothe" the metaphor, as the rhetoricians put it. Cities and forests, mountains and islands, palaces and prisons, trees and flowers—all translate the external world into a spiritual vision and reduce the universal genus to the univer-salized species. If details of allegorical machinery (signet rings, scales of justice, magic mirrors, etc.) appear appliquéd on a two-dimensional surface and seem lost in space, the separation is often the painter's or the poet's wish to underline the separate level of reality they symbolize. If, on the other hand, details of imagery appear humanized to the point of our con-fusing them with autobiography, we must not assume that the poet is any more empirical or factual in his narrative than the primitive mythmaker who personifies inanimate nature in order to identify with it, to gain control over it, and to reinvest it with the same benevolence or malevo-lence that he finds in the great book of nature.

Some of the most important questions that we can ask ourselves about *La Concorde* do bear on the persona of the poet we see there, but they have to do with his universalized self-knowledge. They also deal with the imagery he selects to convey that knowledge, and derive from the ways in which successful allegorical metaphor develops a complex network of images that comment on one another. Knowing the model in whose image he has been created is for the poet ultimately an exercise in self-knowl-edge.[11] Limitations of space disallow all but a minute reading of the poem and prevent us from pursuing some of the many intriguing questions posed by the work, such as the secondary rank of particular historical fact com-pared to the permanence of essential poetic truth; or the deep strain of

Pythagorean learning which informs the work from beginning to end, especially in the symphonic ode to Venus in which the mystery of prime numbers is reflected in the play of language. No universe can be explicated or even read completely. But by examining some of its key image patterns we can at least see that the way in which allegorical metaphor translates meaning from one level to another, from macrocosm to the literary microcosm, is governed by the system of universal correspondence which the divine maker has embroidered in the fabric of his cosmic poem. In *La Concorde des deux langages* these correspondences are thematically harmonized through the leitmotiv of *Discordia concors*.

The mental picture of a poet rediscovering and refashioning the infinite connections of a reality whose basic structure and conditions have already been given may run counter to our fascination with the posture of poets as solitary and unacknowledged legislators of the world. But when Sidney, for instance, speaks of revolving "in the zodiac of [his] own wit," he is referring to searching out links between the known and the unknown, the old and the new. The poet's task is to discover something already prescribed in the bountiful book of nature and to find the golden key that unlocks mysterious correspondences. His creative impulse lies in his talent to select shrewdly and arrange appropriate, prefabricated metaphors that allow him to extrapolate from the microcosm to the macrocosm, where novel and deep expressiveness is sought above pure uniqueness.

In "De la dame infortunée" Lemaire stipulates the unity of rhetoric and music, as well as the consanguinity of Latin, Italian and French "comme une petite trinité," after which he alludes to the *Illustrations de Gaule* as a singular description of "les merveilles tant antiques que modernes" (III, 197-98). The Italian connection is again coincidental, for it was in Italy that the role of *meraviglia* in forging metaphor was first propounded: "È del poeta il fin la meraviglia," as Marino later put it. This primacy came from the earlier formative presence of Aristotle, although his first significant commentator, Francesco Robortello, scored his master for having mishandled the transitions from genus to species and for having confused metaphor and synecdoche. In line with the unvarying task of rhetoric to teach, please and move, metaphor must instruct the reader and give pleasure through its marvelous connections. The capacity to perceive analogies and similarities among dissimilars and the power to reconcile them with "parole armonizate" are at work here. *Meraviglia*, then, treads the thin line between the obvious and the contrived, between traditional metaphors that risk being shopworn and the discovery of unknown and unsuspected affinities that risk being obscure, idiosyncratic and fantastic. The line is maintained by the natural gifts of *acutezza* and *sottilità d'ingegno*.[12]

These later Italian discussions have the advantage of formularizing what is only implicit in France in 1511, but again there is no need to marshal examples from across the Alps. The theme of *Discordia concors* has roots extending back to late neolithic myth, is the grand theme of the *Iliad*, and among the pre-Socratics is most clearly associated with Heraclitus. Heraclitus argued that warring pairs of opposites are ultimately one, are themselves the connections of things ("an unapparent connection is stronger than an apparent one"—fragment B54; cf. "les choses opposites se monstrent mieux quand elles sont approchées l'une de l'autre," III, 233). Tracing the history of this idea would be tantamount to sketching the history of Homer (and Vergil!), would bog us down in Migne, and also involve the parallel traditions of arcane learning, especially alchemy and astrology.[13] Lemaire was of course conversant with all of this and reconciled the Christian and pagan with ease. His making Priam's cousin, King Bavo, an adept of the triple magical sciences (Religion, Medicine and Astronomy) in the *Illustrations* (I, 119) might invite us to explore a possible impact of the alchemical literature of *Mirabilia*—the search for hidden sympathies and antipathies in animate and inanimate nature as a means of averting chaos and enthroning moral virtues. The diligent reader would not have to roam through Lemaire's complete canon to show that his concern for the repulsion and attraction running through and expressing all creation extends to these three domains and far beyond, for countless examples are ready at hand. The poet discovers the marvels that have been fabricated by God, the master "Faiseur de merveilles," as he is described for restoring Marguerite to health (IV, 90). The opening of the *Illustrations de Gaule* proposes the multiple reconciliations of Gaul and Troy, France and Italy, but like the *Iliad* begins with an oxymoronic "merveilleuse dissension" (I, 12). On the other hand, in *La Concorde du genre humain* the poet is visited by a spirit (the demiurge "Concorde du genre humain") who is "gaillard et angelin" and whose epiphany is attended by the traditional symbols of reconciliation (rainbow, olive branch) down through the marvelous chain of being, all culminating in the mind's eye of the poet with the "louables merveilles" of paradise. So essential is the context for apprehending the reach of metaphoric meaning in *La Concorde des deux langages* that we should scrutinize the pages preceding and following the image of these praiseworthy marvels. "Concorde" goes on to appeal to the "prudence celeste" of the Emperor Maximilian to weigh the difference between feminine and virile attributes, and, repeating God's grace-in-action, to recall that Marguerite has served the *res publica* by banishing Discord through political treaties. The demigoddess extends her "lyens invisibles et plus que adamantins" among mankind, just as "minerve prudente et pacifique" (i.e., Marguerite) metaphorically derives her general but partial attributes from the universal and specific manifestations of Peace.[14] Just before the apparition of dame Concord the narrator speciously derives the name of Cambray from a Trojan antecedent, "non sans mistere," in order to "faire conference fructueuse des choses antiques aux modernes." The overarching concordance in this long passage, which the narrator labels as "nostre methaphore," extends through a vast spectrum—gifts of the magi, treaties, tribes, estates of society, countries ancient and modern, parts of the world—and arises from the Pythagorean capacity of prime numbers to embrace and perpetuate the order of the world and make it prosper: "ce nombre sacré de trois a quelque merveilleuse efficace latente . . . la mirabilité de ce nombre ternaire." Apart from the numerous variations in *La Concorde des deux langages* on the theme of "accordant sons discordz," no word is used with more mutations than *merveille*. The style "subtil et mirifique" (v. 297) used to picture the symphony to Venus is too close to "sottilità meravigliosa" to be discounted. In fact, her excessive "arroy merveilleux" suggests that her presence is metaphoric and is placed in perspective by the subverting rhyme word "perilleux" (vv. 46-48). In close proximity, the poet's isolation and his goal of Minerva's temple are couched in the same terms, leading him to seek "aulcune chose estrange, merveilleux et antique."

It is the extrapolated and reconstructed connections that give the concordances *du genre humain* and *des deux langages* their most palpable meanings, since their literal "plots" are trite and virtually meaningless. Yet the latter work has usually been read as an imaginary conversation on the relative merits of French and Italian, held by two disembodied figures who are immediately interrupted by the narrator's autobiography and dream of Venus. In this vision all of nature symphonically greets her arrival and beautifies her temple until her archpriest Genius delivers a sermon on *carpe diem* and on the reconciliation of Venus and Mars; but he then extorts valuables from the parishioners and rejects the painting offered by the narrator. The downcast hero takes the harsh path to the Temple of Minerva where honor reigns supreme. Next, he is consigned to his Beatrice, ponderously named "Labeur historien," who directs him to the summit where in "ung miroir artificiel, fait par art magique," he will find the image of the two languages somehow reconciled.

To be sure, any allegory can be reduced to absurdity simply by summarizing its plot. But since each metaphor of the literary microcosm is synecdoche for yet another metaphor in an unending chain of connections, we should be alert for exceptionally expressive images that synthesize disparate connections yet stand apart in order to summon our attention. The first and most seminal of these occurs at the close of the initial paragraph, after the introduction of the two interlocutors and their assignment of locating the points at which French and Italian coincide. Duality becomes trinity since Latin is the "tronc et racine" of both languages, "toute ainsi comme les ruisseaux procedent de la fontaine et doibvent vivre et perseverer ensemble en amoureuse concordance." Mimetically, the image is ill prepared, mixes tree and fountain without offering any justification, and then appears to drop from sight. Allegory, however, teaches us that appearances can be deceptive. The arboreal image is immediately transformed into the motif of "blossoming" and extends its reach to embrace a broad variety of subjects that crosshatch the poem and one another. The flowering of Italy (p. 4), after a pause to consider "Troy reflourissant" (p. 13), lends itself to etymological banter at the end of the work where the "franchise" of the French and the "flourissance" of the Florentines are joined and arrested in the permanence of the similar heraldic devices of French and Italian ruling houses (pp. 44-45). The first verse of the "Venus" section which introduces the poet's "flourissant aaige" prepares the central image of the sermon of Genius with its likeness of the ravages of time to gnarled bark and twisted branches (p. 25). In this section the first quadrant of the zodiac, "de flourettes armez," reconciles divergent qualities and manifests its "sphere of virtue" through association with the image of the sheltering tree (p. 10). Not until the final appearance of the tree image at the end of the Minerva section does it rejoin the fountain and allow us to see that the original mixture of metaphor was actually an understated yet highly economical use of language leading to an enriched network of related meanings:

> Et ou fin beau milieu, sur ung tertre plaisant,
> Du quel souëf descend maint ruissel arrousant
> La racine fertille à tout fructueux arbre,
> Est ung palais construit de dur et riche marbre. (p. 41)

The reminder that at Minerva's temple we are in "ung paradis terrestre" and various recollections of Genesis 3 along the way, such as Genius's seductive reference to his listeners as "tous demy dieux / Et qui sçavez le bien du mal tirer" (p. 24), all make it apparent that this tree is meant to be understood as the Tree of Knowledge of Good and Evil and that the streams are facsimiles of the Rivers of Paradise. One can only hint at the symbolic range of the tree image, probably the most universal metaphor in human culture and creative myth for expressing the idea of an *axis mundi* where all pairs of opposites (male/female; active/passive; life/death; time/eternity) are reconciled.

From Genesis through the life of Moses, through Isaiah, the Crucifixion, Pauline theology and the apocalyptic mysteries, the Tree of Life has come in the Western tradition to symbolize the most profound and most consequential dimensions of our lives. But so does it in Buddhist symbolism and, some three thousand years before the earliest Hebrew writing, among the Sumerians who, in addition to the imagery of Genesis, gave us writing, history, mathematics, the zodiac and other systems for ordering time and space and categorizing human story. Far more than Egyptian myth, it was ultimately Sumerian iconology that furnished the alchemical symbolism of Mercury, the balance point of the seven planets, in the 16th century— Mercury that is praised for mystically balancing opposites in the *vas mirabile* of alchemy and is even called the Fruit of the Tree of Immortal Life. In the Augustinian tradition, the Tree of Life is wisdom, while the *fons gratiae spiritis* and the rivers are associated with the baptismal rivers flowing from Christ's side, with the Evangelists, and especially (since the syncretizing Philo and Ambrose) with the four cardinal virtues of Fortitude, Prudence, Temperance and Justice. Shaped by the belief in a unified micro- and macrocosm, the Rivers are often associated with all cosmogonic tetrads (elements, virtues, etc.).[15] In the Romanesque capitals of Cluny, for example, the Rivers are variously linked with the four virtues or the four seasons. In 14th-century France and Italy the cardinal and three theological virtues were often combined to make the mystical number seven, gifts of the Holy Ghost.

Since moral allegory in the Renaissance dramatizes the eternal war between vice and virtue, the virtues can combine the idea of manliness (*virtù*), the pagan notion of strength and the Christian sense of purity, even of the awe-inspiring. They can exchange properties and can be endlessly subdivided into "the parts of virtue" (ceste Vertu Animosité bonne; prudence Politique), "afin que des choses terrestres je puisse monter aux celestes et spirituelles" (IV, 42, 63, 72-74, 79, 97, 128).[16] Overlooking the interaction of mundane and celestial values has led some critics to superimpose a flat rejection of *La Concorde*'s Venus in preference for the chaste Minerva, while sharper readers have lingered quizzically over Lemaire's obvious attachment to the mother of Eros. But the desire for resolution into opposites violates the work's guiding principle and the compromise the author has effected with his models. The exhortation to reproduce addressed to mankind by Jean de Meung is an appropriate synecdoche of a general exhortation that lovers should follow virtue (*Roman de la Rose*, 17087-91); his master Alanus used the sexual synecdoche, precisely, to inspire revulsion toward vice. For Lemaire these positions are mutually transcending. When in the "Conte de Cupido et d'Atropos" Mercury

appears on the scene to banish "faulse Discorde" by the magic of his cadu-
ceus, he praises Jupiter, "lequel par sa prudence / Met tout discord en
bonne concordance," for supporting "Venus l'aimable" in her effort to
restrain rampant sensuality (III, 65-66). The point is that life is full of true
and false Florimels, genuine and inauthentic Melissas, and both allegory
and romance teach us the difference while reminding us of their productive
interchange. In fact, the 616 verses of the Venus episode orchestrate[17] a
repeated succession of blame and praise, depending on whether we are
seeing the merely voluptuous Venus or the dispassionate leader of the
Graces, on whether gifts are extorted or freely given, and so on. Our part
as readers is to synthesize and visualize an actual transmutation proposed
in "Tous elementz de joyë transmüerent" of the "coustumiere danse / De
l'ordre humain"; for when "Les elementz les ungs aux aultres riient"
their cooperation mirrors the balance of humors, "Comme gentilz, bien
complexïonnéz, / Sanguins, joyeux" of civilized courtiers who are born
under the benevolent sign of Venus "Par qui tous biens nous sont multi-
pliez" (pp. 12, 15, 23, 27, 31). Unless one takes account of the dynamic
function of the "parts of virtue," it is difficult to make sense of why the
debater in the "tumulte amoureux" who takes the French side is "mar-
velously" gifted with "un hault cueur virile et masculin" but speaks in
"nobles termes amoureux et prudentz par elegance feminine"; or why
Minerva combines beauty and virtue when she is conceived as the "parfaite operation de prudence, paix et concorde"; or why the narrator's gift
—his work—to Minerva is rejected by Genius *malgracieusement* but finally
reappears actively flanking the passive Repos in Minerva's magic mirror
(pp. 4, 6, 35, 46). Does it not accentuate the work's many-leveled sym-
metries to recall that it begins under the sign of Aries, the astrological
patron of the mind; that Aries is the sign of creation, and the sun (Divine
Illumination) was in Aries at the time of its creation (Genesis 1:14-19);
that prudence draws together the three moments of time, as in Titian's
famous allegory; and that from Cicero through Alanus to, for instance,
Chastelain, prudence is the quality to which artists are most beholden?

If we extend the concept of metaphor to include the poet's entire
canon, we encounter numberless analogies to this dynamic. In the "Couronne Margaritique," for instance, Isidore of Seville is made to liken the
Graces to the theological virtue as "une faveur humaine procedant de
celeste influence." As the antipode of ingratitude, grace is the daughter
of Justice, sister of Concorde, and so on, and like them has active and
passive functions (IV, 83). Although the Graces attending Venus play a
relatively marginal role in *La Concorde*, their aspect and suggestive actions
again show that the theme of the microcosm may be grasped and epitomized
in any of its variations:

Lors Patithée, en regardz extrinsecques,
Attrait maint homme, et sa seur Egÿalle
Les Entretient par maintz plaisans obsecques.
Eufrosina, gentille et curÿalle,
S'adonna toute à ce que sejourner
Long temps les face en amour socÿalle.

The attraction and accommodation of the first two Graces is reflected throughout the work, in the depiction of Venus, in the sensual and social magnetism of courtiers, and in the ebb and flow of anonymous characters (pp. 9, 30, 31, 34). The appearance of the Graces is foreshadowed in verses that place them under the aegis of Mercury, "le dieu d'engin," and at the wellspring of creative inspiration:

Et de là sont toutes graces infuses
Aux clers engins, et le don celestin
De la liqueur et fontaine des Muses. (vv. 265-67)

But what arrests our attention is the way Eufrosina ("good cheer") is set off from her sisters, framed in a 2:1 ratio. This is similar to the configuration and "infolding" of the Graces that Edgar Wind explicated in his auroral reading of Botticelli. A more extensive look into Pythagorean numerical lore would show that this is also the double proportion of the diapason—the precise mathematical ratio that must obtain between two strings of equal weight and tension to produce two notes exactly an octave apart—as the key to establishing concordant musical intervals. When extrapolated, it is also the sine curve used to mark the path of the sun through the zodiac for the vernal equinox when it enters the sign of Aries (cf. Peter Apian, *Cosmographicus liber*, ed. Frisius [Antwerp, 1533]). This clearly informs the reference to Pythagoras—now integrated into the Heraclitean concordant universe—and the immediate mention of "monocordes" and "decacordes" (p. 17, cf. IV, 324-25), for the decad $(1 + 2 + 3 + 4)$ delimits yet regenerates the physical Pythagorean universe. And the mediation of extremes through a combination of their outstanding features also undergirds and exemplifies the narrator's search for "noms concordans a l'effect" (p. 31). Reciprocity and interchange of the Graces are mirrored in the sound distribution of certain verses:

Cifflans, bruyans, vous feront escroler,
Flastrir, fener | voz fleurs | et vos verdures,
Lors verrez vous voz feuillettes voler (vv. 434-36)

and the lockstep of the vaunted *terza rima* is transformed into covert quatrains (cf. vv. 598-601). Like many another Renaissance composer, Lemaire gives us a final clue of this in the uncompleted rhyme scheme of the Venus section (v. 616), just in case we may have missed the point.

So much more could be said about this small detail of imagery and about many others. For example, the initial description of Eufrosina recalls the "gentillesse et courtoisie humaine" that concludes the narrator's statement on cultural interchange (p. 5) and anticipates the debate between French *courtoisie* and Italian *gentilezza* that Henri Estienne made so much of in the first *Dialogue du nouveau langage françois italianizé*. Her final attribute sends the reader to Lemaire's rambling disquisition on "Urbanité, moyeneresse de deux extremes" as a prospective example of French lower case "gentillesse ou courtoisie" under the protective nimbus of Prudence and dame Temperance (IV, 102-07). A detail in the microcosm can be a window to the universe.

So mirror, tree, fountain, Graces all participate in a universal harmony where diversity is reconciled by a Providence that composes and conducts. In *La Concorde* the balance of opposites by which God establishes a cosmos out of the chaos of the elements is matched in the individual's life by an equilibrium of passions. Meaning is forever deferred in this microcosm where we retrace our steps endlessly. But we risk missing meaning altogether if we fail to approach the artifact on its own terms, if we discount its *integritas*, as Joyce put it. Like "Danger," Anachronism might be capitalized since it too leads to our misfortune. What greater misfortune is there than to lose touch with a world in which the good of literature is synecdoche for virtue, where manners are synecdoche for morals? As the Word is miraculously "near" and yet "with" God according to St. John and other Greeks back to time out of mind, in the eyes of the Creator poetry and morality lose their trivial differences to become one.

NOTES

1. Patterson, *Three Centuries of French Poetic Theory* (New York, 1966), I, 107-08; Guy, I, 173. It would be inaccurate to "credit" Guy's bird's-eye survey with shaping the modern prejudice toward allegory. For this we must go back to Coleridge's influential definition of allegory as the translation of a non-poetic structure of abstract ideas into poetic imagery (*The Portable Coleridge* [New York, 1950], pp. 398-401). This bad idea misled Huizinga, directly or indirectly, to the laconic and indefensible view of late medieval allegory that "Symbolism is a very profound function of the mind, allegory a superficial one" (*The Waning of the Middle Ages* [New York, 1954], p. 205). Angus Fletcher offers an elegant correction of this view in *Allegory, The Theory of a Symbolic Mode* (Ithaca, 1964), pp. 314-15.

2. *Dark Conceit* (Providence, 1972), p. 114. Among the most influential partial readers, C.S. Lewis typically insists on the continued clarity of allegory (*The*

Allegory of Love [London, Oxford and New York, 1971], p. 166) while Rosemond Tuve makes broad allowance for enigmatic qualities induced by intellectual complexity (*Elizabethan and Metaphysical Imagery* [Chicago, 1965], pp. 105-09).

3. I, 231. The Stecher edition of Lemaire's *Oeuvres* (Louvain, 1882-91) will be designated in the text by Roman followed by Arabic numbers. Due to its clear superiority, however, the Frappier edition of *La Concorde des deux langages* (Paris, 1947) will be indicated in the text by page and/or verse numbers. And, for the sake of economy, this work will occasionally be referred to as *La Concorde*.

4. "De copia" in *Opera omnia* (Leyden, 1703-06), I, Cols. 18F and 90F.

5. Lemaire gives an idea of this richness when he praises Cretin for the moral dimension of his poetic fictions, quickly raising the question of poetry's association to history and then to the influence of astrology (IV, 188). Much remains to be said about this connection throughout his works between allegory and astrology.

6. The best summary I know of is given by an anthropologist, Edmund Leach, "Michelangelo's Genesis: Structuralist Comments on the Paintings on the Sistine Chapel Ceiling," *TLS*, No. 3914 (18 March, 1977), 311-13.

7. *Oeuvres poétiques de Guillaume Cretin*, ed. K. Chesney (Paris, 1932), pp. 31-32. These ideas are all part of a vast network of commonplaces that become even more crystallized in Bodin and Sidney. One of the "Plato Four," Cristoforo Landino, puts it nicely in his commentary on Dante, "Et e idio sommo poeta: et e del mondo suo poema," while Magny phrases it in language that we will take up later: "L'Architecteur du grand Palais des Cieux, / Voulant remplir de merveille le monde" (*Les Amours*, 19).

8. *De planctu naturae*, trans. Douglas Moffat (New York, 1908), Prose III, 72-84.

9. The Renaissance "world picture" has been rehearsed, with varying emphasis, many times. For unfocused comments, yet highly suggestive for the bipartite structure of *La Concorde*, for the Pythagorean "deep kinship throughout all nature" (but in modern literature), and for the way in which the images and agents are "placed in a symmetrical relationship to each other" in allegories of micro- and macrocosm, see Fletcher, *Allegory*, pp. 184, 192-93, and esp. S.K. Heninger, *Touches of Sweet Harmony* (San Marino, 1974). Helen North briefly points out that in medieval iconography the micro-macrocosm explicitly embraces the "divine quaternities" of the cardinal virtues, the elements and the Rivers of Paradise (*From Myth to Icon* [Ithaca, 1979], p. 202).

10. E.g., Paul Imbs, "Jean Lemaire de Belges: *La Concorde des deux langages*," *Bulletin de la Faculté des Lettres de l'Université de Strasbourg*, 26 (April, 1948), 183.

11. In his oration on the dignity of man, Pico della Mirandola, who styled himself as the "Concordiae Comes" and waxed eloquently on the need to follow Heraclitus and assist in the birth of Harmonia from Venus and Mars, proposed that "he who knows himself, knows all things in himself."

12. *Aristotelis de arte poetica* (Florence, 1548), pp. 245, 256. See also Ludovico Castelvetro, *Poetica d'Aristotile* (Vienna, 1570), pp. 271, 327, and Alessandro Piccolomini, *Annotazioni della Poetica d'Aristotile* (Venice, 1575), pp. 325, 356-57. Analogous examples abound in French poetry. Cf. Ronsard, *Oeuvres complètes*, ed. Laumonier (Paris, 1914-60), IV, 108-09; VII, 244-46; XVII, 136, 208-09, 219-22, 262-63; Marot, *Pseaume* 9, vv. 1-4; Du Bellay, *Sonnets divers* 28, vv. 5-6; Garnier, *Les Tragédies* (Heilbronn, 1882-83; rpt. Geneva: Slatkine, 1970), p. 384.

13. Edgar Wind's *Pagan Mysteries in the Renaissance* (New York, 1958) is

exceptionally pertinent here, suggesting as I think it does that the organizing structural principles of "The School of Athens" and "Primavera" are fundamentally iden-
tical to those at work in *La Concorde* (see pp. 40, 198, 211 and 220). A careful look
at late 15th-century Sienese painting, especially the work of Lorenzetti, makes the
comparison obvious.

14. Jodogne's note in his excellent edition correctly sends the reader to a
passage in the *Illustrations* where Minerva speculates on the etymological derivation
of Pallas and Bellona, and he might also have mentioned the last sentence of *La Concorde* in which her capitalized titles draw together the various attributes in lower case
that the poem has just illustrated.

15. According to patrology, virtue or sin issues from the concupiscible, iras-
cible or rational faculties of mind. In overseeing the actions of her three Graces and
in bestowing grace on mankind, Venus in *La Concorde* is disposed "A tout conjoin-
joindre en amour melliflue, / Leur propinquant vertu concupiscible" (p. 24; cf. I,
247).

16. At the beginning of Meschinot's *Lunettes des Princes* the narrator is visited
by dame Reason bearing a book of "grand merveille" in one hand and, in the other,
spectacles with lenses labeled Prudence and Justice which are held together by Force
and Temperance.

17. "Tistre" is the verb used to describe Nature's marriage of heaven and earth
in celebration of Venus, and in Minerva's temple as well, and indeed *braiding* might
be the best way to describe the interchange of conflation and deflation. If that is so,
the reader may wish to consult the brilliant essay of Ananda Coomaraswamy, which
deals with the mystery of hidden principles that reconcile archetypal opposites
(Right and Sinister) and with the etymology of con-cords whose plaited filaments
can regenerate a map of the universe ("Dürer's Knots and Leonardo's Concatena-
tions," *Art Quarterly*, 7 [1944], 109-25.

Saint-Gelais and the Epigrammatic Mode

Donald Stone, Jr.

No one, to my knowledge, has ever maintained that research in the area of literary history constitutes the only worthwhile activity for a professor of literature. However, when we elect to study an author like Mellin de Saint-Gelais, such research does have the interesting advantage of placing before the fertility of the critical imagination the richness of an historical reality with which we must contend, regardless of established or personal responses to the material at hand.

Consider, for example, a recent general assessment of Mellin: "one is tempted to think that today he would be lucky to obtain employment as a writer of mottoes for Christmas crackers."[1] Through its reference to "Christmas crackers," this judgment summarizes much critical reaction to Saint-Gelais's poetry: it is trivial and precariously close to doggerel. Moreover, given that Saint-Gelais wrote a great number of epigrams and that the *Deffence* dismissed the epigrammatists of the day as "un tas de faiseurs de comtes nouveaux, qui en un dizain sont contens n'avoir rien dict qui vaille aux ix. premiers vers, pourveu qu'au dixiesme il y ait le petit mot pour rire,"[2] the "Christmas cracker" analogy is not without precedent. But what does the literary history of the period tell us about the analogy?

It tells us that like Saint-Gelais himself the epigram enjoyed a place of singular prominence among French poets who preceded the Pléiade even though we would not divine this from reading the *Deffence*, which pits ballade and rondeau and virelai against sonnet and ode and Roman elegy when discussing what genres must be renounced or embraced by the new national literature. An appreciative contemporary of Saint-Gelais knew better. Of the various forms commented upon by Thomas Sébillet in his *Art poétique* of 1548, the epigram receives pride of place and for good reason: "Je commenceray a l'Epigramme comme le plus petit et premier œuvre de Pöésie."[3] Only when we reach Chapter III, which is reserved for the rondeau, do we understand the precise meaning of the phrase "premier œuvre de Pöésie": "pource que la matiére du Rondeau n'est autre que du sonnet ou épigramme, lés Pöétes de ce temps lés plus frians ont quitté lés Rondeaus a l'antiquité, pour s'arrester aus Epigrammes et Sonnetz" (p. 120). The volumes of poetry produced between 1540 and 1548 prove Sébillet's point beyond any doubt.[4]

The same documents that affirm the importance of the epigram also confront us with the very difficult problem of how to define what to Saint-Gelais's generation constituted an epigram. Even Sébillet confuses more than he enlightens. On the one hand his discussion of the epigram maintains that fluidity and a witty conclusion are its cardinal traits; yet in the body of the same chapter he alludes to epitaphs written by Marot and calls them "épigrammes sépulchrauz" (p. 104). Were all of Marot's epitaphs witty and had the poet eventually reprinted them with his epigrams, we might conclude that the period considered "epigram" to be the general term for any relatively short, clever poem. But the vast majority of Marot's epitaphs were not to be subsumed under the heading of "epigram" and if some are witty, many are not.

Michel d'Amboise appears to offer us some assistance when, in one of the earliest volumes to employ the word "épigramme" (c. 1533), he pens a poem entitled "Qui a contraint lacteur faire Epigrames."[5] D'Amboise recounts how Apollo urged him to give up drinking of Parnassus' sacred fountain. Then Venus came forth and directed him to drink at Paphos, and, indeed, most of the poetry that follows treats of love. But other cords are struck: encomiastic pieces to royal personages, pietistic reflections on this earthly life. Moreover, the majority of the poems d'Amboise composed for this volume—including "Qui a contraint lacteur faire Epigrames"—he translated from the Latin of Girolamo Angeriano. If d'Amboise's translation contains any personal conviction about the appropriate subject matter for an epigram, the surrounding poems give the lie to the assumption that the form treats exclusively of love.

Marot adds to the confusion when in 1538 he decides to use the heading "Deux Livres d'Epigrammes" in the Dolet edition of his *Oeuvres* and gathers under this heading a number of poems previously entitled dizain, blason, envoy, huictain, huictain pour Estreines.[6] As a result, it can come as no surprise that in the course of the 1540s the rubric "épigramme" introduces a variety of forms and subjects. Charles de Sainte-Marthe's *Poésie françoise* appeared in 1540. The first book is presented as "contenant des Epigrammes." In this section we find poems of love, poems addressed to friends and important personages, poems that are didactic in tone—all categories reminiscent of Michel d'Amboise. But there is more. Some of Sainte-Marthe's epigrams such as his paraphrase of psalm 120 are stanzaic in nature. To a variety in subject matter must be added variety in form as well.

The posthumous 1544 edition of Bonaventure Des Périers's *Oeuvres* also contains the rubric "Epigrammes." Here, however, no stanzaic poems appear and the general uniformity in structure only accentuates the lack of conformity we encounter elsewhere under that same heading. Bonaventure's "Blason du Nombril" and other works in *rimes plates* precede the "Epigrammes," of which twenty-three are dizains. The remaining pieces include three huitains, two quatrains, and one example each of poems of seven, eleven, twelve, fourteen, and sixteen lines. In content, most might be termed brief epistles. Since only two of the thirty-three poems contain fewer than eight lines, the Des Périers volume serves as a pertinent reminder that although the period knew of the historical relationship between epigram and inscription, that briefest manifestation of the genre was not the preferred one.

Peletier du Mans's *Oeuvres poétiques* of 1547 brings us to a volume in which some of the earliest verse of the Pléiade was printed, but no less "Aucuns épigrammes dudict Autheur" (f. 86^V). Again we are treated to a mixture of themes and structures. Flattery addressed to the powerful shares the stage with poems of love and satire. If none are stanzaic, two are written in *rimes plates*. Some bear the title "Dizain" and "Huittain," but others are called "Estreines" or "Epitaphe." The two poems in *rimes plates* are a blason and a contreblason. Like Marot and Sébillet, Peletier appears to make no firm distinction between the epigram as a shortish poem of unspecified function, such as the huitain or dizain, and a mode of witty verse varying in length and inclusive of forms associated with quite specific ends such as the étrenne or épitaphe.

Judging by the *Deffence*, these complexities arise, in part at least, for want of a proper classical model. Do not practice the epigram as do today the "faiseurs de comtes nouveaux," writes Du Bellay, but rather "à l'imitation d'un Martial" (p. 110). This suggestion as to a lack of familiarity with, or perhaps insufficent regard for the Roman poet must, however, be discounted. The period knew of Martial and frequently imitated him. The very year Marot grouped his dizains, huitains, blasons, and envoys anew under the title of "épigramme," he offered a manuscript to Anne de Montmorency part of which contains his "Epigrammes à l'imitation de Martial." In the section of Peletier's *Oeuvres poétiques* devoted to his translations, we find the French version of an epigram by Martial. Let me suggest, therefore, that the complexity surrounding the form, content, and definition of the epigram constitutes aspects of a broad program of experimentation undertaken by a world that had already downgraded the medieval *formes fixes* and yet only begun to explore alternate avenues of expression.

To some degree, this idea is not new. Early in our century, a student of Charles Fontaine wrote: "As time passes, it becomes more and more evident that only when all the secondary writers of the [first half of the 16th century] shall have been treated can a definitive history of the Pléiade be written."[7] The ensuing investigation emphasizes ideas on the poet and the French language held in common by the Pléiade and Fontaine, to wit, "his learning, his imitation of Italian models before 1549, his Platonism" and use of "some of the poetic forms recommended by Du Bellay" (p. 233). A slightly earlier study on Charles de Sainte-Marthe stresses many of the same points.[8] In both instances the argumentation rests on points of similarity, a phenomenon not to be disparaged, but not necessarily the only gauge of the period's vitality.

It was a period that had discovered the sonnet, or to be more precise, "le sonnet-épigramme, . . . chose légère, faite vite pour peu d'instants"[9] but in the hands of many the sonnet did not remain such. In Jean Maugin's 1546 translation of the romance of Palmerin d'Olive, a poem entitled "Chanson" appears as part of chapter 126[10]—nothing untoward since the mixing of verse and prose occurs frequently in romances of the day. However, this chanson is composed of two sonnets. Each contains the same rhyme scheme but no rhyme is repeated in the second sonnet. Thus each sonnet may legitimately be called a stanza of the song. In Forcadel's *Chant des Seraines* (1548), a major division of the collected poems bears the rubric "Les Complaintes." The initial poem under this heading, "Sur le trespas d'vne Damoyselle," has a lyric structure: quatrains with no repeated rhymes. But then we encounter the first of several other "complaintes," all sonnets, to which Forcadel gives the sub-heading "Sonnet plaintif" (f. 51ᵛ).

Twice now I have had occasion to refer to the absence of repeated rhymes between stanzas. This feature derives its importance, of course, from the fact that the medieval *formes fixes* proceed differently and another means to underscore the strangeness of Du Bellay's emphasis in the *Deffence* on ballade, rondeau, and virelai is to observe how early 16th-century poets began to move toward stanzaic verse without repeated rhymes. Brian Jeffery's *Chanson Verse of the Early Renaissance* (2 vols., London, 1971 and 1976) provides invaluable information on this subject by reproducing pertinent works that date from before 1530.

The texts reprinted by Jeffery are of the musical chanson, a genre whose influence on the lyric forms to come has never been doubted. At the same time, the musical chanson shares with the epigram a lightness of touch that frequently degenerated into obscenity. Marot knew how to be naughty in both genres, but as his translations of the psalms testify, he also knew how to create new patterns for lyric expression on a much higher plane. Ronsard later observed that in the 1540s the two models for lyric verse he studied were Marot's psalms and Horace's odes[11] but we do not have to await Ronsard to note the influence of these works. The number of translations from the psalms, now in French (Sainte-Marthe, Scève), now in Latin (Bourbon, Salmon Macrin) suffices to signal just one aspect of the concerted effort before 1549 to experiment with the freer lyric forms.

As the decade made the sonnet into epistle, encomium, song, and elegy, and saw the lyric mode express both the sacred and the scatological, so the epigram could be satire, epitaph, blason, étrenne but also a vehicle for more elevated expression.[12] Dorothy Coleman has convincingly argued that by his phrase "durs Epygrammes" Scève wished to distinguish between the "*dolcezza* of Petrarch and the petrarchists" and "the seriousness of the poet of high-style love."[13] Innumerable studies devoted to Scève's love cycle testify to Scève's success in this endeavor. Such success is a tribute to his talent, to be sure, but it points as well to a willingness to explore the potential of the dizain and gives substance to Sébillet's otherwise surprising statement in his *Art poétique* that "Le Sonnet suit l'épigramme de bien prés, et de matiére, et de mesure: Et quant tout est dit, Sonnet n'est autre chose que le parfait epigramme de l'Italien, comme le dizain du Francois" (p. 115). That Scève was not alone in treating the epigram diversely Saint-Gelais demonstrates very well.

Of the poet's works published in his lifetime, the proportion of "Christmas cracker" verses to his longer poems is unexpectedly small. The short, witty pieces remained for a long time in manuscript form.[14] Moreover, prominent among the longer works in question are his translations, a facet of his writing to which the title of the one collected edition of Saint-Gelais's poems printed before the poet's death called special attention: *Saintgelais, Oeuvres de luy tant en composition, que translation, ou allusion aux Autheurs Grecs, & Latins*. Obviously not only was use made of classical models before the *Deffence*, but that use was advertized and, one presumes, comparisons encouraged. (In a work of 1550 entitled *Traductions de latin en francoys, imitations, et inventions nouvelles* which contains adaptations by Saint-Gelais from Second's *Basia*, on occasion the Latin poems appear with the French translations.) Three years before, a reader of the 1547 edition of Saint-Gelais's *Oeuvres* would have found a version of an epigram by Martial, of an epigram by Claudian, and of an ode of Horace. The title of each poem identifies the source and, in the cases of Horace and Martial, the incipit of the source is also provided.

The epigrams of Martial and Claudian translated by Saint-Gelais have nothing in common save their form. Though both are presented in a single, non-stanzaic unit, Martial tells of a bereaved young girl whose loss turns out to be not the familiar dead pet but an adolescent "dont le priape n'avait pas encore un pied et demi" (Ep. XIV). Claudian writes of the fortunate old man of Verona who has lived all his days in the house in which he was born, untempted by foreign adventures and military exploits. The same sermonizing informs the Horatian ode, in which the change of the seasons mirrors, the poet reminds us, the mutability of all things and the fact that about tomorrow we can never be certain.

The range in tonality could hardly be greater but, as we have seen, it constitutes no novelty in the literary world of the 1540s. Of greater interest to us must be the worth of Saint-Gelais's choice of models and mode of execution.

To learn that Marot, also, translated the Martial epigram teaches us nothing new about Saint-Gelais or Marot. But what of the revelation that Ronsard incorporated the same Claudian epigram in a poem to the Cardinal de Châtillon and that Du Bellay inserted lines from the Horatian ode in his "Du retour du printens"? Or that a poem by Menander adapted by Saint-Gelais attracted Ronsard as well? Or that an octave from the *Furioso* which inspired Saint-Gelais to produce the dizain "Si j'ay du bien" returns in *L'Olive* in the sonnet "Ce que je sen', la langue ne refuse"? Surely these facts suggest that, in the eyes of the two finest poets of the brigade at least, Saint-Gelais's choice of models could not always be faulted.

His execution, too, has its impressive side. Consider, for example, the first few lines of a blason addressed to a lock of hair:

> Cheveux, seul remede et confort
> De mon mal violent et fort;
> Cheveux longs, beaux, et desliés,
> Qui mon cœur tant plus fort liez,
> Que plus il veut tendre et tacher
> A se distraire et destacher,
> Plus il est pris et mieux estraint,
> Plus est de demeurer contraint.
> (*Oeuvres*, ed. Blanchemain, I, 191)

In addition to its clear and flowing syntax, the segment brings into play a significant variety of poetic touches from the musicality of "Cheveux longs, beaux, et desliés" to the mimetic movement that, through enjambement, accentuates the heart's effort to break its bonds ("plus il veut tendre et tacher / A se distraire et destacher"), only to emphasize the

futility of the effort by completing the phrase with clauses that are cir-
cumscribed by the concluding conjunction and a rhyme that repeats the
notion of emprisonment: "Plus il est pris et mieux estraint, / Plus est de
demeurer contraint"). To be sure, the octosyllabic lines of the blason
betray the period of their composition but for that, as with the choice of
models, we cannot dismiss the poetic sense displayed by Saint-Gelais. His
capacity to produce such clear, cleverly balanced lines explains in large
measure, I suspect, his success as a writer of epigrams, but the blason was
also intended to evoke the beauty of its subject and the lyric quality of
certain of its lines points to a further aspect of Saint-Gelais's art that must
be touched upon.

   Like other poets of his day, Saint-Gelais willingly applied such talent
to non-epigrammatic subjects and won for himself further acclaim. His
"Laissez la verde couleur," a lyric work on the death of Adonis, achieved
phenomenal success throughout the 16th century.[15] As presented by one
Paris manuscript, the poem bears the title: "Lamentation de Venus en la
mort d'Adonis, pour reciter en façon de conde clare d'Espagne." This
reference to the Conde Claros air calls attention to an interesting pecu-
liarity of the rhyme scheme of "Laissez la verde couleur." Just as in the
Spanish *Romance del Conde Claros de Montalvan* the rhyme -ar appears
in alternate lines with distinct, if not absolute regularity, so in "Laissez la
verde couleur" not only do the second and fourth lines of each quatrain
rhyme, but the same rhyme appears in these two lines throughout the
poem's fifteen quatrains.

   Although this technique cannot be compared to verbal acrobatics in
the vein of Marot's

> Ce Rimailleur, qui s'alloit enrimant,
> Tant rimassa, rima et rimonna,
> Qu'il a congneu quel bien par rime on a,

we might decide from the rhyme scheme of "Laissez la verde couleur" that
Saint-Gelais did not escape the tendency among the rhétoriqueurs to add
ever more difficulties to the ordinary demands of prosody. This is one
possible conclusion; however, in light of the Conde Claros allusion, one
could argue also that the poet wished to give the repetition the quality of
a subtle refrain. In the chanson form, the repetition of even entire lines
within the new stanzaic structures will survive long after the eclipse of the
ballade, rondeau, and virelai. Equally relevant to this alternate conclusion
is the fact that, contrary to Marot's procedure in the lines just quoted,
"Laissez la verde couleur" does not call attention to the phenomenon of
the repeated rhyme. In a truly impressive way, the substance of the poem
dictates its development as, I believe, the concluding quatrains will reveal:

Au son de ses cris indignes
Respond Echo tourmentée,
Et mesme ses deux blancs cygnes
Chanson piteuse ont chantée.
    Mais voyant l'obscure nuict
Estre ja presque arrivée,
Ont doucement et sans bruit
Leur maistresse en l'air levée.
    Plus elle approche des cieux,
Plus tient la teste baissée;
Et eust volontiers ses yeux
Et sa veue en bas laissée.[16]
(Blanchemain, I, 132)

What strikes in these quatrains is the combination of appropriateness and effectiveness. Whether the poet alludes to the falling of night or to Venus' dejected state as she is driven upwards by her swans, we are hard-pressed to espy any cheville occasioned by the necessity to repeat the single -ée rhyme. Instead, the three quatrains give evidence of an effort to gather together the essential elements of the story's conclusion: cries and piteous song to accentuate the central theme of lament; allusion to night and Venus' soundless elevation to effect the transition from event to closure in which the scene of Adonis' dramatic death is contrasted with darkness, cries, with silence, presence, with withdrawal; and finally, Venus' bowed head, through which Saint-Gelais captures the saddest contrast of all—a bereft goddess who cannot follow her mortal lover, who, Olympus bound, can only wish that her eyes belonged here below.

Such activity by Saint-Gelais and his contemporaries is important in itself and deserves to win for these poets greater measure of respect but it can serve another function, that is, to help us understand better why the strident voices of the brigade did not drown out all that had been said in the preceding decade.

The *Quintil Horatian* shows us that at least one reader of the *Deffence* could distinguish between fact and distortion in the manifesto. Of Du Bellay's invocation of Martial as a model for the epigram, Aneau is quick to observe (with considerable justification) that Martial often gives evidence of that very failing Du Bellay scorns in the contemporary French epigram, to wit, no substantial content save "le petit mot pour rire à la fin." More important perhaps is the shock expressed by Aneau at the Pléiade's denigra-tion of the French language: "en tout ton livre n'y a un seul chapitre, non pas une seule sentence, monstrant quelque vertu, lustre, ornement, ou louange de nostre langue Françoise, combien qu'elle n'en soit degarnie non plus que les autres, à qui le bien scait cognoistre" (quoted in Chamard's edition of the *Deffence*, p. 28 n.). Is this outburst not a plea for "knowing" what poets like Scève and Saint-Gelais had accomplished? Eventually relations between Saint-Gelais and Ronsard in particular would take on a friendly air and produce declarations of mutual admiration. Documents exist to suggest that their society repeated the reconciliation.

A 1556 Lyon reprint of Sébillet's *Art poétique* and the *Quintil Horatian* also contains a treatise entitled "Autre Art poétique réduit en bonne méthode" (p. 229). Given the company this treatise is keeping in the volume, we feel no surprise when poems by Saint-Gelais are cited as models for the six- and seven-syllable line or for "rimes croisées" (pp. 235, 237). But what to make of further statements by the author to the effect that, "maintenant ie diray seulement de noz François, lesquels (ie dy sans flaterie) commencent à piller l'honneur des anciens approchans si pres du souuerain degré de la gloire poetique, que ie puis esperer (& n'est mon esperance vaine) les voir faire honte aux anciens" or that "Ronsard, en ses Odes, le Caron en son Demon & Odes, monstrent desia que la poesie Françoise est digne de philosophie" (pp. 261-62)? Clearly not everyone felt it necessary to choose between the old and new schools, a fact borne out by an even later work. A 1571 Paris anthology of memorable French verse called *Le Parnasse des poètes françois* quotes the Pléiade extensively but includes also thirteen works by Marot and as the example of the theme of "Homme Rustique bien heureux," it quotes Saint-Gelais's translation of the Claudian epigram mentioned above.

Scholars who have studied the music of the century chronicle a comparable phenomenon. Despite the attacks launched by Du Bellay against the poetry of his day (and especially against "Laissez la verde couleur" and a second lyric piece by Saint-Gelais which are excoriated in the *Deffence*), Thibault notes that "Il ne semble pas que ces attaques, toutes littéraires, aient ému les musiciens; Certon n'hésitera pas, dans son recueil de 1552, à introduire les deux pièces de Saint-Gelais."[17] He could have added that Le Roy did not hesitate to do the same in 1573, nor Jehan Chardavoine, when preparing his *Recueil des plus belles et excellentes chansons* of 1576.

Such, in very summary form, are some of the many facets of the century that research unearths for our consideration. Since this essay began with an observation about research and its usefulness, the time has perhaps arrived to relate that observation to the substance of what has just been presented. The achievement of the Pléiade dazzles, but as with all that dazzles, the achievement also blinds. We see dimly the exceptional success of the epigram in the 1540s; we have perceived even less clearly the breadth of activity in which the poets of the same period engaged or the acceptance of that activity well beyond the publication of the *Deffence*. How often, for example, does criticism record that Ronsard penned an "Epitaphe de la barbiche de Madame de Villeroy" (*Oeuvres complètes*, ed. Laumonier, XVIII, 162-64) or that Du Bellay translated into Latin an epigram by Saint-Gelais in which the poet explains why red-headed individuals do not get along? As lovers of great—or at least good—poetry, we are likely to sympathize with these oversights. Yet they have made it easier to ignore the forces in the century that both doomed such experiments as Ronsard's pindaric odes and kept the epigrammatic mode alive, very much alive.

That long-recognized disciple of Ronsard, Amadis Jamyn, appears to have had a solid grasp of the nature of the epigrammatic form. Gone in his *Oeuvres poétiques* of 1575 is the variety of structures that we find earlier in the century under the rubric of "épigramme." To that heading Jamyn relegates only quatrains, dizains, and the like. At the same time all that is epigrammatic in Jamyn the poet did not call an epigram. Read in the same volume such poems as "Amour bandoit son arc comme vn croissant voûté / Quand il veit ma Deesse" (f. 138^r), or "Ha! malheureuse Main qui me rends malheureux" (f. 100^v) and its companion piece "Quoy? m'ozes-tu blasmer d'auoir bien commencé?" (f. 101^r), all of which happen to be sonnets. The line of thought from Sébillet ("Et quant tout est dit, Sonnet n'est autre chose que le parfait epigramme de l'Italien") to Jamyn is unswerving, and it continues. "Le sonnet, et l'Epigramme est quasi tout de mesme, si ce n'est que quand une Epigramme est de quatorze vers, en rime platte, c'est Epigramme; et si la rime est autrement disposée, elle est appellée Sonnet," writes Laudun d'Aigaliers in his *Art poétique français* of 1597 (ed. Dedieu, p. 95). We could not be farther here from the *Deffence*, which associates the sonnet with the ode, not the epigram (p. 121), whereas the blurred lines of pre-Pléiade practice continue to surface, as they will do again in a work of the 17th century, Colletet's *Traitté de l'épigramme* (1658).[18]

To Colletet also "le Sonnet n'est autre chose qu'une Epigramme bornée d'un certain nombre de Vers" (p. 124). He recognizes the epigram as a distinct genre, yet notes that its range of subject matter forges links with the elegy, the epic, tragedy, comedy, and satire (p. 24). In addition to tracing with these remarks a network of ideas reminiscent of the world of Scève and Saint-Gelais, Colletet injects into his discussion this provocative statement: "ce n'est pas un moindre defaut à un Poëte de ne pouvoir aux occurrences abbaisser son Genie et son style, que de ne les pouvoir élever quand il en est besoin" (p. 57). Since the evidence of our preceding discussion suggests that Colletet's remarks constitute the expression of a general, as well as personal belief and that that belief was held before as well as after the coming of the Pléiade, it is on certain implications behind Colletet's pronouncement that I should like to conclude.

The *Deffence* was produced by a group of young, inexperienced poets. Because of their talent and eventual successes, we have willingly forgiven them the brashness of their manifesto and I dare say our tolerance can be defended. It can also be criticized to the extent that such tolerance perpetuates certain distortions of fact present in the *Deffence*. More serious still, it tacitly dismisses a poetic mode to which the literate world held fast and made to coexist throughout both the 16th and 17th centuries with the elevated brilliance of Ronsard and Racine.

When in 1692 Fontenelle published his *Recueil des plus belles pièces des poëtes françois*, among the thirty-four poems by Saint-Gelais included in the anthology we find the same "Du rousseau et de la rousse" that had once inspired Du Bellay. When Colletet refers to Saint-Gelais as "l'Esprit le plus raffiné dans la Science Epigrammatique," he follows the remark with reference to the same epigram translated from Claudian that is reproduced in the 1571 *Parnasse des poètes françois* (pp. 46-47). These reprises are no accident. The signs abound as to continued interest in a poetry "fluide" and "facile," or to use Colletet's definition of the epigrammatic style, in "un langage naïf, naturel, et sans fard, net et familier" (p. 54). Researching the years that precede the *Deffence* reminds us that the gains for French poetry achieved by the Pléiade, though real enough, follow closely upon the heels of earlier efforts to examine and perfect the same medium. The survival of that contribution over a significant span of French literary history should suffice to justify the assumption that gain followed gain. But one final point may also be in order.

Studying the epigram brings us face to face with poems *and* attitudes. Over time not everyone has shared La Bruyère's surprise that the works of Marot, "si naturels et si faciles," could not make of Ronsard a better poet,[19] and we may be tempted to say that this remark reveals more about La Bruyère than about Ronsard. Yet La Bruyère gives voice here to a conviction that is neither new nor isolated since the days of Ronsard. Moreover, that curious mixture of wit and elegance to which the epigrammatists bear witness binds not only 16th and 17th centuries but also poetry and prose of that same period and sets the literary miracles wrought by Rabelais and Montaigne within a context that actively encouraged the mind to show its ability to "aux occurrences abbaisser son Genie et son style." The dignity that the *Deffence* called upon its readers to restore to the national literature has its place in the chronicles of French letters, but it is a place that must be shared with rather different and singularly persistent criteria for excellence.

NOTES

1. I.D. McFarlane, *A Literary History of France: Renaissance France 1470-1589* (London, 1974), pp. 130-31.

2. Joachim Du Bellay, *La Deffence et illustration de la langue francoyse*, ed. Henri Chamard (Paris, 1966), p. 110.

3. Thomas Sébillet, *Art poétique françoys*, ed. F. Gaiffe (Paris, 1910), p. 103.

4. Of volumes of previously unpublished poetry printed in the 1540s we have found only one—*La Poésie françoise de Charles de Sainte-Marthe* (1540)—that contains a section reserved specifically for "Rondeaux, Ballades, et Chants royaux" (pp. 81-112). Elsewhere, an occasional ballade, rondeau, or virelai may appear, but their frequency cannot even begin to compare with the quantity of elegies, epigrams, chansons, and épîtres offered to the public in the same period.

5. Michel d'Amboise, *Les Cent Epigrames*, in *Les Cent Epigrames avecques la vision, la complainte de vertu traduyte de frere Baptiste Manuan* (Paris, s.d.).

6. For a detailed discussion of this aspect of Marot's career, see C.A. Mayer's introduction to his critical edition of Marot's epigrams (London, 1970).

7. Richmond L. Hawkins, *Maistre Charles Fontaine parisien* (Cambridge, Mass., 1916), p.v.

8. See Caroline Ruut-Rees, *Charles de Sainte-Marthe (1512-1555)* (New York, 1910), pp. 222-26.

9. Max Jasinski, *Histoire du sonnet en France* (Douai, 1903; rpt. Geneva, 1970), p. 38.

10. The poem appears on leaf CXXVIII[r]. In the 1525 Seville edition of the Spanish romance the comparable chapter (CL) contains no equivalent poem.

11. See Pierre de Ronsard, *Oeuvres complètes*, ed. Paul Laumonier (Paris, 1914), I, 44.

12. The epigram could even be a chanson. Antoine Du Moulin introduced in 1547 a number of new poems into the collection of chanson verse he had originally published two years earlier under the title *Déploration de Vénus sur la mort de bel Adonis* (the title also of the first piece in the anthology, Saint-Gelais's "Laissez la verde couleur"). One of the poems added in 1547 is called "Vent d'esté." The work comes from Jean Martin's translation of Bembo's *Gli Asolani* and although Du Moulin's decision to include the work in an anthology of chansons is, in a sense, justified by the sentence that precedes the poem—"Et ce dict, il se print a chanter ainsi" (f. 61v)—"Vent d'esté" proves to be a dizain. (It might be noted here that the previously mentioned chanson in which sonnets comprise the two stanzas of the song is also reproduced by Du Moulin in his 1547 anthology.)

13. Dorothy Coleman, *Maurice Scève: Poet of Love* (Cambridge, England, 1975), p. 50.

14. The 1574 edition of Saint-Gelais's works is the first to incorporate some of this manuscript material; in the collected edition of 1719 an entire section is devoted to "Vers de Mellin de S. Gelais non imprimez jusqu'à présent" (p. 225).

15. In addition to the many 16th-century manuscripts that contain the poem, I have found no fewer than thirteen reprintings in the century of the complete poem and three incomplete reprintings (for song books of the day).

16. Although large segments of "Laissez la verde couleur" are borrowed from Bion and Pseudo Theocritus, these quatrains show no significant reflection of these and other poets Saint-Gelais imitated in his poem.

17. G. Thibault, "Musique et poésie en France au XVIe siècle avant les 'Amours' de Ronsard," in *Musique et poésie au XVIe siècle* (Paris, 1954), p. 84.

18. I quote from the P.A. Jannini edition (Geneva, 1965).

19. *Les Caractères*, ed. Charles Louandre (Paris, 1869), p. 18.

Clément Marot: une poétique du silence et de la liberté

Gérard Defaux

"Ubi spiritus, ibi libertas—Où est l'esprit, là
est la liberté."
Marguerite de Navarre, *Les Prisons*

"Ut instrumenta ad opus, non opus ad instrumenta":[1] partons de cet
axiome ou plutôt de ce credo, à mon sens fondamental, qu'il ne saurait
y avoir de bonne lecture, de lecture digne de ce nom, sans une adéquation,
aussi parfaite que possible, des moyens de notre investigation critique à
l'objet de notre investigation. Adoptons ensuite comme postulat qu'en
dépit de sa diversité et de son morcellement, son caractère résolument
événementiel, anecdotique et pour ainsi dire fortuit, l'œuvre de Marot,
dans ce qu'elle a d'éminemment *singulier*—je veux naturellement dire son
style—, est susceptible d'une interprétation tout à la fois cohérente et tota-
lisante. Et posons-nous alors la question suivante, l'inévitable question:
étant donnée la nature si particulière de cette œuvre, son indéniable singularité, quelle est l'approche critique, quelles sont la problématique et la
stratégie qui se révéleront, en dernière analyse, de la plus grande valeur
opératoire *possible*—qui s'avéreront finalement capables d'en rendre compte
au mieux?

En guise de réponse toute provisoire à cette question—comme dans
L'Adolescence clementine, il ne s'agit ici que d'un hésitant "coup d'essay"
—, mon propos sera, dans les pages qui suivent, de suggérer qu'une telle
approche gagnerait peut-être considérablement à s'articuler autour et en
fonction du concept, alors si dense et si riche, de LIBERTÉ; que c'est tout
bien pesé ce dernier et son contraire, la PRISON ou l'EXIL, qui semble
non seulement informer la vie de Marot, structurer son expérience la plus
significative de l'histoire et du monde, mais aussi bien son activité poétique, au quadruple niveau des formes dans lesquelles cette activité s'inscrit,
de l'idéologie clairement contestataire qu'elle véhicule, de la conception,
pour nous étrange et inattendue, que le poète semble se faire de lui-même

et de sa fonction et, *last but not least,* de l'attitude nettement réticente qu'il manifeste vis-à-vis du langage, cet instrument tout ensemble indispensable, incontournable et dangereux.

> "Maudit soit le premier dont la verve insensée
> Dans les bornes d'un vers renferma sa pensée,
> Et donnant à ses mots une étroite prison,
> Voulut avec la rime enchaîner la raison."
>   Boileau, *Satires*

Je prendrai comme point de départ de ma lecture essentiellement deux poèmes de Marot, tous deux liés à l'épisode très connu de l'emprisonnement au Châtelet du printemps 1526: l'épître X, "A son Amy Lyon," et le rondeau LXIV, baptisé "Rondeau parfaict A ses Amys apres sa delivrance."[2] Comme l'épître IX, adressée à l'énigmatique "Monsieur Bouchart, Docteur en Theologie," ces deux poèmes n'apparaissent ni dans *L'Adolescence clementine* de 1532, ni dans la *Suyte* de la dite *Adolescence* (début 1534, nouveau style), mais dans la seconde édition du *Premier Livre de la Metamorphose d'Ovide*, qui sort des presses d'Estienne Roffet au printemps ou à l'été de la même année. On suppose généralement—c'est par exemple le cas de Claude Mayer—qu'en dépit de leur publication tardive ces deux poèmes ont été composés à l'époque même de l'emprisonnement auquel ils se réfèrent, c'est-à-dire—comme *L'Enfer*—au printemps 1526. Cette supposition s'en double inévitablement d'une autre, qui consiste à expliquer le délai apporté à la publication par des raisons de prudence, le poète ne se décidant à rendre publiques ces pièces pour lui compromettantes qu'à partir du moment où, après la campagne de dénonciations et les persécutions de l'hiver 1533-34, l'Evangélisme croit avoir définitivement gagné la partie, le Roi multipliant alors les contacts avec Melanchthon et les Princes protestants d'Allemagne.[3] Pour vraisemblable que soit cette hypothèse, je préfère cependant croire, après Villey, que ces poèmes sont de composition nettement postérieure à l'événement qui leur sert de cadre. Et suggérer en outre que s'ils ne figurent dans aucune des cinq éditions de *L'Adolescence* qui voient le jour, à Paris ou à Lyon, entre 1532 et 1534,[4] c'est pour la raison bien simple que ni l'un ni l'autre ne sauraient en aucun cas rentrer dans la catégorie de ces "coups d'essay," de ces "miennes petites jeunesses" et autres "arbres, herbes & fleurs" dont Marot nous dit lui-même avoir exclusivement orné son premier jardin poétique;[5] mais que, bien au contraire, plutôt qu'"Oeuvres de jeunesse," et l'un et l'autre constituent déjà l'œuvre de la maturité.

Ce qui par dessus tout me pousse à préférer nettement cette hypothèse, c'est que l'intérêt des deux poèmes en question me semble résider ailleurs que dans leur dimension référentielle, anecdotique et narrative: c'est que, sans doute pour la première fois dans l'œuvre de Marot, cette dimension référentielle se double d'une dimension non seulement *allégorique*, mais encore *réflexive*. Pour la première fois, et sans rien perdre de ses vertus, le discours marotique s'étage, il se dédouble et s'approfondit. Sa *lettre* y révèle un *esprit*, sa transparence une métaphore. Il n'est plus seulement ce qu'il nous énonce, mais aussi bien ce que, parallèlement, il nous dit de lui. Somme toute, en racontant, il *se* raconte, il se prend soi-même pour objet. Relisons d'abord, pour nous en convaincre, une partie de l'épître "A son amy Lyon":

> Je ne t'escry de l'amour vaine & folle,
> Tu voys assez s'elle sert ou affolle;
> Je ne t'escry ne d'Armes ne de Guerre,
> Tu voys qui peult bien ou mal y acquerre;
> Je ne t'escry de Fortune puissante,   5
> Tu voys assez s'elle est ferme ou glissante;
> Je ne t'escry d'abus trop abusant,
> Tu en sçais prou & si n'en vas usant;
> Je ne t'escry de Dieu ne sa puissance,
> C'est à luy seul t'en donner congnoissance;   10
> Je ne t'escry des Dames de Paris,
> Tu en sçais plus que leurs propres Maris;
> Je ne t'escry qui est rude ou affable,
> Mais je te veulx dire une belle fable,
> C'est assavoir du Lyon et du Rat.   15
> Cestuy Lyon, plus fort qu'un vieil Verrat,
> Veit une fois que le Rat ne sçavoit
> Sortir d'ung lieu, pour autant qu'il avoit
> Mangé le lard & la chair toute crue;
> Mais ce Lyon (qui jamais ne fut Grue)   20
> Trouva moyen & maniere & matiere,
> D'ongles & dentz, de rompre la ratiere,
> Dont maistre Rat eschappe vistement,
> Puis mist à terre un genoul gentement,
> Et, en ostant son bonnet de la teste,   25
> A mercié mille foys la grand Beste,
> Jurant le Dieu des Souriz et des Ratz
> Qu'il luy rendroit. Maintenant tu verras
> Le bon du compte. Il advint d'aventure
> Que le Lyon, pour chercher sa pasture,   30
> Saillit dehors sa caverne & son siege,
> Dont (par malheur) se trouva pris au piege,
> Et fut lié contre un ferme posteau.
> Adonc le Rat, sans serpe ne cousteau,
> Y arriva joyeulx . . .   35

On peut certes lire cette épître comme on lit les autres, comme on lit par exemple l'épître XI ("Au Roy, pour le deslivrer de prison") ou l'épître XXV ("Au Roy, pour avoir esté desrobé"). On se trouve alors plus ou moins rapidement réduit au silence ou, ce qui est encore pire, à l'insignifiance; confronté à un objet dont la transparence est telle qu'il échappe irrémédiablement à la prise, à un message d'une telle efficacité, d'une telle perfection littérale que son sens s'épuise tout entier dans l'acte même de sa communication. Dans son "naturel" et son "esprit," son "élégance" et sa "simplicité" d'écriture, l'épître marotique offre si peu de résistance à l'exploration que tout commentaire critique en devient pratiquement impossible. A cet égard antithèse parfaite du dizain scévien. Le regard la parcourt avec ce genre de plaisir que procure un paysage familier. Il y cherche en vain des raisons de retarder l'annexion à laquelle il se livre sans y penser, une aspérité, une épaisseur, une densité capables, ne serait-ce que pour un instant, de le retenir. N'en découvrant aucune, il la traverse. Et en ressort tout à la fois charmé, dépourvu et inquiet. Charmé, parce que le fameux *badinage* est une réalité qui ne saurait laisser quiconque indifférent. Dépourvu, parce que Boileau a fait depuis longtemps le voyage, et qu'il lui a suffi d'une formule pour exprimer l'essentiel. Inquiet, parce que la facilité même de son progrès le conduit à s'interroger. Puisqu'il n'a rien vu qui véritablement mérite, comme on dit, le commentaire, puisqu'il n'a pu voir que le déjà vu, de deux choses l'une. Ou bien c'est lui qui est aveugle, qui a la vue trop basse pour voir ce qui ne demande qu'à être vu. Ou bien c'est l'œuvre elle-même qui n'a rien à montrer, rien de plus que cette transparence et cette aimable linéarité qui la caractérisent. Et qui du coup pâtit, sa place, son importance et son statut se trouvant soudain remis en question.

Comme je l'ai déjà fait comprendre, la poésie de Marot me paraît pouvoir générer un autre discours. Sa transparence ne se traverse pas. Elle pose au contraire un problème de lecture extrêmement difficile à résoudre—aussi difficile, en son genre, et plus problématique, que celui constitué par l'admirable densité du style scévien. Elle est en effet, comme cette perfection secrète et fragile qui informe les rondeaux de Charles d'Orléans ("Que pensé je? dictes le moy / Adevinez je vous en prie"),[6] non pas vide ou absence, donnée négative et déserte, irrémédiable manque: mais bien au contraire présence, indice positif et parlant, plénitude conquise, silence habité: marque, pour tout dire, d'une liberté. Ce que donc il s'agit de lire dans cette transparence, c'est ce qu'elle a justement pour fonction d'occulter: les raisons esthétiques et/ou idéologiques qui la font être, le cheminement créateur, l'*epistémè*, la poétique qui la sous-tendent. Ce que donc il s'agit de lui faire dire, c'est le non-dit qui la structure et qui la fonde. Non-dit dont l'épître X, entre toutes précieuses, nous donne une idée. Car la prétérition anaphorique par laquelle elle commence n'a pas seulement valeur ornementale. Cette fleur de rhétorique, que Marot utilise ailleurs,[7] est ici figure du refus: refus d'une présence que l'on écarte mais qui, par sa dénégation même, continue d'exister; d'un ensemble de discours possibles qui, bien qu'absents, participent activement à l'élaboration du sens. Elle fait ironiquement songer à certains sonnets du début des *Regrets*, la série de ses "Je ne t'escry" trouvant un écho dans les "Je ne veux" de Du Bellay. Et ce que, comme les "Je ne veux" du rival de Ronsard, les "Je ne t'escry" du futur "Rat pelé" nous énoncent, c'est une volonté proclamée de prendre ses distances, de se situer par rapport à un modèle menaçant, à une tradition dont on ne veut plus. Le ton primesautier adopté par le poète, sa démarche apparemment inconséquente, sa feinte naïveté, le sourire complice qu'il adresse à son correspondant, ne sauraient ici épuiser notre lecture: ni même le fait, souvent noté, que les quinze premiers vers de l'épître renferment des allusions aujourd'hui encore transparentes à certains événements de caractère personnel ou public. L'essentiel, cette fois, est ailleurs: dans la prise de conscience qu'à travers la série de ses prétéritions le poète désigne nommément, l'un après l'autre, tous les grands thèmes du répertoire poétique du temps, tous les "sujets" traditionnels que lui-même, imitant en cela ses maîtres les Grands Rhétoriqueurs, a jusqu'à présent traités: l'amour, la guerre, la fortune, les abus du monde, Dieu et la religion, les Dames de Paris.[8] Et que, ce faisant, il désigne du même coup, indirectement, les *genres* dans lesquels ces sujets se cultivent traditionnellement, les règles et les conventions qui les régissent, le code et les contraintes formelles qui président à leur élaboration. Par quoi prend soudain tout son sens le mécanisme vite prévisible de la répétition, la rigidité parfaite des six premiers couples de rimes plates, la reprise insistante et monotone des mêmes formes verbales, l'alternance des pronoms personnels Je/Tu, l'assujettissement obséquieux des structures grammaticales à la structure métrique, celle-ci régnant en maîtresse absolue, chaque unité syntaxique remplissant exactement, sans en déborder, le moule étroit du décasyllabe, l'absence d'enjambement qui en résulte donnant toute sa force au jeu contraignant des rimes, et faisant d'autant mieux ressortir celui, rythmique, des parallélismes binaires qui occupent l'espace situé après la césure du quatrième pied. On ne saurait, je crois, souligner avec plus d'éloquence l'importance accordée aux considérations formelles, la prééminence que le "facteur" leur accorde traditionnellement dans l'écriture du poème, la façon, aurait déjà pu dire Marot, dont la rime enchaîne la raison, asservit à soi les mots, s'impose finalement comme la raison de la pensée. Si bien qu'au terme de cette analyse, le lecteur se trouve confronté à la possibilité d'une double interprétation. D'un côté, et à un premier niveau, Marot, dont l'imagination a été mise en branle par les hasards de l'homophonie (son ami s'appelle *Lyon* Jamet) et aussi par les particularités de sa situation (il est accusé d'avoir "Mangé le lard et la chair toute crue"), utilise une vieille fable d'Esope pour faire comprendre à cet ami qu'il est en prison et que toute aide extérieure serait en l'occurrence la bienvenue. De l'autre, et à un second niveau, à un niveau cette fois *allégorique* et non plus *littéral*, le poète met à profit sa situation et la thématique dont elle est porteuse—la prison, le désir de liberté—pour justement se situer par rapport à la tradition, aux conventions et aux pratiques d'écriture de son temps. Ce qu'il évoque ainsi dans la première partie de son épître, ce qu'il nomme et refuse en même temps, ce qu'il *représente* métaphoriquement, c'est en somme son Châtelet poétique, une véritable *prison formelle* dont son discours est en train, sous nos yeux, de se libérer.

Déjà, je crois, suffisamment justifiée en soi par l'éloquente juxtaposition des structures antithétiques qui composent le poème et le divisent, l'une résolument rigide, contraignante et close, l'autre allègrement, spirituellement souple et ouverte, cette lecture allégorique trouve une justification supplémentaire dans le "Rondeau parfaict" dont Marot régale ses amis "apres sa delivrance." Ce rondeau offre d'abord l'étrange particularité d'être le seul de son espèce. Et ceci non seulement dans l'œuvre de Marot lui-même, mais aussi bien dans toutes celles de ses prédécesseurs et des maîtres qu'il se reconnaît. Aucun des *Arts de seconde rhétorique* que j'ai pu consulter—ceux, par exemple, que Langlois a rassemblés dans son *Recueil*—ne signale son existence. P. Fabri, pourtant très représentatif de ce qui se pratique alors dans ce domaine, n'en souffle mot. Seul, naturellement, Thomas Sebillet en dit quelque chose. Et ce quelque chose vient tout entier de Marot. Il a beau affirmer que "ce Rondeau estoit estimé souverain entre lés anciens"—et pour cette raison, dit-il, "appelé parfait" —, nous inviter à en "essayer" la forme "en reverence de l'antiquité," le seul exemple qu'il nous en propose est justement celui qui nous occupe ici:[9]

> *En liberté maintenant me pourmaine,*
> *Mais en prison pour tant je fuz cloué.*
> *Voylà comment Fortune me demaine!*
> *C'est bien & mal. Dieu soit de tout loué.*
>
> Les envieux ont dit que de Noé
> N'en sortirois; que la Mort les emmaine!
> Maulgré leurs dentz, le neud est desnoué.
> *En liberté maintenant me pourmaine.*
>
> Pourtant, si j'ay fasché la Court Rommaine,
> Entre meschans ne fuz oncq alloué.

Des bien famez j'ay hanté le dommaine;
Mais en prison pourtant je fuz cloué.

Car aussi tost que fuz desavoué
De celle là qui me fut tant humaine,
Bien tost apres à sainct Pris fut voué.
Voylà comment Fortune me demaine.

J'eus à Paris prison fort inhumaine;
A Chartres fuz doulcement encloué.
Maintenant voys où mon plaisir me maine;
C'est bien & mal. Dieu soit de tout loué.

Au fort, Amys, c'est à vous bien joué
Quand vostre main hors du parc me ramaine.
Escript et faict d'ung cueur bien enjoué
Le premier jour de la verte Sepmaine
En liberté.

Autre particularité, non moins troublante, ce rondeau est décrit par Sebillet d'une façon qui ne correspond pas exactement au modèle qu'il nous propose. On lit en effet dans l'*Art poétique françoys* que ce type de rondeau "admet autant de coupletz qu'il y a de vers au premier couplet"; que, par ailleurs, "à la fin de chaque couplet suivant son ordre se répéte un vers du premier couplet l'un aprés l'autre"; et que, pour finir, "la reprise de cestuy [i.e. vers du premier couplet] n'est pas abondante hors du couplet comme les autres," mais que, au contraire, "le vers repris est du nombre des constituants du couplet" (ibid., p. 128). Or il est clair, à comparer le rondeau à sa description, que Sebillet n'a saisi qu'une partie du jeu formel auquel se livre Marot. S'il a bien vu que les quatre vers constituant le premier quatrain sont successivement repris à la fin de chacun des quatre quatrains qui suivent, et intégrés, non ajoutés, à la structure de ces derniers, en revanche il ne dit rien, sans doute parce qu'il ne sait qu'en dire, ni de la présence, apparemment en surnombre, du sixième quatrain, ni du rentrement sur lequel ce dernier se termine. Loin, comme Sebillet l'affirme, d'admettre "autant de coupletz qu'il y a de vers au premier couplet," ce rondeau admet en fait "autant de coupletz qu'il y a de vers au premier couplet," *plus un.*

Somme toute, à prendre conscience et de la singularité de ce rondeau, et de l'impuissance évidente à laquelle il réduit Sebillet, le lecteur, amusé, finit par se demander en quoi ce rondeau peut bien être *parfaict.* Voici, en fait, un rondeau qui n'est pas un rondeau; un rondeau qui n'obéit à aucune des lois du genre; un rondeau qui ne ressemble à aucun rondeau connu. Au mieux, une variante de rondeau, un rondeau éloigné, à la mode de Bretagne, inventé par Marot pour les besoins de la cause, pour fêter dignement sa liberté recouvrée. Mais en tout cas, pas un rondeau parfait. L'ironie, donc, est patente. A moins que peut-être il ne faille lire: "Rondeau à ses Amys, *parfaict* (c'est-à-dire *complété*) apres sa delivrance"? Lecture qui, si elle est moins immédiate et aussi moins plausible que la lecture tradition-nelle de Sebillet (ce rondeau est dit "parfaict" parce que les Anciens l'esti-maient "souverain" plus que nul autre), a cependant pour elle l'indiscuta-ble mérite de suggérer que la "perfection" du dit rondeau réside justement dans son imperfection même, c'est-à-dire dans le fait qu'il a été "complété" d'un sixième quatrain surnuméraire à rentrement. La règle du jeu, inventée, semble-t-il en l'occurrence, par le poète lui-même, indique en effet que le poème devrait en bonne logique se clore à la fin du cinquième quatrain, puisque c'est précisément à cet endroit-là que le premier quatrain, épuisé, n'est plus susceptible de fournir un autre vers de reprise. C'est cette logique évidente qui fait dire à Sebillet, d'ailleurs au mépris de toute évidence, que ce genre de rondeau "admet autant de couplets qu'il y a de vers au premier couplet." Et si, contre la logique qu'il a lui-même instituée, contre la règle qui, clairement, gouverne sa structure et son fonctionnement, le poème s'ajoute un quatrain supplémentaire, un quatrain dont le rentrement est justement constitué par l'expression "en liberté," c'est bien évidemment parce que cette fois encore, comme dans l'"Epistre à son amy Lyon," toute la stratégie du poète consiste en définitive à libérer sous nos yeux son discours de la prison formelle dans laquelle il l'avait d'abord enfermé. Rondeau au total "parfaict," puisque sa forme même, entre toutes impar-faite, exprime métaphoriquement et parfaitement son thème—*réfléchit* parfaitement ce dernier.

C'est bien en tout cas quand on l'envisage dans cette perspective résolu-ment réflexive que l'opposition si nettement établie entre les deux parties de l'épître X prend son sens le plus plein. Cette opposition est d'abord et bien évidemment celle de deux poétiques. La première d'entre elles est indiscutablement la poétique des Grand Rhétoriqueurs, celle dont Marot est l'héritier. Elle porte, entre autres, le nom du père. C'est elle qui a fait le Marot de *L'Adolescence clementine*, celui de la "Premiere Eglogue," du "Temple de Cupido," des rondeaux, des ballades et de "L'Espitre du Des-pourveu." A cette poétique, Marot certes doit beaucoup. Il ne cessera pas, d'ailleurs, de proclamer ses dettes, de saluer bien haut le talent de ceux qui l'ont formé. Mais nous savons bien que ce genre de bienfait est toujours un fardeau. Marot a beau se vouloir bon fils et bon disciple, "exempt d'ingra-titude," vite il regimbe et se sent à l'étroit. Dès 1518-19, par exemple, la fameuse "Petite Epistre au Roy" atteste en lui sinon l'existence d'un ma-laise à tout le moins celle d'une volonté de prendre ses distances, de ne pas être dupe. Le poète renchérit. Et du coup l'équivoque n'existe pas seulement dans les jeux laborieux de la rime, elle est aussi dans le ton même de l'épître, dans l'attitude mi-complice mi-réticente qui informe ces jeux. De même, la non moins fameuse "Deploration sur le trespas de feu messire Florimond Robertet," qui date, elle, de 1527, peut aussi, comme l'a bien vu Mario Richter,[10] s'interpréter dans un sens contestataire et au fond subversif. Tout en adhérant extérieurement aux conventions du genre, Marot en métamorphose totalement, de l'intérieur et sans le dire, la signification sociale et la portée. Rien d'étonnant, donc, à ce que nous lisions finalement dans l'épître X une volonté d'échapper, un désir de libération cette fois clairement formulé.

La seconde de ces poétiques, que Marot nous présente essentiellement par l'intermédiaire de la fable d'Esope, entretient avec la première des relations tout à la fois directes et ambiguës. Motivée comme nous l'avons dit par un désir de libération, elle est avant tout l'antithèse de l'autre, son *à rebours*. Il s'agit, pour être, d'être d'abord tout ce que l'autre n'est pas. La poétique traditionnelle est prison, lieu d'une parole contrainte et figée dans le moule artificiel de l'*écrit*. La nouvelle poétique sera donc vécue comme le lieu par excellence de la parole vivante et libre: d'une parole proprement *dégelée* et qui, se jouant des contraintes, fuyant notamment les artifices de l'écrit, est présence immédiate, expression authentique, directe et spontanée du moi. Nous sommes évidemment ici en pays de connaissance, au cœur même de cette "illusion logocentrique," de cette "métaphysique de la présence" qui, selon Derrida, caractérisent la pensée humaniste occidentale. Tout, à vrai dire, y est exactement à sa place. L'écriture y est clairement perçue comme extériorité artificielle et "dangereux supplément." Le *dit* est au contraire valorisé, considéré comme seul moyen d'accès à la vérité de l'être et du sens. Il serait facile de déconstruire cet utopique échafaudage, le dit restant pour cause prisonnier de l'écrit, le désir de présence se médiatisant, se laissant prendre en charge par un discours aussi vieux que le monde,[11] retombant du même coup dans les artifices et les conventions qu'il cherchait à fuir. Mieux vaut, je crois, épousant la "logique" du texte et jouant son jeu, faire remarquer que ce désir de présence et de liberté aboutit pratiquement, dans ses moments de plus grande intensité, à une déstructuration totale du vers, à un effacement si radical de la rime que le lecteur se voit finalement, comme Jourdain, contraint d'avouer sa perplexité. S'il est patent que tout ce qui n'est point vers est prose et, inversement, que tout ce qui n'est point prose est vers, dans quelle catégorie ranger ce discours hybride et fabuleux? Il ne saurait être prose, puisque la rime n'y est pas toujours sacrifiée, puisqu'elle continue de régner dans la plupart des cas, imposant son rythme à la diction intérieure, riche et équivoque à souhait:

> Auquel a dit: tays toy, Lyon lié,
> Par moy seras maintenant deslié;
> Tu le vaulx bien, car le cueur joly as;
> Bien y parus, quand tu me deslias.
> Secouru m'as fort Lyonneusement;
> Ors secouru seras Rateusement.
>
> (vv. 41-46)

Inversement, il ne saurait non plus être vers puisque, soudain escamotée, la rime disparaît, et que, proprement désarticulée, la structure métrique n'arrive plus cette fois à s'imposer, à morceler et à scander la diction, la phrase ainsi libérée n'obéissant plus qu'aux seules exigences, toutes prosaïques, de la syntaxe, glissant, courant, sautant allègrement d'un décasyllabe à l'autre par une série concertée d'enjambements. Le conte, ici, n'est plus véritablement "rimassé." Il se fait littéralement, pour utiliser le langage des Arts de seconde rhétorique contemporains, *à bâtons rompus*:[12]

> Cestuy Lyon, plus fort qu'ung vieulx Verrat,
> Veit une fois que le Rat ne sçavoit
> Sortir d'ung lieu, pour autant qu'il avoit
> Mangé le lard & la chair toute crue;
>
> (vv. 16-20)
>
> Et, en ostant son bonnet de la teste,
> A mercié mille fois la grand Beste,
> Jurant le Dieu des Souriz et des Ratz
> Qu'il luy rendroit. Maintenant tu verras
> Le bon du compte. Il advint d'aventure
> Que le Lyon . . .
>
> (vv. 25-30)
>
> Lors sire Rat va commencer à mordre
> Ce gros lien; vray est qu'il y songea
> Assez long temps; mais il le vous rongea
> Souvent & tant qu'à la parfin tout rompt;
>
> (vv. 62-65)

Marot fait non seulement porter le chapeau de la rime à des éléments grammaticaux qui bien évidemment ne s'en accommodent pas, mais il s'ingénie en outre, par une habile disposition des articulations logiques de son récit, à briser systématiquement les couples de rimes plates.[13] De telle sorte que, aussi bien par son insistance que par la variété des moyens qu'il met en œuvre, ce jeu en apparence espiègle et sans conséquence devient jeu subversif.[14] Car remettre ainsi en question la suprématie et le rôle de la rime n'est pas, dans le contexte où opère Marot, un geste innocent. La poésie, on le sait, ne jouit pas à l'époque d'un statut clairement défini. Elle n'a pas encore su, à proprement parler, s'imposer dans sa différence, se faire reconnaître par les autres *artes sermocinales*. Elle n'a rien encore du langage des dieux. Comme en témoignent les *Arts*, les *Regles* et autres *Instructifs* du temps,[15] elle reste entièrement tributaire de la rhétorique. Baptisée en fait "Rhétorique seconde," "vulgaire," "rithmique" ou encore "metrifiée," elle ne se distingue au fond de cette dernière que par les contraintes métriques, le jeu des assonances et des rimes.[16] S'attaquer à ces contraintes, prendre ainsi la rime, et lui tordre son cou, c'est donc ni plus ni moins disposer de tout ce qui, *stricto sensu*, constitue alors l'être même du langage poétique. C'est, sous couvert de libérer ce dernier, de le rendre à la présence et à la vie, porter atteinte à son existence même.

> "Ex abundantia enim cordis os loquitur."
> Matthieu (XII, 34)

Ce qu'il s'agit par conséquent maintenant d'interroger, c'est ce paradoxe d'un poète qui semble trouver dans la prose l'instrument rêvé de sa poétique; d'un poète qui, très certainement autant qu'un autre soucieux de s'affirmer, de faire "style à part, sens à part, œuvre à part," tire et son style, et son sens et son œuvre non pas, comme après lui Ronsard, vers le "brave" et le "haut" mais, contrairement à toute attente, vers le médiocre et le bas, vers cette "commune maniere de parler" que Du Bellay lui reproche amèrement dans sa *Deffence*; d'un poète d'ailleurs suffisamment conscient du caractère paradoxal de son entreprise, de l'insurmontable contradiction qu'elle renferme, pour nous dire lui-même, dans l'un de ses rondeaux (XXI), qu'il "RIME EN PROSE (& peult estre en raison)" (IV, 88). D'où la question qui doit maintenant nous retenir: pourquoi, quand on se veut poète, et bon poète, "rimer en prose"? quelle raison Marot peut-il bien avoir de vouloir ainsi dépouiller son langage de ses ornements les plus visibles et les plus rares, de toutes ces "fleurs" et "couleurs" de riche rhétorique dont les poètes embellissent généralement le leur? quel motif peut ainsi le pousser à vouloir libérer son discours, son "stille mesuré," de toutes ces contraintes sonores et formelles qui en assurent justement la mesure, qui seules le distinguent en définitive de la "commune maniere de parler"?

Il est je crois possible de trouver un premier élément de réponse à cette question dans la *persona* même du poète, c'est-à-dire d'invoquer le topos, entre tous rhétorique, de l'humilité et de la modestie. En ce sens aussi, l'épître X est paradigme. Marot constamment prend la pose du Rat. Fréquentant les Grands, et nourri à leur table, il se fait petit ("le plus petit de tous," Cantique VI, v. 5, III, 295), il ne cesse de rappeler sa roture et son insuffisance, de se dire "plomb bas & humile" auprès d'"argent mieux resonnant." Sa muse est naturellement "foible" et "debile," sa plume "lourde, essorée & rustique," son œuvre "grossiere, mal faicte & mal escripte."[17] Rien d'étonnant donc à ce que le style lui-même trahisse ses origines, qu'il soit comme l'homme "dur," "rude" et "trop mince."[18] Marot souligne d'ailleurs lui-même, dans son épître "Au Reverendissime Cardinal de Lorraine," le caractère inévitable de ce déterminisme. Petite clochette a beau s'agiter, vouloir être la cymbale du monde, elle ne saurait produire "grand son":

> L'Homme qui est en plusieurs sortes bas,
> Bas de stature et de joye & d'esbas,
> Bas de sçavoir, en bas degré nourry,
> Et bas de biens, dont il est bien marry,
> Prince tresnoble, à vostre advis, comment
> Vous pourroit il saluer haultement?
> Fort luy seroit: *car petite Clochette*
> *A beau branler, avant que ung haut son ne jecte.*
> Puis qu'il n'a donc que humble & basse value,
> Par ung bas style humblement vous salue.
> (Epître XV, v. 1-10, I, 144)

Si convention il y a—et il y a convention—, Marot s'y établit et y évolue avec une telle aisance qu'il finit par faire sien ce langage emprunté. Sa modestie paraît d'autant plus authentique qu'elle se double en lui d'un sens aigu de sa valeur. L'essentiel pour ce qui le concerne n'est point, au fond, de flatter les Grands, il est, comme pour Horace, de bien se connaître, de savoir ce dont on est capable, de choisir sa matière et son sujet en fonction de ses moyens: *parvum parva decent*. Quoi qu'en pense l'oreille, Marot sait qu'il n'est pas Maro. Mais cette constatation ne l'empêche pas de se situer cent coudées au-dessus de ces "Rymasseurs nouveaux" qui le jalousent, ou de ces "beaulx Retoriqueurs" et autres "gentils veaux" dont on lui attribue à tort les "Ouvrages mal lymés."[19] "Bas" sans doute, mais "Poete de Roy," dispensateur d'immortalité et bon artisan du vers. "Petit" certainement, et d'un génie limité, mais grand en ceci qu'il se sait petit, qu'il a conscience de ses limites, et qu'il s'y tient. Une même sagesse mesure la vie et la poésie, l'utopie de Marot: "Plus hault qu'on n'est ne poinct vouloir actaindre."[20] Son œuvre est, en ce sens, tout entière illustration, parabole et figure du "Riche en pauvreté"; amplification concertée de la devise de notre "Homere gregeois," Jean Lemaire: "DE PEU ASSEZ ha cil qui se contente; / De prou n'a riens celluy qui n'est content."[21]

Pour exemplaire qu'elle soit, cette volonté au fond très "humaniste" et très "classique" de ne pas être dupe, de se voir tel qu'on est, de s'estimer à son juste prix, ne me paraît cependant fournir qu'une partie de la réponse que nous cherchons. L'essentiel, je crois, est ailleurs. Comme le suggère en effet fortement l'épître X, le choix du "bas style," de la "rime en prose," n'est pas seulement chez Marot fruit de la connaissance de soi. Il est aussi, à l'égard du langage, celui d'une méfiance qui sourdement affleure, d'un malaise qui n'ose ou ne sait dire son nom. Il participe moins, en fait, d'un désir "temperé" et somme toute naturel de poser *sa* voix, de chanter *sa* partie—et non pas celle d'un autre—, que d'une attitude fondamentalement ironique et réticente envers tout ce qui est "parolle fardée," "hault stile," ou "grande levée / De Rhetorique."[22] L'équation, pour Marot, va de soi. Elle a la force de l'évidence, l'incontournable poids de la donnée. La hauteur est nécessairement artifice et "enflure," la "rime" antithèse obligée du "cœur" ou de la "raison."[23] Quand le sujet traité requiert "plus hault stile," ce dernier n'est jamais immédiatement assumé, accueilli, développé dans le présent de l'écriture. Il est au contraire toujours révoqué et tenu à distance, toujours situé soit dans un espace clairement parodique, soit dans un futur irréel ou hypothétique.[24] C'est que Dame Rhétorique est aux yeux de Marot décidément suspecte. Outil de Rhadamante, arme de Folle Amour, elle est "Diable cornu en forme d'un bel Ange," fauteur de mensonge, d'erreur et d'illusion, "faincte doulceur," obstacle fatal à la communication idéale, à la parfaite communion que Marot rêve d'établir entre son lecteur et lui.[25] Ce dernier ne cesse d'ailleurs de le répéter dans son œuvre. Le langage n'existe à ses yeux que pour exprimer directement le moi, que pour être l'être du moi. Hors de cette fonction, il n'a point à proprement parler de légitime raison d'être. Il compte seulement dans la mesure où il rend immédiatement *présents* le "cœur" ou le "vouloir," l'être le plus authentique et le plus intime du sujet parlant. Il est moralement pernicieux et dangereux chaque fois qu'il introduit une béance entre lui et sa source vivante, chaque fois qu'il revendique une certaine autonomie, qu'il entend se déployer suivant ses propres lois, non suivant celles du sujet en qui seul il se fonde. Ce que par exemple le poète, entre autres choses, reproche à l'Eglise romaine, la "grande Symmonne," c'est de chanter "jour & nuict maintes choses / Qui ne sont pas dedans son cœur encloses." C'est de "farder" son "doulx langaige" encore plus lourdement qu'elle ne farde son visage. Marot reconnaît au contraire sa déesse "la Belle Christine" à la rareté, à la densité et à l'efficacité du sien. Cette dernière a l'art d'exprimer l'essentiel en peu de mots. Elle sait, elle, donner au langage l'épaisseur de l'être, se mettre tout entière en lui, devenir, en l'investissant, l'autre qu'elle parle. Le peu qu'elle dit n'est pas alors à proprement parler langage, mais action. Ce peu suffit à communiquer irrésistiblement la liberté qui le constitue. Et c'est alors le langage même du poète qui se fait soudain lui aussi liberté, métamorphosé qu'il est par la grâce de la Parole évangélique:

Tant chemina la belle qu'elle vint
Au fleuve Loyre, où des fois plus de vingt
Jecta son œil sur moy la premiere,
Car mes gros yeulx n'avoient propre lumiere
Pour regarder les siens premierement;
S'approche pres & me dit seullement:
Resveille toy, il en est temps, amy;
Tu as par trop en tenebres dormy!
Resveille toy! A sy peu de parler
Je la congneuz, et si sentoys aller
Hors de mon cœur une pesante charge
De griefz tourmentz, dont me trouviz au large
Et en repos de franche liberté,
Où paravant n'avoys jamais esté.[26]

On voit du coup, tant cet exemple est éclairant, en quoi cette conception éthique et substantialiste du langage ne peut que poser à Marot, à Marot le poète et "l'enfant d'Apollo," des problèmes insurmontables. Si elle permet d'attacher une signification particulièrement riche à toute forme de dialogue et de correspondance, si elle constitue en l'occurrence un cadre idéal au déploiement de l'épître personnelle, elle paraît en revanche, et a priori, extrêmement peu propice à l'épanouissement d'un discours proprement poétique, au moins au sens où vaguement aujourd'hui nous entendons ce terme. En admettant qu'il soit à la limite possible de concevoir et d'accepter comme viable l'idée d'une poésie fondée sur une recherche de la simplicité, de la sincérité et du dépouillement, d'une poésie refusant aussi bien toute contrainte sonore que formelle, toute artificialité rhétorique, d'une poésie visant au fond, par le biais de ses refus, à l'invention d'un nouveau langage—et c'est je crois précisément dans cette perspective simultanée d'une libération et d'une création qu'il conviendrait d'interpréter les fameux "Coq-à-l'âne"—, que dire alors d'une poésie qui, informée et comme structurée par une sourde méfiance à l'égard du langage, perpétuellement travaillée par le désir du "sy peu de parler," subrepticement tend au silence comme à sa propre fin? Car, au-delà de toutes ces conventions qui le figent et l'aliènent du sujet, le rendent impropre à l'expression du vécu personnel, c'est bien en définitive de soi que, chez Marot, le langage cherche à se libérer.

Cette entreprise bien évidemment chimérique et irréalisable rend compte, à mon sens, non seulement du paradoxe de la "rime en prose," mais encore de toutes ces déclarations sibyllines faites par Marot regardant l'absolue priorité du "cœur" sur le langage. Si en effet ce dernier n'a pour seule fonction légitime que de communiquer immédiatement la vérité de l'être, et sa présence, s'il n'existe que pour et dans cet acte même, et s'y épuise tout entier, s'il est en un mot toujours perçu comme moyen, et non comme fin, il est alors inévitable qu'une fois atteinte cette fin même ne le condamne, en quelque sorte, à l'insignifiance et à l'oubli. Il n'était là, après tout, que comme un pis-aller. Ayant accompli sa tâche, il devient superflu. Peut-être même eût-il mieux valu se passer de ses services. Car décidément la vraie vie est ailleurs. Seul le "vouloir" importe, ne cesse de répéter Marot à ses amis poètes. Et je l'"estime" bien davantage que vos "escriptz," votre "Raison," votre "Rime."[27] Lui seul les "faict valoir." D'un poème à l'autre, la permanence du thème est telle, et celle du vocabulaire dans lequel ce thème s'inscrit, que le lecteur finit par y voir plus qu'un badinage de convenance. Comme à son habitude, Marot parle du cœur. Comme par exemple à son ami Vignals, Toulousain:

> Quand Dieu m'auroit aussi bien presenté
> Le bon loysir et l'entiere santé
> Que *le vouloir*, ta Response alongée
> Seroit du tiers, et beaucoup mieulx songée;
> Ce neantmoins (Vignals) je pense bien
> Que tu congnois que *le souverain bien*
> *De l'amityé ne gist en longues Lettres,*
> *En motz exquis, en grand nombre de Mettres,*
> *En riche Rime, ou belle invention,*
> *Ains en bon cueur et vraye intention . . .*
> (Epître XXIX, v. 1-10, I, 180)

Ou encore à Anne et à Renée de Parthenay. "Ce Cueur là," leur dit-il, "c'est ma richesse vraye"; "C'est le tresor le meilleur de mon Coffre"; "Le demeurant n'est rien où je me fonde."[28] Déclarations qu'il convient certes de replacer dans leur contexte érotique conventionnel, et qu'il faut se garder de trop solliciter—dans chacun de ces deux derniers cas, Marot fait don de son cœur à une Dame—, mais dont cependant la terminologie, dans sa technicité même, ne saurait passer inaperçue. Car si le "cueur" est bien évidemment ici métaphore courtoise (et souffrante) de l'Amant, il est aussi et surtout *pectus*, siège de l'inspiration du Poète, lieu par excellence de la *copia*, de la plénitude et de l'authenticité du discours. De la même façon, le "vouloir," dont Marot parle à ses amis, est *vis mentis*, énergie et clarté de la pensée s'énonçant dans les mots. Et le "coffre" auquel il fait allusion ne peut alors être que le *thesaurus* de Quintilien et de la rhétorique classique, le "magasin des mots et des figures" dont parle Montaigne en son chapitre *Sur des vers de Virgile*.[29] Ce que donc Marot, à travers son badinage poétique, finalement nous redit, ce que, dans un langage somme toute précis, il reprend à son compte, c'est le vieux thème platonicien de la parole comme présence—de cette parole "vivante et ani-

mée" dont, nous dit Phèdre, "le discours écrit n'est qu'un simulacre."
C'est l'idée que tout ce qui dans le langage est rhétorique, arrangement,
ornement, psychagogie, ne saurait qu'être nuisible à l'irruption de cette
présence. C'est au fond que, dans son refus de l'artifice et sa volonté
d'effacement, son désir d'être non seulement *speculum animi*, "miroir
trespur" de l'âme de son auteur,[30] mais encore cette âme même actualisée
et communiquée à autrui, d'être non pas signe opaque et interposé, présence substitutive, moyen de représenter, mais *res*, chose elle-même, être
et matière, vie, souffle et mouvement, la parole utopique dont il rêve
débouche, étrangement, sur le silence.

On doit bien sûr lire cette "rhétorique de la présence"—je dirais plutôt,
en l'occurrence, cette "contre-rhétorique"—dans sa dimension historique
et collective. Comme l'ont en effet déjà et par avance montré Michel Jeanneret et Terence Cave, le rêve de Marot est celui d'une époque.[31] La *Moria*
d'Erasme reprend elle aussi le vieux mythe platonicien de l'invention
blâmable de l'écriture. Et elle évoque cet Age d'or où la parole n'avait
encore pour seule fonction que de communiquer l'immédiateté de l'être et
du sens.[32] A l'autre bout du siècle, Montaigne découvre son esthétique
idéale dans une "naturalisation de l'art." Son modèle est Socrate, celui qui
n'écrit pas. Parfaitement mimétique, son langage se veut "consubstantiel"
au vécu, il se moule étroitement sur lui pour le reproduire. Mais cette
lecture est, je crois, insuffisante. Il faut aussi, pour ce qui concerne une
juste compréhension de l'attitude de Marot face au langage, dépasser cette
problématique platonicienne, aujourd'hui très en vogue, de l'*écrit* et du
dit, en l'intégrant dans un radicalisme d'origine essentiellement mystique
et religieuse. Car, comme le montrent les textes jusqu'à présent cités, il
ne suffit certainement pas de dire que, parce qu'il croit au dit comme
instrument de la présence, Marot privilégie constamment celui-ci par
rapport à l'écrit. Le principe premier de sa poétique, son but ultime—et
peut-être inconscient, inavoué—semble bien plutôt être, à la limite, de
contourner le langage: non seulement de *le* libérer, mais surtout de *se libérer de lui*. Si, dans son absence de fard et d'artifice, la prose vaut mieux
que la rime, si, par la spontanéité de son jaillissement, le dit l'emporte sur
l'écrit, la parole reste cependant, aux yeux de Marot, trop imparfaite et
trop déchue pour vraiment, en soi, le satisfaire. Il y a toujours en lui,
au-delà de ce dit qu'il préfère, un "sy peu de parler" qu'il ne pourra jamais
atteindre, qui lui est d'ailleurs pratiquement interdit—il est Poète, il faut
qu'il parle—, mais vers lequel cependant obscurément il tend; un désir très
augustinien de présence et de communication en dehors, en-deçà ou au-
delà de tout langage.

Comme je viens de le suggérer, ce désir s'ancre bien évidemment dans le religieux. Il participe d'une attitude et d'une mentalité qu'on peut sans errer qualifier de mystique. Cette attitude et cette mentalité sont, à mon sens, celles de ce groupe d'Evangéliques qui, précisément dans les années où Marot compose, gravite d'abord autour de Guillaume Briçonnet, puis de Marguerite de Navarre. Ce groupe—j'ai encore récemment essayé de le montrer[33]—manifeste une méfiance profonde, un scepticisme radical à l'égard de tout ce qui, en l'homme, est présomption, prétention à la possession et à l'expression de la vérité. Il ne cesse, pour anéantir en lui le "Cuyder" et le précipiter au bas du cheval d'orgueil, de lui mettre devant les yeux l'impuissance de sa raison, la vanité et l'imperfection de son langage. La parole a beau "mener le jeu" du monde, elle n'étreint que du vent. Elle est caquet, babil, *vaniloquium*. L'essentiel, c'est-à-dire l'Etre, et sa Présence, est à jamais hors de sa portée, proprement indicible, inattingible, incompréhensible. C'est pourquoi, comme le dit, dans son *Cymbalum*, Bonaventure des Périers, à propos d'ailleurs de la querelle Marot-Sagon, il vaut beaucoup mieux "prendre garde à l'utile silence de vérité" que "s'amuser à la vaine parolle de mensonge" (p. 26). Double équation qui, ainsi posée, a force de Loi. Et qui peut encore s'exprimer de la façon suivante: "Dieu et sa parolle sont tout et l'homme et sa parolle ne sont rien."[34] Seule la Parole de Dieu est proprement parole. Celle de l'homme n'est pas parole, sinon en la Parole de Dieu. Le pire qui puisse donc se produire, rappelle Lefèvre d'Etaples en tête de sa traduction française des *Evangiles*,[35] est de "mesler la parolle de l'homme avec la parolle de dieu, pour parolle de dieu." Parallèlement, et par voie de conséquence, le mieux pour l'homme est d'être ce rien qu'il est, c'est-à-dire de s'effacer et de se taire, de laisser Dieu, le Tout, parler en lui. *Nam silentium dicit, et tacet voces:*[36] comme la théologie de saint Paul et celle du pseudo-Denys, l'Evangélisme est "Maître de silence," *magister silentii*. Et comme celui de Lefèvre d'Etaples, le cheminement spirituel de Marguerite de Navarre, aussi bien dans son *Oraison à nostre seigneur Jesus Christ* que dans son *Miroir de l'ame pecheresse*, aboutit au double et complémentaire aveu de l'inadéquation du discours et de la nécessité du silence. Pourquoi la créature essayerait-elle de "parler oultre," de commenter un mystère dont lui-même l'Apôtre s'est tu? Faire en soi l'expérience de l'Etre, être envahi par sa Présence, c'est du même coup perdre définitivement non seulement le pouvoir, mais encore le désir de dire, c'est à jamais prendre conscience de l'inanité de tout langage humain.[37] Marguerite le dit à la fin de son *Oraison*:[38] "Mon long parler, trop inutil, mal sonne. / En ceste Foy ferme et seure je me taiz; / Et pour penser, le parler j'abandonne." Par quoi certain vers de Marot soudain affleure à la mémoire, pour s'y lester d'un sens inattendu. Exemplaire, en ceci que sa structure même symbolise et reflète l'hésitation fondamentale, la tension essentielle à l'œuvre, le paradoxe qui la fonde et qui nourrit sa transparence: "Ceste escripture, où je impose silence" (Epître XXXVIII, v. 80, I, 213). Lorsque Marot parle, c'est au fond toujours en rêvant qu'il vaudrait mieux se taire. La liberté qu'il espère se trouve en dehors des mots. Elle est, dans le silence, la fille de l'Esprit.

NOTES

1. Voir, sur cette question, les solides études de C.A. Mayer: "Le Texte de Marot," *BHR*, 14-15 (1952-53), 314-28 et 71-91; "Les Oeuvres de Clément Marot: l'économie de l'édition critique," *BHR*, 29 (1967), 357-72.
2. J'utilise ici l'édition critique en six volumes de C.A. Mayer: 1) *Les Epîtres* (Univ. of London: The Athlone Press, 1958); 2) *Oeuvres satiriques* (ibid., 1962); 3) *Oeuvres lyriques* (ibid., 1964); 4) *Oeuvres diverses* (ibid., 1966); 5) *Les Epigrammes* (ibid., 1970); 6) *Les Traductions* (Genève: Editions Slatkine, 1980). "Epistre à son amy Lyon," in Vol. I, pp. 127-31; "Rondeau parfaict A ses Amys apres sa delivrance," in Vol. IV, pp. 133-34.
3. Voir à ce sujet mes deux études: "Rabelais et les cloches de Notre-Dame," *Etudes Rabelaisiennes*, 9 (1971), 1-28; et "Les Dates de composition et de publication du *Gargantua*," *Etudes Rabelaisiennes*, 11 (1974), 137-42.
4. Nous possédons ici, pour dater ces deux poèmes, une indication précieuse. On comprendrait en effet que Marot, prudent, omette de les faire figurer dans les éditions *parisiennes* de son *Adolescence*: la Sorbonne n'est pas loin. Mais pourquoi les omettre aussi bien dans l'édition *lyonnaise* donnée par F. Juste le 12 juillet 1533? Cette dernière édition contient, par exemple, le rondeau "En l'eau, en l'eau," trop anti-sorbonnique pour apparaître à Paris, mais apparemment publiable à Lyon. Sur ce rondeau, voir Mayer, IV, 40 et 273.
5. Mayer, I, 95: "Ce sont Oeuvres de jeunesse, Ce sont coups d'essay. Ce n'est (en effect) autre chose qu'un petit jardin que je vous ay cultivé de ce que j'ay peu recouvrer d'arbres, d'herbes & fleurs de mon printemps . . ."
6. Voyez à ce sujet G. Defaux, "Charles d'Orléans ou la poétique du secret: à propos du rondeau XXXIII de l'édition Champion," *Romania*, 93 (1972), 194-243.
7. Par exemple, dans la mordante épître "Aux Dames de Paris," Mayer, II, 80, v. 79-86: "Brief, pour escrire y a bien d'autres choses / Dedans Paris trop longuement encloses. / Tant de Brouillis qu'en justice on tolere, / Je l'escriroys, mais je crains la colere; / L'oysiveté des Prebstres et Cagotz, / Je la diroys, mais garde les Fagotz! / Et des abus dont l'Eglise est fourrée, / J'en parleroys, mais garde la Bourrée!" Le fait que cette épître, composée en juin 1529, trouve apparemment un écho dans l'épître X "A son amy Lyon" (v. 11-12) constitue un indice supplémentaire de la composition relativement tardive de cette dernière.
8. On ne peut en effet s'empêcher de penser, par exemple, au "Temple de Cupido," aux Elégies et aux Chansons (l'Amour), à "L'epistre du Camp d'Attigny" (la Guerre), aux Rondeaux XXIII et XXIV, aux Complaintes I et III (la Fortune), à "L'Enfer" (les Abus du monde), aux Chants royaux I, II et IV, à la Ballade XIII, à "L'Oraison contemplative" et aux "Tristes vers de Philippes Beroalde" (Dieu et la religion). On sait par ailleurs à quel point abondent, dans la poésie des Grands Rhé-

toriqueurs, les "Temples de Mars," les "Haults Sieges d'Amours," les "Labyrinthes de Fortune," les "Abuz du monde," et les "Chappelets des Dames."

9. Thomas Sebillet, *Art Poétique Françoys*, éd. Félix Gaiffe (Paris: E. Cornély et Cie, 1910), pp. 128-29. Sans doute pour mieux dissimuler encore son ignorance, Sebillet ajoute: "Tu en pourras faire d'autres qui ne reprendront en fin de leurs coupletz que lés simples hémistiches dés vers du premier couplet, mais n'en atten de moy exemple, car je te vœil retenir aux specifications de cés exemples plus prolixes que profitables, pource que mon but est de te montrer lés élémens et fondemens de Pöesie le plus clérement et brévement que je pourray." Voire. F. Gaiffe n'en est d'ailleurs nullement inpressionné, qui interroge ("De quels Anciens s'agit-il?") et qui constate: "Nous n'avons rencontré aucune description ni aucun exemple de cette forme de rondeau chez les prédécesseurs de Sebillet . . ."

10. Mario Richter, "L'Evangelismo di Clément Marot: lettura della 'Déploration de Florimond Robertet,'" *BHR*, 35 (1973), 247-58.

11. Le fait est à noter: pour parler à son ami, Marot a recours à une fable d'Esope. Il n'échappe en somme à une tradition que pour en rencontrer une autre. Et s'il se montre par là bon poète, expert en "poetrie," en "science qui aprent à faindre," il souligne cependant, et du même coup, l'impossibilité d'échapper au langage de l'autre, l'impuissance totale du sujet à faire sien le langage qu'il parle. Sur ce concept de "poetrie," voir F. Rigolot, *Poétique et onomastique: l'exemple de la Renaissance* (Genève: Droz, 1977), pp. 50-53.

12. Le vers est en effet, dans les *Arts* de l'époque, fréquemment appelé *baston*. Voyez par exemple le *Recueil d'Arts de seconde rhétorique*, publié par E. Langlois (Paris: Imprimerie Nationale, 1902), p. 4: "Si doiz sçavoir que ung chacun rondel a tout le moins doit contenir cinq *bastons* . . . Oultre pluz, dois sçavoir que aucuns rondeaulx sont doubles, les quelz se font ne plus ne moins de la façon dessusdicte, excepté que l'en double les *bastons* en faisant deux pour ung . . ."

13. Cf. les vers 14-15, 33-34, 61-62, 71-72. Chacun de ces "couplets" est brisé par la présence d'une pause correspondant à une articulation logique de la narration.

14. Je m'écarte ici des conclusions de R. Griffin, pour qui (*Clément Marot and the Inflections of Poetic Voice* [Berkeley: Univ. of California Press, 1974], p. 83) "Subverting of rhyme ending through enjambement does not represent a revolt from strophic constraints toward free form." Je les suis au contraire totalement lorsqu'un peu plus loin (p. 89) il souligne "Marot's apparent inability, or at any rate *his methodological unwillingness, to emprison his thought within the confines of verse lines of any length*." Et lorsqu'il intitule "Formlessness" la troisième partie de son étude.

15. Outre le *Recueil* de Langlois, cité *supra*, on peut mentionner *Le grand & vray art de plaine rethoricque* . . . Compile & compose par tresexpert / scientifique et vray orateur maistre Pierre Fabri (Paris: Denys Janot, 1539). Edition moderne de A. Héron (Rouen: E. Cagniard, 1889-90), en trois volumes.

16. Par exemple, le second livre de Fabri, consacré à "lart de rithmer," est occupé tout entier par une description, à prétentions normatives, d'abord "des differences des rithmes en fin de ligne" (équivoque, léonine, croisée, enchaînée, entrelassée, annexe, couronnée, rétrograde, etc.), puis des différentes formes poétiques pratiquées par les Grands Rhétoriqueurs (lai, virelai, rondeau, bergerette, pastourelle, chapelet, chant royal, ballade, chanson, serventois).

17. Respectivement, IV, 81 (rondeau XIV); I, 179 (épître XXVIII, v. 18); ibid., p. 165 (épître XXII, v. 4 et 7); ibid., p. 105 (épître III, v. 1) et p. 159 (épître XX, v. 116), etc.

18. I, 154 (épître XVIII, v. 55); p. 111 (épître III, v. 138); p. 165 (épître XXII, v. 7).

19. II, 77, satire III (épître "Aux Dames de Paris"), v. 7; et satire II ("Epistre des excuses de Marot"), p. 75, v. 11-12.

20. V, 222. Epigramme CLV ("De soy mesmes"), v. 13.

21. Ibid., p. 248. Epigramme CLXXXVIII ("Sur la devise de Jan Le Maire de Belges, laquelle est: De peu assez"), v. 1-2.

22. Respectivement III, 385 ("Le Balladin & dernier œuvre de maistre Clement Marot," v. 117-18); I, 149 (épître XVI, v. 22-23); II, 81 ("Aux Dames de Paris," v. 101).

23. I, 176 (épître XXV, v. 122); V, 124 (épigramme XXXVI, v. 7-8); I, 182 (épître XXXI, v. 1-4), etc. Je ne puis, ici encore, partager l'opinion de R. Griffin, lequel affirme (p. 92) que "rime" et "raison" sont chez Marot *synonymes*. Il est clair, au contraire, que la *rime* a toujours chez Marot connotation formelle, et que la *raison* renvoie à la pensée, à l'argumentation, c'est-à-dire au "sens" et au contenu. Pour une variante de cette opposition, voyez l'épigramme CCXLVII (V, 299).

24. Je n'ai pas trouvé d'exception à cette règle. Voyez par exemple I, 149 (épître XVI, v. 22-23): "Et *eusse faict* une grande levée / De Rhetorique . . ."; ibid., p. 176 (épître XXV, v. 122): "Et ce faisant mon style *j'enfleray* . . ."; ibid., p. 278 (épître LVII, v. 72): "Ains *sonneray* la Trompete bellique . . ."; IV, 127 (rondeau LVIII, v. 1 et 10-11): "*En attendant* que plus grand œuvre face / . . . / Ce *sera* lors que ma Muse trop basse / *Se haulsera* . . ."; V, 218 (épigramme CLIII, v. 4-5): "lors *fera* son devoir / D'escripre vers en grand nombre & hault style . . ." Sans oublier l'épître "Aux Dames de Paris" (II, 81, v. 101): "Ou *parlerois* (usant de plus hault style) . . ."

25. I, 267 (épître LIII, v. 48-50): où "Folle Amour" est qualifiée "Tresdoux parleur en faincte Rethorique"; II, 64 ("L'Enfer," v. 240-42): où Rhadamantus "mitigue & pallie / Son parler aigre, & en faincte doulceur / Luy dict ainsi . . ."

26. III, 388 ("Le Balladin," v. 222-35). Je ne vois personnellement aucune raison de ne pas attribuer ce poème à Marot. Sur ce thème du "Sy peu de parler," consulter aussi le rondeau XIX (IV, 87, v. 7-8): "Brief, ta façon en peu de Ryme embrasse / Raison fort grande . . ."

27. I, 182 (épître XXXI, v. 3-4): "Quand ton vouloir (lequel trop plus j'estime / Que tes escriptz, ta Raison, ne ta Rime) . . ."; ibid., p. 256 (épître XLVIII, v. 46-50): "Le bon zelle / D'amytié / La moytié / Plus j'estime, / Que ta Rime . . ." Etc.

28. V, 167 (épigramme LXXXV, v. 5-6) et p. 209 (épigramme CXLVI, v. 7).

29. Je fais ici allusion au beau livre de Terence Cave, *The Cornucopian Text: Problems of Writing in the French Renaissance* (Oxford: Clarendon Press, 1979). La fameuse sentence de Quintilien (*Institution Oratoire*, X, vii, 15) y est citée et discutée pp. 37-38: "Pectus est enim, quod disertos facit, et vis mentis." Sur le *thesaurus*, se reporter aussi à Quintilien (*Institution Oratoire*, XI, ii, 1): "*memoria* . . . thesaurus hic eloquentiae dicitur." Et à Cave, p. 6.

30. Sur ce thème du langage comme miroir de l'âme, T. Cave, p. 43 et ss., apporte de précieux renseignements. Voyez aussi *The Prefatory Epistles of Jacques Lefèvre d'Etaples and Related Texts*, ed. Eugene F. Rice, Jr. (New York and London: Columbia Univ. Press, 1972), "Epistle 149," p. 520: ". . . mais la seulle parolle discerne l'homme de la beste et est le caracter et miroir du couraige et pensee. . . . Leiz les Psalmes, qui te representent non seulement l'exterieur, mais aussy l'interieur

David plus expressement que luymesme en presence n'eust peu se descripre par aulcunes parolles . . ."

31. T. Cave, "*Enargeia*: Erasmus and the Rhetoric of Presence in the Sixteenth Century," in *The French Renaissance Mind. Studies Presented to W.G. Moore, L'Esprit Créateur*, 16 (1976), 5-19; M. Jeanneret, "Rabelais et Montaigne: l'écriture comme parole," ibid., pp. 78-94.

32. Erasme, *Moriae encomium*, in *Opera omnia*, éd. J. Clericus (Lugduni-Batavorum, 1703-06), IV, 433-34. Version anglaise du passage chez T. Cave, p. 144.

33. Voyez G. Defaux, *Le Curieux, le glorieux et la sagesse du monde dans la première moitié du XVIe siècle: l'exemple de Panurge (Ulysse, Démosthène, Empédocle)*, French Forum Monographs, 34 (Lexington, KY: French Forum, 1982).

34. *Jacques Lefèvre d'Etaples et ses disciples. Epistres et Evangiles pour les cinquante et deux dimenches de l'an*, Texte de l'édition de Pierre de Vingle, éd. Guy Bedouelle et Franco Giacone (Leyde: E.J. Brill, 1976), pp. 37 et 199.

35. *Prefatory Epistles*, éd. citée, p. 453 ("Epistle 137"). Cette épître dénonce elle aussi la "parolle fardée": "Et sachez que ce que plusieurs estiment elegances humaine is inelegance et parolle fardee devant dieu, et que la parolle de dieu en chasteté et simplicité de esperit est vraye elegance devant dieu et aux yeulx spirituelz, lesquelz luy seul enlumine."

36. Voir Guy Bedouelle, *Lefèvre d'Etaples et l'intelligence des Ecritures* (Genève: Droz, 1976), pp. 64-65, 126-31: "L'esprit se tait dans la méditation de l'immensité et de l'incompréhensibilité divines, reconnaissant qu'il est impossible de louer en disant quelque chose de celui qui est tellement supérieur à toute louange" —*cum mens in meditatione immensitatis et incomprehensibilitatis divinae silet / agnoscens quicquam dicendo non posse eum laudare qui omni laude in immensum superior est (Quincuplex Psalterium*, éd. citée, f° 92 v°).

37. *Marguerites de la Marguerite des Princesses* (Lyon: Jean de Tournes, 1547) —rpt. S.R. Publishers, Johnson Reprint Corporation and Mouton and Company, 1970, I, 69-70: "Si nous possedons Dieu par la Foy: / . . . tel est l'avoir, / Que de le dire en nous n'est le pouvoir."

38. Ibid., p. 147; voir aussi p. 138: "mieux vault que je me range / A humblement aymer ce que doy craindre, / En me taisant, considerant ma fange: / Et par taiser, de louenge me ceindre."

Clément Marot and the Face in the Gospel

M.A. Screech

Renaissance authors are set in a culture which supplies roots to our own. It is always thus with developed cultures. When Mussolini pranced into Greece, Metaxas cited Aeschylus; Chamberlain returning from Munich cited the *Book of Common Prayer*. Taken in ignorant isolation, "Now the battle is for your all," or "Peace in our time" may mean little or much; but what such words seem to mean will be inevitably off the mark if the cultural context of the author who cites them is not shared by the reader. Meaningful reading and writing within developed cultures presuppose a cultural communion, with meanings being conveyed by allusion, echo, reference, quotation, parody. Not to share in that communion is to fail to understand—to fail, that is, to grasp vital elements of the purport of the words employed. We can help our students to enter into that communion or we can, for whatever reason, fail to help them or even prevent them from doing so.

Marot is an author such that, if we cannot meet him halfway, we shall get him wrong. It is a fairly tall order to recover the cultural communion which Marot presupposes; but it is not an impossible one: books survive; philology helps to recover lost meanings and shades of meaning; the slightest semantic discomfort on our part or apparent awkwardness on his part can be the starting point of a journey towards a deeper, wider, richer appreciation of what he wrote and what we read.

In the case of Marot the main area of symbolic communion which we need to share in if we are to understand and enjoy whole tracts of his writings consists in Scripture and Liturgy. Neither Jew nor Christian speak of God without calling on authority, myth and imagery. Marot was an heir to this cultural fashioning and wrote for others who were so, too. It is a coarse view of religion, let alone of poetry, which assumes that imagery, myth or authority are so unimportant that it does not matter if we fail to recognize the allusive language through which a poet sings of religious experiences, individually savored or collectively celebrated.

Marot used the Bible and Liturgy in two main ways. They are—in outline—the subject of this study. I shall not repeat here what I have written elsewhere, especially in my *Marot évangélique* (Geneva: Droz, 1967).[1]

Marot and the Blessed Virgin: Riches Shared

Marot—like Luther—venerated the Virgin Mary. Examples speak louder than generalizations: the *Chant-Royal* "for the conception of our Lady" (1521) will serve as one here. What students make of it on their own is anyone's guess; editions of Marot either have no notes on it at all or, so far as exegesis is concerned, only have misleading ones.

This *Chant-royal* tells of "the King" who set out to "vaincre Ennemys" and to rescue "ceulx de son Ost à grands tourments submis." We are within the Judaeo-Christian myth of God the King who sets the captives free by vanquishing Satan, the Fiend (who is here given his French name, *Ennemys*, with an Old French "s" for epic savor). At one level Marot is echoing *Hebrews* 2, 14-15, where Christ conquers the devil to free the elect from death and slavery. But on to this Marot grafts evocative images and metaphors taken mainly from *The Song of Songs, Ecclesiasticus* and *Proverbs.* In the *Envoy* we are given a key:

> Prince, je prends, en mon sens puerile,
> Le pavillon pour Saincte Anne sterile,
> Le Roy pour Dieu qui aux Cieulx repos a,
> Et Marie est (vray comme l'Evangile),
> La digne Couche où le Roy reposa.

Within the poem Marot declares that St. Anne's immaculate conception of her daughter has been vouched for *en plein Concile.* Similar declarations can be found in sermons and commentaries on the pericope for the Feast of the Conception (when *Proverbs* 8, 22-35 stands for the epistle):

omnes qui dicunt ipsam [Mariam] fuisse conceptam in peccato originali mentiuntur: quia nihil determinatum fuit in conciliis nisi quod verum: sed determinatum fuit in concilio Basiliensi quod Virgo Maria non fuit concepta in peccato originali: igitur non fuit concepta in peccato originali. (*Postillae majores totius anni,* with notes from Lefèvre d'Etaples, Lyons 1529, fol. clxxviii Ro—*In festo conceptionis gloriosę virginis Marię*)

Commentaries on *Proverbs* 8, 22-35 show that Divine Wisdom (the literal subject of this passage) is being interpreted in the Liturgy as prefiguring the Church, and, increasingly, as authorizing the veneration of the Blessed Virgin. In Scripture it is Wisdom who declares that, "from all eternity, *jam concepta eram"* (*Proverbs* 8, 24); reading these words at the Feast of the Conception made it inevitable that, liturgically, they should be taken as applying to the Virgin as immaculately conceived by St. Anne.

Such themes are delicately but powerfully evoked by Marot when he writes of Mary as:

> Le jardin clos, à tous humains promis,
> La grand cité des haulx Cieulx regardée,
> Le Lys Royal, l'Olive collaudée.

Marot presents Mary as the *hortus conclusus* of the *Song of Songs*, interpreted as a veiled prophecy of her purity and virginity: "A garden shut up is my sister, my bride: / A garden shut up, a fountain sealed" (*Song of Songs* 4, 12). Marot was drawing upon knowledge which he shared in a communion of devotion not least with the judges of *Le Puy de la Conception* for whom he wrote this poem. The hold that the *Song of Songs* has exerted on Christian imagery is very momentous and still lingers on in such phrases as *Trahe me post te* (in the carol) or in Black Virgins illustrating *Nigram sum: sed formosa*, some conveniently painted by angels. This latter is a favorite text of Marot's but there is no *Nigra sum* in this particular poem where it would be inappropriate since Marot, by images of whiteness and blackness, stresses that Mary was without sin: "Aulcuns ont dit noire la Couverture; Ce qui n'est pas."

The *hortus conclusus* is then supported by an earlier verse of scripture, Marot's "Tour de David immobile" referring to the only mention of that tower in the Bible (*Song of Songs* 4, 4): *Sicut turris David collum tuum*. This was taken as foretelling the fortitude of Mary and of the Church. As for the "grand cité," in context it probably alludes to the *civitas* of *Song of Songs* 3, 2-3 and of *Revelations* 21, 3—once more, therefore, to the Virgin and Church.

This is the very stuff of Marian veneration. So too is "l'Olive collaudée" which, from its source in *Ecclesiasticus*, leads on to the refrain of this *Chant-royal* and so lends color to the whole poem. *Ecclesiasticus* 24, 8-15, serves as the epistle at the Feast of the Assumption. It contains the words: "I was exalted like a palm-tree in Cades, . . . / And as a fair olive-tree in the plain." This peaceful *Oliva speciosa in campis* is the Virgin who supports the elect of the Church militant, toiling along the road to heaven. If you know this context, the *Oliva speciosa* reveals the allusions behind the poem as a whole with its military metaphor of the King who, setting out to vanquish *Ennemys*, finds a temporary resting-place in the *digne Couche* who is Mary, the *jardin clos*, who was herself enclosed through St. Anne in the protecting cloud of immaculate conception: "C'estoit la nue, ayant en sa closture / Le jardin clos . . ." So the *hortus conclusus* of *Song of Songs* 4, 12 is itself enclosed in the *nebula* and *nubes* of *Ecclesiasticus* 24, 6-7 (*Vulgate*): "I came forth from the mouth of the Most High . . . and covered the whole earth as a cloud (*nebula*). I dwelt in high places and my throne was in the pillar of the cloud (*in columna nubis*). Marot then leads us triumphantly to the Refrain, *La digne Couche où le Roy reposa*, which draws its force from *Ecclesiasticus* 24, 12: "He who created me rested (*requievit*) in my tabernacle." Marot sees this in terms of the prophecy of Christ's birth piously found in Virgil's fourth Eclogue: the phrase *Mettant en fin le dict de la Sybille* refers to that "last age" sung by the Cumaean Sybil: *Jam redit et Virgo* . . . But that is an enrichment of this *Chant-royal* rather than its framework, which may be found in the *Postillae Majores* for the Feast of the Assumption. As well as the usual terms for the *Theotokos—domicilium* for example—we find in the *Postillae* the basic theme of this *Chant-royal*:

Creator hujus Virginis Deus est, qui requievit in utero ejus novem mensibus et sex diebus, in quo utero sicut miles in tabernaculo et armaturam nostre humanitatis accepit, contra diabolum pugnaturus.

The marginal note dots this i: "*in tabernaculo meo, i. utero virginali.*"

Poetry such as Marot's *Chant-royal* draws upon hallowed imagery shared by an entire culture in its liturgical cycle. The shared knowledge was such as to allow steps to be jumped. In *Ecclesiasticus* 24, Wisdom is not only *sicut oliva* but *Quasi cupressus in Monte Syon*. Marot draws on notions associated with this when he writes "L'Aspic hostile, Pour y dormir, approcher n'en osa." The *Postillae Majores* comment: "Serpents flee from the odour of the cypress." It is therefore appropriate to apply this term to the Mother of Christ "who expels demons with the odour of her name."

Personal Zeal

In Marot's case this tranquil world of shared liturgical image was in a highly unstable balance with a more disturbing one: that of an elect group of *amants de vérité* who were set ablaze by the *ipsissima verba* of Christ, who (as Marot put it in his Epistle 35, *A Deux sœurs savoisiennes*, line 15) were convinced that, through their very sufferings "Jesus . . . nous aconplist ses parolles escrites." *Parolles escrites*! The term screams out for commentary. Evangelicals of Marot's sort were persuaded, with even more certainty than the Church at large, that what they found written in their Bibles—in both Testaments—was Christ's own *written* words. As Lefèvre d'Etaples asserted in his *Epistre hortatoire* to his *Seconde partie du Nouveau Testament* (A3v°-4R°), the Scriptures "ne sont pas des hommes mais sont de Jesuchrist parlant en et par eulx." Similarly Augustine, in the last chapter of the first book of *De Consolatione evangelica* maintained that Christ had ordained that whatever needed to be known about himself should be written down *tanquam suis manibus*. (Hooker cites this to good effect in *The Laws of Ecclesiastical Polity*, I, 13, 1.) Through these "written words" of Jesus Marot discovered meaning in his suffering and exile, assurance of divine guidance, rapture and certainty. (He needed such comforts with the Inquisition closing in on him in Renée's little court at Ferrara.) In so doing he found himself within an intensely pious group (which included Marguerite de Navarre and, perhaps, Rabelais) for whom the language of Scripture was at times the very form of their expression, and for whom the truth of the Gospels and the Pauline theology of adoption and grace were completed by God, the Spirit of Truth, inspiring them directly.

Such groups have their passwords: *la dame sans si* and *la belle Christine*, for example. Even holy texts can be applied to their own private affairs. Renée of Ferrara (meaningfully "reborn") has a child who leaps in her womb, as Elizabeth had (Epistre 37, 12; *Au Roy*; cf. *Luke*, 1, 41); Renée, like the Virgin, is *sicut lilium inter spinas* (Epistre 42, 37-38) and Eléonore of Austria, in Epistre 21, 16, is the *pretiosa Margarita* of *Matthew* 16, 46. But above all, of course, they find scriptural texts which they form into chains of meaning, argument or authority. The end of Rabelais's *Enigme en Prophétie* is one example; Marguerite de Navarre's *Miroir* and *Prisons* are others; Marot's epistles, written during exile, are choice examples of the genre.

But the Bible is a *mer des histoires*. What you find in it depends partly on what you bring to it. In it Marguerite found, above all, freedom. Her *Prisons* end with the "vehement" (that is, the enrapturing) freedom of the Spirit: "Où l'esprit est divin et vehement / La liberté y est parfaictement." *Ubi est spiritus Domini*, according to St. Paul (*2 Corinthians* 3-17) *ibi est libertas*. Marot was also sure that he was vouchsafed guidance by *l'Esprit de Dieu* (Epistre 42, *A Madame de Ferrare*, lines 8-9). But what Marot found was not so much freedom as Truth. Indeed, for Marot, it was for revealing Truth that Christ suffered and died; his followers may have to do so too. Marot found that lesson in Jesus' adage, "The disciple is not above his master" (*Matthew* 10, 25 f.; *Luke* 6, 40; 6, 25):

> Et pour apprendre aux autres à souffrir
> Droit à la croix premier se vint offrir.
> Au serviteur n'est [pas] besoing qu'il failhe
> Se repouser, quant le maistre travailhe.

> Il a le premier verité descouverte,
> Et tous ceulx là qui comme luy diront
> Peine audjourd'uy come luy souffriront.
> (Epistre 35, *A deux sœurs savoisiennes*, line 19 ff.)

In context Marot emphasizes that "Tous ces maulx et poynes que j'é dictes / Promist aux siens par son nom precieulx." With this these lines become a telling echo of *John* 15, line 20 ff. All this travail and suffering is undergone *propter nomen meum* (verse 121). But persecuted, zealous Christians like Marot have hidden strengths. They know that "leur loyer est grant ès cieulx" (line 18). This assurance comes straight from the Beatitudes: (*Matthew* 5: 12): *Merces vestra copiosa in coelis*, which Lefèvre translates just as Marot does: "Vostre loyer est grant aux cieulx."

Miré me suis: *The Clear Stream of Truth*

> Je ne suis pas si laid comme il me font;
> Miré me suis au cler ruisseau profont
> De verité . . .
> (Epistre 37, *Au Roy, nouvellement sorty de maladie*, line 57 ff.)

Marot saw his face reflected in a stream of truth. He is appealing in part to the theme of the *speculum* found in the epistle for the 5th Sunday after Easter (*James* 1, 23-24): it is idle to behold your "natural face *in speculo*." A man must look into "the perfect law of liberty." Here Pole's *Synopsis criticorum* cites Erasmus and others to show that the *lex perfecta* is the *Evangelium, sive verbum Dei*. Erasmus, in his *Paraphrases*, adds that it is the *Evangelicae doctrinae speculum*. But for Marot this is less the *lex libertatis* than revealed Christian Truth, including truth about himself, sought and found outside himself. He was, I suspect, syncretizing *James* 1, 23-24 with the myth of Narcissus, which could be taken to mean, *Nosce teipsum*. That is not certain. But what is certain is that Marot found his own self reflected deep within the *speculum* formed by this Evangelical stream of Truth. In this way the Bible became very different for him from that key to a wider world of shared liturgical symbols which opens up for us his Marian writings. He was not alone though. With his patroness Marguerite he shared the theme of the Scripture as a means of self-reflexion, as, that is, his own *Miroir de l'ame pecheresse*. In Marot's case the reflexion showed, a sinner no doubt, but a sinner purified by suffering, justified—and possessed of revealed truth. Like Narcissus, the face he saw reflected back to him pleased him. It was by no means as "ugly" as his accusers alleged.

In the Gospel following the epistle for the 5th Sunday after Easter
(*John* 16, 23-27), Christ stresses the right and duty of Christians to make
supplications to the Father *"per nomen meum."* In Marot's case this fell
upon willing ears. His Evangelical writings give pride of place to the "name"
of Christ and to prayers and requests made "in that name." There is full
Scriptural authority for this. Marot often insists that he is an adopted son
of the Father and so, in Christ's name, is enabled boldly to call on the
Father as a son. Interestingly, this same link between the themes of the
Epistle and Gospel for the 5th Sunday after Easter is specifically brought
out in Lefèvre's *Exhortation* on this pericope:

Doncques mes freres il se fault mirer en la parolle de Dieu qui est la parolle de Jesus-
christ, qui est la loy de parfaicte liberté des enfans de dieu, la loy evangelique: &
toujours l'avoir devant soy, estre permanent en soy mirant . . . .[2]

It was precisely as a son of God that Marot made sense of his suffering and
exile:

> Ne voys tu pas comment Dieu eternel
> Par un courroux de zelle paternel
> M'en veut chasser?
> (Epistre 42, *A Madame de Ferrare*,
> lines 10-12)

Marot's *Chant-royal chrestien* (written, it seems, in the full zeal of such
meaningful suffering) also proclaims that ". . . quand Dieu, Pere celeste,
oppresse / Ses chers enfants, sa grand bonté expresse" (line 45 ff.). That is
the standard appeal to *II Samuel* 7, 14: "Ego ero ei in Patrem et ipsi erit
mihi in filium; . . . arguam eum in virga virorum." It is a sobering doctrine,
one which gives strength to Marot in two ways—as it did to so many Renaissance Christians in their agony. Persecution and suffering were a sign of
God's love—a tender mercy, in fact, analogous to an earthly father whack-
ing his son for his own eventual good. But there was also the joy of antici-
pating the even greater, endless torments awaiting those who persecute
you and which may be continued in their descendants. Marot can leave his
enemies to the Lord; his divine Father will avenge his son Marot on those
toughs of Ferrara who

> Se sont ruez dessus l'enfant d'un Pere
> Qui des meschants fait vengeance condigne
> Jusqu'à la tierce et la quarte origine;
> Doncques à luy je laisse le venger.
> (Epistre 42, *A Madame de Ferrare*,
> line 21 ff.)

I know of no other author who complacently turns *Exodus* 20, 5; 34, 7 and *Numbers* 14, 18 so comfortingly to his own favor. Nevertheless delight at the thought of God's revenge on one's enemies is quite Scriptural. Marot treats the chaff that will perish in the fire—those destined to be damned at the Judgement—with cool satisfaction:

> Tu sentiroys Enfer dedans ton cueur . . .
> Tu periroys comme paille en la flamme
> Sans nul espoir de jamais recevoir
> Santé au Corps et Paradis à l'Ame.
> (*Chant-Royal Chrestien*, lines 37-44)

Marot was comforted by the thought that, as a son of God, his sufferings, unlike those of his persecutors (if they did have any in this world) were part of God's plan:

> Si ton Pere est, tu es donc son enfant,
> Et heritier de son Regne prospere,
> S'il t'a tiré d'eternel improance
> Durant le temps que ne le congnoissoys,
> Que fera-il s'en luy ton cueur espere?
> (*Deploration de F. Robertet*, line 343 ff.)

That is a close appeal to *Galatians* 4, 6-8, where Paul (as Marot in the *Epistres*) goes on to make this the explanation of the suffering of the elect: "If children, then heirs; heirs to God and joint heirs with Christ, if so be that we suffer with him . . ."

Divine Guidance

Marot claimed direct guidance from God. When he fled to Italy, "Dieu qui me guydoit / Dressa mes pas . . ." (Epistre 36, *Au Roy, du temps de son exil à Ferrare*, lines 199-200). At first he was not sure that he had been counselled to flee; the divine warning which sent him on to Venice was a probable not a certain one (Epistre 42, *A Madame de Ferrare*, line 18). But after he arrived in Venice his doubts vanished and he talks to the King, no less, of "Le departir que Dieu me conseilla" (Epistre 44, *Au Roy, de Venise*, line 24).

Marot further showed he was moved to ecstasy by his religious zeal. This aspect of his religion, clear enough then, is harder to grasp now that the vocabulary of ecstasy has to be re-learned from scratch. By far the clearest example of ecstatic transport comes during and after the prayer with which Marot interrupts his sermonizing to François Ier (Epistre 36,

Au Roy, du temps de son exil à Ferrare, lines 103-20): if Leviathan, the *serpens tortuosus* of *Isaiah* 27, 1, can worship God, so can he! Marot prays God not that he be excused suffering but that his suffering may be for God's own cause, not for a foolish one like the 1535 *Placards*. That would make him numbered with the elect; he would be suffering "Pour vous et pour vostre parolle"—like, that is, those blessed souls in *Revelations* (20, 4) martyred *propter testimonium Jesu et propter verbum Dei*. These are the ones "who did not worship the Beast." (Marot certainly did not!) He prays that any torture visited on him should not be "vehement." Vehement torture "carries the mind away," producing a true ecstacy (a real dislocation of body and soul) but a bad one in that the pains of the body are so ghastly that they impede the worship of the soul. Marot prays to be privileged to persevere unto the end—to invoke God "jusque au dernier souspir," so echoing the prayer of the appallingly tortured righteous man who, in *2 Maccabees* 7, 9, expressed his faith in the resurrection *in ultimo spiritu*, "au dernier souspir").

In this Epistre, *Vous* is God: *Tu* is François Ier. Princes rightly take second place to God. When Marot affirmed that his poetic talent was a divine gift he twice made that clear (Epistre 12, *Au Roy, pour succeder en l'estat de son pere*, line 63 ff. and Epistre 34, *A la duchesse de Ferrare*, line 63 ff.). But there are ways to do—and not to do—such things. Here Marot goes beyond that just subordination of king to God which Christian kings acknowledged. He presents himself as so carried away by his prayers and supplications that he is shown as actually forgetting his king entirely. When he "comes back" to his theme at the end of the prayer for martyrdom he adds: "Que dys-je? où suis-je? O noble Roy Françoys / Pardonne moy, car ailleurs je pensoys." Ever since *Phaedrus* 263 was suitably adapted to Christian theology by the early Church, confused semi-amnesia such as this is *the* hallmark of the man who has "come back" from an ecstatic rapture.[3] Marguerite would have understood. She ends her *Miroir* with appeals to St. Paul's rapture; and Rabelais made her triply ecstatic in his liminary poem to the *Tiers Livre*. But kings—like Bishop Butler faced by Wesley—tend to find complacent claims to such a rapture "a horrid thing: a *very* horrid thing."

"A real, if minor, poet?"

G.B. Elton calls Marot such in *Reformation Europe*. Marot was rated far more highly in early times. Sleidan thought he *longe superabat* all poets in the vulgar tongues.[4] His renown as a force in religion can be seen from the engraving of *La Balance*, where all of Rome's seeming power and holiness weigh nothing against the Bible, alongside which stand a group including John Huss, Calvin, Luther, Melanchthon . . . and Marot. The success of Marot's psalms troubled the Catholic Pléiade; Beelzebub himself greeted Huguenot singing of them with a sneer about "jolly little songs that I helped to write . . ."[5] Metrical psalms, in imitation of Marot, became typical of Reformed worship everywhere.

Damião a Goes (the intimate of Erasmus) wrote from Padua to Amerbach in Basle, on 24 September 1536, asking him to help Marot "on whom God has deigned to bestow such gifts and grace that he excells all French poets as much as Virgil tells us that the city of Rome excells all others." On receiving the letter Amerbach learned from Grynaeus that this *praestantissimus poeta* had changed his mind.[6] Was this one of the occasions when Marot proposed and God disposed?[7] Anyway Damião a Goes' letter suggests that the Marot/Maro pun was by no means always a joke.

Cooler Counsels

Somehow Marot was brought to cool down—for a while. The influence of Celio Calcagnini in this process may have been important. He was a convinced Erasmian. Was it he who led Marot to elaborate his exile poetically in terms of Ovid's *Tristia*? I think he did. Did he encourage him to translate Erasmus? Certainly Marot wanted to study under him. Calcagnini was a pious scholar, a protonotary, tolerant and by no means a prude. His *Descriptio cunni* and *Descriptio culi* are no great shakes as poetry but no worse (perhaps wittier) than similar *Blasons du Corps feminin*. I find it hard to believe that there is no connection at all between Calcagnini's *Descriptiones* and the French *blasons* arising from the *Beau Tétin*. I wonder who influenced whom... In graver matters, if Calcagnini led Marot in the direction of Erasmian catholicism and away from Lutheranism, that would go a long way to explain Marot's wavering recantation. One way of reaching a compromise between the triumphalist evangelism of the *Epistres* and the triumphalist catholicism of Marot's trible-crownèd Beast of the Apocalypse could be through wit, transposing criticisms of vice and error away from the world of biblical texts, concatenated with passionate zeal, to one which afforded a place for Marot's laughter and humor.[8]

But will our students even be able to ask such questions, if we do not help them to enter into worlds they may not even know to exist?

NOTES

1. All texts are taken from Claude Albert Mayer's edition of Marot for the Athlone Press of the Univ. of London: *Les Epitres*, 1958, for all allusions to the Epistres; the *Oeuvres lyriques*, 1964 for the *Deploration de Florimont Robertet*; the *Oeuvres diverses*, 1966, for the *Chants-royaux*.

2. Jacques Lefèvre d'Etaples, *Epistres et Evangiles pour les Cinquante & deux sepmaines de l'an*, ed. M.A. Screech, THR (Geneva: Droz, 1964), facsimile, cxliiii; or ed. Guy Bedouelle and Franco Giacone (Leiden: Brill, 1976), pp. 192-93.

3. I have treated this in my book *Ecstasy and the Praise of Folly* (London: Duckworth, 1980).

4. G.R. Elton, *Reformation Europe*, 1517-1559, Fontana History of Europe, 1963 (later impression used, 1970, p. 286); Joannes Sleidan, *Commentarii de statu Religionis & Reipublicae . . .* (Strasbourg, [1612]), p. 425.

5. D.P. Walker, *Unclean Spirits* (London: Scolar Press, 1981), p. 25.

6. Alfred Hartmann, ed, *Die Amerbachkorrespondenz* (Basle, 1953), IV, 446 ff. and 458 ff.

7. Cf. Epistre 44, *Au Roy*, line 23 ff., and his translation of Psalm 33, *Exultate justi*.

8. For the *Descriptiones* see Johannes Baptista Pigna, *Carmina* (with poems by Calcagnini) (Venice, 1553), p. 53. Oddly, Clément Marot seems to have been the second *Maro poeta* helped by Calcagnini. There is a poem *Ad Maronem* in the Pigna volume (pp. 172-73) concerning a contemporary poet neglected by his monarch and called Maro. Who this "Maro" was I do not know, except that he was mentioned several times in Calcagnini's letters in 1518, from Agria (Hungary). In one dated "Pridie idus Januarii M.D.XVIII" (12 January 1518), writing to Bishop Franciscus Perrenus of Petrovaradin in Serbia—called *Vuaradinensis*—Calcagnini refers to "Maro ille meus, planè natus & educatus in Musarum sinu" (*Opera, aliquot, Basle*, 1544, p. 76), adding later, "Habebitis posthac Maronem virum clarissimum, & planè ad poeticam natum apud te." (No other poet than "Clemens Marotus" is listed under a name anything like "Maro" or "Virgilius" in Lilius Gregorius Gyraldus Ferrarensis, *Dialogi Duo de Poëtis nostrorum temporum*, dedicated to Renée of Ferrara, p. 77.)

Louise Labé et le genre élégiaque

Michel Dassonville

Il est surprenant qu'on n'éprouve aucune hésitation à placer dans la production poétique antérieure à la Pléiade les œuvres que Louise Labé publia
en 1555,[1] à Lyon il est vrai, mais bien après la *Deffence*, après les *Odes*, la
Cléopâtre captive et peut-être les *Hymnes*, et surtout après la plupart des
canzonieri néo-pétrarquisants des poètes de la nouvelle vague. On ne peut
pas même invoquer un décalage entre composition et publication: s'il est
vraisemblable qu'elle ait écrit quelques-uns de ses sonnets dès 1545, les
critiques s'accordent pour dater de 1553-1555 la composition de ses trois
élégies, ce qui les rend exactement contemporaines de celles que publiaient
Du Bellay dans le *Recueil de poesie* (1553) et Ronsard dans le *Bocage* et
les *Meslanges* (1554).[2]

Si paradoxal que cela puisse paraître, on a pourtant raison. Mais c'est
que la Pléiade est en retard sur elle-même. Malgré la définition qu'il en
donnait dans la *Deffence*, Du Bellay ne s'inspire pas d'Ovide, de Tibulle ni
de Properce pour écrire son élégie de 1553 pas plus que celles de 1558 et
n'y entremêle aucune de "ces fables anciennes, non petit ornement de
poésie."[3] Ce sont "des épîtres dolentes, des plaintes d'amour sous la forme
de lettres adressées anonymement à une maîtresse, en décasyllabes à rimes
plates, écrites en un style élégant sans trop d'apprêt."[4] Bref, ce sont des
élégies marotiques. Il n'en est pas de même toutefois de celles que publie
Ronsard dans le *Bocage* et les *Meslanges* de 1554. Elles sont au nombre
de neuf. Sept d'entre elles sont déjà explicitement intitulées "Elegie," les
deux autres (VI, 61 et 73) ne portant ce titre ou n'étant rangées parmi les
Elégies qu'à partir de l'édition de 1567 sans avoir subi pour autant de
remaniements sensibles. Cette première floraison révèle déjà le souci
qu'avait Ronsard de faire ici encore "euvre apart" et de prendre ses
distances à l'égard des marotiques. *L'Elegie* (déplorative) *sur le trepas
d'Antoine Chateignier* (V, 243) présente non seulement une tentative
d'adaptation française des distiques élégiaques en faisant alterner un à un

alexandrins et décasyllabes mais elle suit le plan de la *Consolatio ad Liviam Augustam* qu'on attribuait alors à Ovide, paraphrase en ses vingt-huit premiers vers l'élégie d'Ovide sur la mort de Tibulle et emploie, dans les idées comme dans l'expression, de nombreuses réminiscences antiques.[5] Trois autres élégies non amoureuses élargissent les limites du genre: l'*Elegie à la Peruse* (V, 259) traite d'histoire littéraire,[6] l'*Elegie à Pascal* (VI, 61), écrite en alexandrins, est une suite de (fausses) confidences autobiographiques, l'*Elegie à Brinon* (VI, 165) fait l'éloge du verre—et de son contenu éventuel pour lequel le destinataire avait une certaine prédilection. La fable d'Hercule sous-tend l'*Elegie à Muret* (V, 224) et celle de Narcisse l'*Elegie à Charbonnier* (VI, 73) écrite elle aussi en alexandrins. Quant aux élégies proprement amoureuses, l'une adressée au même Brinon (VI, 149), est une apologie pseudo-philosophique de l'amour, l'autre, adressée à Janet (VI, 152) énumère une nouvelle fois "les beautez" que Ronsard "voudroit en s'amie." Enfin, dans l'*Elegie à Cassandre* (VI, 57) le poète feint de regretter qu'il lui faille accrocher sa lyre au clou afin d'écrire la *Franciade* que lui commande, paraît-il, le roi Henri II. Par les sources autant que par les thèmes, par la variété des rythmes comme par la diversité des tons, on constate que Ronsard s'efforce de faire éclater les cadres de l'élégie marotique. Quoi qu'en pensât Verdun L. Saulnier,[7] on sent nettement qu'un renouvellement est en cours bien que les poètes de la Pléiade ne se soient pas encore fait, en 1555, une idée précise de l'élégie, si tant est qu'ils s'en feront jamais une. Mais c'est une autre histoire.[8]

Louise Labé, quant à elle, gravite résolument dans l'orbite marotique tout au moins dans la mesure où l'élégie marotique a été définie par Thomas Sébilet dans son *Art poetique françois* en 1548. "Triste et flebile (*qui fait pleurer*), elle traite singulierement des passions amoureuses."[9] Mais quand on y regarde d'un peu plus près, on ne tarde pas à s'apercevoir des différences fondamentales qui distinguent les élégies de la belle Cordière de celles de Clément Marot.

Qu'on accepte ou non l'interprétation qu'en proposait naguère Saulnier,[10] il faut convenir que les élégies que Marot avait publiées en 1534 et 1538 ne sont pas des cris du cœur, des chants désespérés—on sait que "les plus désespérés sont les chants les plus beaux / Et j'en sais d'immortels qui sont de purs sanglots." Sans être aussi sévère qu'Henri Chamard qui n'y voyait que "des badinages d'amour gracieux, mais un peu vides, faits de galanterie et de préciosité, . . . des discussions d'ordre subtil sur de menus problèmes de casuistique amoureuse,"[11] on doit reconnaître que les élégies de Marot nous présentent "une galerie de cas typiques sur le propos du malheur d'amour" et que, s'inspirant des héroïdes ovidiennes à la mode plus que des *Amores* elles sont "loin de nous livrer des sentiments intimes." N'en faut-il pas conclure avec C.A. Mayer qu'"une poésie élégiaque impersonnelle implique contradiction"?[12] Or cette impersonnalité par où s'explique la médiocrité des élégies de Marot fait place à une authenticité du cri, à la liberté d'"une langue charnelle, vraie jusque dans ses naïvetés,"[13] à une sincérité où gît le principal mais non le seul intérêt des élégies de Louise Labé. A la différence de son illustre prédécesseur, elle avait découvert un siècle avant Boileau qu'"il faut que le cœur seul parle dans l'élégie."[14]

Là n'est pourtant le trait le plus caractéristique de l'élégie et comme son attribut essentiel. Quel que soit le thème qu'il aborde, en majeur ou en mineur, tout poème lyrique suscite des émotions, engendre des sentiments, s'adresse au cœur du lecteur qu'il fait vibrer à l'unisson du cœur du poète. Par une sorte de communion—d'autres diraient: contagion—le poème lyrique rassemble, rapproche, unit les membres de la grande famille humaine dont chacun se sent solidaire par l'entremise de l'un des siens. C'est en ce sens qu'on a traditionnellement défini le lyrisme comme l'expression (rythmée) de sentiments personnels, i.e. de sentiments que tout être humain éprouve ou doit éprouver dans la mesure même où il est humain. Le poème élégiaque prétend au contraire témoigner d'une expérience unique, incomparable, vécue par un être d'exception—le poète—dont le cœur, de plus fine facture que tout autre, éprouve des douleurs ou des joies, mais le plus souvent des douleurs extra-ordinaires en des circonstances de temps et de lieu—"Un soir, t'en souvient-il?"—qu'il est indispensable de narrer avec précision sous peine de ne pas être cru des lecteurs qui, eux, n'ont jamais connu ni ne connaîtront jamais de tels tourments. Ainsi le poète élégiaque se dit-il souvent victime d'une torture qui fait ses délices car elle le place hors du commun. Il entre toujours une part de masochisme dans l'élégie qui décrit une expérience, exprime des émotions et des sentiments proprement individuels. "Il est doux de pleurer des maux qui n'ont été pleurés de personne," avouait Chateaubriand. On comprend que l'élégie ait été si fort en vogue parmi les romantiques au point qu'il nous faut faire effort aujourd'hui pour n'y pas réduire tout lyrisme. On comprend aussi pourquoi peu de critiques résistent à la tentation du biographisme lorsqu'ils se penchent sur une élégie: ils pensent sonder le mystère de la création poétique lorsqu'ils retrouvent et racontent en leurs plus menus détails les circonstances qui présidèrent à l'avènement du poème.[15] C'est la tentation que j'éviterai ici bien qu'il soit indéniable, comme l'a remarqué Albert-Marie Schmidt, que "les *Elégies* de Louise Labé peuvent être tenues pour autant de pages d'un journal intime alors que l'élégie marotique est trop souvent une simple dissertation sur un point de casuistique amoureuse."[16] Il n'est chez elle "aucune solution de continuité entre sa vie affective et sa plume d'oie."[17] Et c'est justement son détachement, sa franchise qui furent jugés "cas pendable."[18] Sa première et sa troisième élégies sont en fait des lettres ouvertes aux dames lyonnaises:

> Quand vous lirez, ô Dames Lionnoises,
> Ces miens escrits pleins d'amoureuses noises,
> Quand mes regrets, ennuis, despits et larmes
> M'orrez chanter en pitoyables carmes,
> Ne veuillez point condamner ma simplesse.

Ainsi débute la troisième élégie qui, comme la première, est un plaidoyer dans l'acception la plus stricte du terme, le plaidoyer d'une femme adressé à des femmes qui, n'ayant pas subi la même douloureuse expérience, auraient tendance à condamner celle qui, par "simplesse" mais aussi par l'ardeur d'un tempérament exceptionnel, a été victime de l'amour.[19] "Dames qui les lirez / De mes regrets avec moy soupirez" (I, v. 43-44), car il est possible malgré tout que vous subissiez vous-mêmes un jour la torture unique dont je brûle en "mon sang, mes os, mon esprit et courage" (I, v. 4). Les arguments féminins mais non efféminés qu'elle avance sont d'autant plus convaincants qu'ils sont adressés à toute la communauté des femmes et d'autant plus désintéressés—et donc sincères—qu'ils sont proférés par une voix de femme. Un Marot, un Ronsard, tout homme conseillant à une mignonne de cueillir dès aujourd'hui les roses de la vie a toujours l'air de prêcher *pro domo*. Dans cette première et cette troisième élégies Louise Labé mène son combat en faveur de la liberté féminine de sentir et d'exprimer, jusqu'à l'indécence, la ferveur d'aimer de tout son cœur, de tout son sang, de tout son sexe.

> Boire, manger et dormir ne me laisse.
> Il ne me chaut de soleil ne d'ombrage.
> Je n'ai qu'Amour et feu en mon courage . . .
>   (III, v. 68-70)[20]

Nulle honte en cette "fille d'amour et de flamme";[21] il semble au contraire que l'amour, si charnel soit-il, lui confère des lettres de noblesse. Les déesses ne l'ont-elles pas connu et les plus grandes dames?

> Leur cœur hautein, leur beauté, leur lignage
> Ne les ont su preserver du servage
> De dur amour . . . ((I, v. 57-59)

Plaidoyers sans vergogne, ces deux élégies sont aussi des confessions sans contrition ni pénitence:[22]

> J'ai de tout temps vescu en son service (*d'amour*)
> Sans me sentir coulpable d'autre vice
> Que de t'avoir bien souvent en son lieu,
> D'amour forcé, adoré comme Dieu.
> (II, v. 45-48)

Si Louise Labé souffre et se plaint, c'est de ne pouvoir jouir pleinement de l'objet de ses désirs. Et l'avertissement qu'elle donne aux dames lyonnaises consiste à ne pas laisser passer l'occasion. A la fin de la première élégie elle développe le thème du "Quand vous serez bien vieille" mais elle le fait avec une cruauté qui n'appartient qu'aux femmes. Le portrait de la vieillarde, frigide en sa jeunesse, qui essaie mais trop tard de "chasser le ridé labourage / Que l'aage avoit gravé sur son visage" et qui plante de traviole une perruque sur son chef gris, cette charge est plus féroce que Ronsard ne l'a faite dans son ode *A Jane impitoiable* ou dans le sonnet *pour Hélène* que tout le monde connaît.

La seconde élégie est elle aussi une épître amoureuse écrite en décasyllabes à rimes plates adressée à un amant anonyme mais réel. Il est parti en Italie, remontant le "Pau cornu" (II, v. 15-16). En Italie, le beau pays mais aussi le pays des belles femmes. Il a bien écrit une lettre pour annoncer son retour mais voilà deux lunes qu'il aurait dû revenir. (Les femmes tiennent volontiers registre du temps par le nombre de lunes.) Elle se morfond et "de la longue attente / Hélas, en vain (son) desir se lamente" (II, v. 7-8). Elle n'a besoin ni d'Ovide ni de Marot pour dire ce qu'elle souffre et elle renouvelle sans effort le thème de l'Absence en confiant au papier ses inquiétudes de femme. D'abord sa jalousie:

> peut estre ton courage
> S'est embrasé d'une nouvelle flame
> En me changeant pour prendre une autre Dame.
> (II, v. 16-18)

Elle écarte momentanément cette pensée insoutenable et trouve des accents quasi-maternels pour plaindre le pauvre chéri: "Tu es, peut estre, en chemin inconnu / Outre ton gré malade retenu" (II, v. 31-32). Mais ce n'est pas possible car elle prie trop bien les dieux (en ce cas il vaut mieux en avoir plusieurs qu'un seul) et ne doute pas d'être exaucée. C'est donc bien qu'il s'est "enamouré en autre lieu." Par un remarquable sursaut de fierté féminine, elle le plaint d'avoir si mauvais goût car

> say-je bien que t'amie nouvelle
> A peine aura le renom d'estre telle,
> Soit en beauté, vertu, grace et faconde
> Comme plusieurs gens savans par le monde
> M'ont fait à tort, ce croy je, estre estimée.
> (II, v. 55-59)

Avec beaucoup de coquetterie, elle vante son renom mondain, sa gloire littéraire et les charmes appétissants de sa personne: "Goute le bien que tant d'hommes desirent / Demeure au but où tant d'autres aspirent" (II, v. 69-70). Elle se flatte de préférer l'absent à "maints grans Signeurs" qui prétendent à lui plaire et elle tente finement de susciter la jalousie de l'inconstant. Elle a toutefois réservé sa meilleure botte pour l'estocade finale: pourvu que je sois encore vivante lorsque tu reviendras.

La pièce rend un son de vérité, de naturel et de simplicité qui serait du très grand art si l'auteur n'avait fait qu'imaginer la situation. Mais on y sent Louise Labé tout entière "dans ces passages furtifs de cœur à phrase, de chagrin à rimes que constitue sa poésie" car lorsqu'on se mêle d'écrire des élégies "C'est peu d'être poète, il faut être amoureux."[23]

Folle ardeur, soupçons et reproches, compassion, inquiétude, cri de bête blessée et confidence de l'âme, il y a là, dans cette seconde élégie, des accents qui ne trompent pas et je ne crois pas qu'il ait fallu qu'elle se souvienne de Tracconaglia, de Pétrarque ou de Serafino Aquilano pour soupirer: "Tu es tout seul, tout mon mal et mon bien. / Avec toy tout, et sans toy je n'ay rien" (II, v. 81-82).

Mais qu'elle n'ait pas eu nécessairement besoin de modèles, antiques ou modernes, pour exprimer sa passion ne signifie pas que ses élégies soient une suite de cris inarticulés, de platitudes épistolaires, une espèce de matière brute dont la seule valeur résiderait en la vérité d'un drame réellement vécu. Et comme les poètes s'y trompent moins que les critiques littéraires, fussent-ils universitaires, c'est encore une fois à Léon-Paul Fargue que je me réfère pour avancer que Louise Labé a écrit "des vers exacts quant à leur substance, d'une sensibilité discrète et prolongée, des vers chargés de pressentiments et de tristesse, et qu'on entend couler comme des filets de rosée et de larmes."[24]

De son propre aveu, Louise Labé était musicienne avant d'être poète et elle devait avoir l'ouïe fine pour jouer aussi subtilement qu'elle le fait avec la musicalité d'une langue qui était encore parfois "scabreuse" (raboteuse). Qu'on saisisse au passage ces harmonies aussi douces que baisers sur l'oreille:

> Ne *m*eritoit sa Royalle grandeur (i.e. *Sémiramis*)
> Au *m*oins avoir un *m*oins fascheus *m*alheur
> Qu'ay*m*er son fils? (I, v. 71-73)

> Tout aparsoy, l'ame d'Amour atteinte!
> (II, v. 26)[25]

> Si *m*eritoient elles estre esti*m*ées
> Et, pour ay*m*er leurs Amis, estre ay*m*ées.
> S'estant ay*m*é, on peut A*m*our *l*aisser
> N'est-i*l* raison, ne *l*'estant, se *l*asser?
> (III, v. 89-92)

Ces douceurs d'expression voisinent d'ailleurs avec des accords plaqués que lui inspirait la passion, le désir, et lui faisait désirer

> que celui que j'estime mon tout,
> Qui seul me peut faire plorer et rire
> Et pour lequel si souvent je soupire
> Sente en ses os, en son sang, en son âme
> Ou plus ardent, ou bien egale flame.
> (III, v. 98-102)

Occlusives et fricatives sont ici chargées de traduire, me semble-t-il, la fièvre du sang et la profondeur du dépit. En ses *Elégies* bien mieux encore que dans ses *Sonnets*, Louise Labé s'est servi pour crier sa passion d'un moyen d'expression "plus naturel, on l'a dit, que la langue maternelle," un moyen qui, selon Thierry-Maulnier, l'égale aux grandes héroïnes raciniennes. Ce n'est pas là mince éloge à lui faire.

NOTES

1. Les notes renvoient au texte des *Oeuvres complètes*, éd. E. Giudici (Genève: Droz, 1981).

2. On les trouvera respectivement dans les *Oeuvres poétiques* de Du Bellay, éd. H. Chamard (STFM), IV^2, p. 215 et dans les *Oeuvres complètes* de Ronsard, éd. P. Laumonier (STFM), V, pp. 224, 243, 259 et VI, pp. 57, 61, 73, 149, 152, 165.

3. Cf. *Deffence*, éd. Chamard (STFM, 1966), II, iv, pp. 111-12.

4. C'est la définition que V.L. Saulnier donnait des élégies marotiques (*Les Elégies de Marot* [SEDES, 1952], pp. 100-10). Nous nous sommes permis de mettre sa phrase au pluriel.

5. Selon les notes de P. Laumonier, éd. citée, lieu cité.

6. Comme Charles de Sainte-Marthe en avait précédemment écrites.

7. Cf. Oeuvre citée, pp. 113-14.

8. Cette histoire du genre élégiaque en France au XVIe siècle est encore à écrire. Aux œuvres citées par V.L. Saulnier (p. 99, n. 3), j'aimerais ajouter la thèse encore inédite d'une de mes étudiantes, Joan Manley-Davis sur *L'Elégie ronsardienne* (Ph.D., Univ. of Texas at Austin, 1966). Je reprends ce sujet dans mon *Ronsard*, V, ch. 2 (à paraître).

9. Livre II, ch. 3, éd. F. Gaiffe (STFM, 1932), p. 154.

10. Oeuvre précédemment citée, *passim*. On se souviendra qu'il suggérait de "lire le recueil comme un roman" (p. 55) où apparaissaient successivement cinq épisodes aux héroïnes différentes: l'oublieuse, la rebelle, l'intéressée, l'empêchée, la malavisée (p. 59) par lesquelles Marot faisait apparaître plusieurs facettes de l'éternel féminin.

11. Dans l'article "élégie" du *Dictionnaire des lettres françaises. Seizième Siècle*, publié sous la direction de G. Grente (Paris: Fayard, 1951).

12. *L'Enfer. Les Coq-à-l'Ane. Les Elegies*, éd. C.A. Mayer, Introduction, pp. xxi et xxiii.

13. Léon-Paul Fargue, "Louise Labé," *Revue de Paris*, février 1950, p. 27.

14. *Art poétique*, ch. II, v. 57.

15. L'un des exemples les plus piquants que je connaisse mais il n'est hélas! pas le seul, est fourni par une note de G. Lanson à l'édition critique des *Méditations poétiques et religieuses* de Lamartine, pp. 137-38 pour la Collection des *Grands Ecrivains littéraires de la France*.

16. *Poètes du XVIe siècle* (Paris: Bibliothèque de la Pléiade), p. 272.

17. Léon-Paul Fargue, p. 26.

18. A.-M. Schmidt, p. 271.

19. On trouve, me semble-t-il, la prétention d'unicité que je disais chère à tout poète élégiaque dans le passage de la première élégie (v. 61-90) où Louise Labé évoque le sort de Sémiramis, reine de Babylone, qui fournit un double, antique et anoblissant, à la belle Cordière. Celle-ci d'ailleurs se présente une autre fois à cheval et en armes (III, v. 37-42).

20. Certain sonnet d'ailleurs n'est pas moins explicite: "Tout aussi tot que je commence à prendre / Dans le mol lit le repos desiré, / Mon triste esprit hors de moy retiré / S'en va vers toy incontinent se rendre. / Lors m'est avis que dedens mon sein tendre / Je tiens le bien, où j'ay tant aspiré" (s. ix, v. 1-6).

21. L'expression est de L.-P. Fargue, p. 24.

22. Mais aussi, faut-il l'ajouter, sans défi ni arrogance. Cf. *Elégie* I, v. 28-30, 91-92 et III, v. 27-29. Et tout le sonnet XXIV: "Ne reprenez, Dames, si j'ay aymé" où vibrent les échos de la "Ballade des pendus" de François Villon.

23. Boileau, *Art poétique*, chant II, v. 44.

24. Art. cité, p. 22.

25. J'ai préféré ici la leçon A, C, D (*atteinte*) à celle de B (*esteinte*) suivi par E. Giudici, éd. citée, p. 134. (Les sigles choisis sont ceux de cette édition critique.)

*The Taming of the Muse: The Female Poetic Voice
in Pernette du Guillet's* Rymes

Lance K. Donaldson-Evans

> In the beginning was the Word and the Word was
> with God and the Word was God. He was in the
> beginning with God: all things were made through
> him, and without him was not anything made that
> was made. (John I: 1-3 RSV)

John's account of the Creation is, unwittingly, an elegant and succinct
statement of what certain modern critics see as the central problem of
Western philosophical and metaphysical thought: its logocentricity. By
this they refer to the primacy which has been accorded to the *Logos*, the
spoken word, the discourse of reason and rationality emanating from
God or some Divine Principle which is seen as the source of wisdom and
spiritual enlightenment. That the Word in John's gospel and the *logos* of
Hellenic philosophy are inalterably and unrelentingly masculine has led
Jacques Derrida, after his attempts at deconstructing the framework of
Western philosophy, to reconstruct the term "logocentric" so that it
becomes "phallogocentric." Whether we applaud or deride such Derridian
derivations, it is impossible to deny the pertinence of this particular neologism (perhaps we should say *neo-log-ism*) to literature and above all to
that privileged literary form perhaps most closely associated with the *logos*:
poetry (since poetry was long thought to be the language used by the gods
to communicate with mankind—Montaigne called it "l'originel langage des
Dieux").[1] With a few notable exceptions, virtually all Western poetry has
been produced by male poets, and while it is true that some of these poets
call upon God or the gods for inspiration, the archetypal model (one could
even venture to say the Idea) of the poet is that of a man, who seeks his
inspiration from an external creative force characterized as female and personified in myth since the Greeks as the Muses. This model is even more
sharply delineated when love poetry is being written since the female

object of male discourse is often either identified with the Muses or becomes a substitute for them. However, although exalted as goddesses, these midwives of poetic utterance have no voice of their own, since their language is that of the male poets who seek their inspiration and who sing their praises. Paradoxically, they become silent female objects inscribed in monumental slabs of male-produced discourse and as such bear (literally) mute testimony to the silence feminist critics see as the role traditionally apportioned to women in literature and indeed in society in general.

There have of course been some notable, if rare exceptions, starting with the celebrated Sappho of Lesbos. Yet the fact that her poetic production was considered as something abnormal or even monstrous is shown by the excessive praise or the exaggerated criticism heaped upon her from ancient times when she was considered either as the Tenth Muse or as a scandalous courtesan, notorious for leading young women astray. Even today she is known less as a poet than as a "right-on woman"[2] or as the bearer of a name from which the term sapphism was created, which puts her in the same league as Sade and Sacher-Masoch. Of course, whether she is placed on a pedestal as the Tenth Muse or denigrated as a meretricious hetaera, the result tends to be the same: her poetry becomes secondary to her person and is thus devalued in a way in which male-produced poetry rarely is. It is perhaps this mistrust of women's writing which is responsible for the fact that the work of the most famous woman poet of antiquity has only been preserved in the form of a few fragments and an occasional complete poem.

Women poets did fare a little better in the history of French literature. We know of at least twenty women troubadours writing during the Middle Ages and then there are Marie de France and Christine de Pisan, the latter being perhaps the first French poetess to express fully and openly her awareness of writing as a woman.[3] However, it is above all in the 16th century that women begin to come into their own in France and that within a relatively short span of time we find three major women poets: Louise Labé, Pernette du Guillet and Marguerite de Navarre, the latter of whom was also writing plays and her unfinished masterpiece, the *Heptaméron*. In addition to these three illustrious women, there were other female writers such as Anne de Marquets, whose sonnets were praised by Ronsard, and Hélisenne de Crenne, the creator of the first *roman sentimental* in French literature. Joan Kelly-Gadol's contention that women did not enjoy the fruits of the Renaissance in 15th-century Italy and in fact lost some of the power and privileges they possessed in the Middle Ages,[4] does not hold true for Renaissance France where women played at least as important a role in French political and cultural life as they had before. It is significant too that of the three best known women writers, one is a *bourgeoise* and that Pernette du Guillet was at most only a member of the *petite noblesse* and probably of bourgeois origin.[5] For this partial democratization of female writing we undoubtedly have to thank the relatively tolerant and open society which had been created in 16th-century Lyons where learning for women was tepidly encouraged, at least among the aristocracy and middle class. However, we should be careful not to paint too rosy a picture, since, as Natalie Davis has shown, even in Lyons a serious education for the women of the *menu peuple* was considered ludicrous. We need to be reminded also that because she knew Latin, Louise Labé was considered "learned beyond her sex" ("dessus et outre la capacité de son sexe").[6] That even the fiercely independent Labé was conscious of the constraints imposed upon women and the necessity of being "a credit to her sex" is shown quite clearly in the preface to her *Oeuvres*, dedicated to Clémence de Bourges:

Estant le tems venu, Madamoiselle, que les severes lois des hommes n'empeschent plus les femmes de s'appliquer aus sciences et disciplines: il me semble que celles qui ont la commodité, doivent employer cette honneste liberté que notre sexe ha autrefois tant desiree, à icelles aprendre: et montrer aus hommes le tort qu'ils nous faisoient en nous privant du bien et de l'honneur qui nous en pouvoit venir . . .

She goes on to encourage all virtuous ladies in the following terms:

Je ne puis faire autre chose que prier les vertueuses Dames d'eslever un peu leurs esprits par dessus leurs quenoilles et fuseaus, et s'employer à faire entendre au monde que si nous ne sommes faites pour commander, si ne devons nous estre dédaignées pour compagnes tant es afaires domestiques que publicques, de ceus qui gouvernent et se font obeïr.

This exhortation, however, clearly underlines the subordinate role of women in contemporary society and the closing sentences, while expressing the conventional topos of authorial modesty and inadequacy, do so in a much more extreme fashion than is usual and lay stress on the uncertain reception women's writing could expect even in Lyons:

Mais depuis que quelcuns de mes amis ont trouvé moyen de lire (mes poèmes) sans que j'en susse rien, et que . . . ils m'ont fait à croire que les devois mettre en lumiere: je ne les ay osé esconduire, les menassant ce pendant de leur faire *boire la moitié de la honte* qui en proviendroit . . .

The prologue closes with a revealing comment on social customs, as Labé encourages her friend to engage in the act of writing and to follow her example: "Et pource que les femmes *ne se montrent volontiers en publiq seules*, je vous ay choisie pour me servir de guide, vous dediant ce petit œuvre . . ."

The restrictions placed on women in social life carry over into the literary domain. The fact that there were a relatively large number of women writing in 16th-century France—yet still very much a minority—should not blind us to the feelings of constraint they felt in a man's world of learning and poetry. Women's writing was still something of an oddity in a basically phallogocentric world.[8]

Of course, some modern feminist critics deny the very possibility of women's writing before modern times and establish a firm distinction between women writing and women's writing. Simone de Beauvoir was one of the first feminist critics to make this point:

(les femmes) n'ont ni religion, ni poésie qui leur appartiennent en propre: c'est encore à travers les rêves des hommes qu'elles rêvent. Ce sont les dieux fabriqués par les mâles qu'elles adorent . . . ; la femme est exclusivement définie dans son rapport avec l'homme.[9]

This idea has been developed by critics such as Hélène Cixous and her disciples, who, paradoxically, ignore most writing by women and concentrate on male authors (such as Genêt, and Kafka) and on male critics (like Derrida and Lacan). The equally influential Luce Irigaray reaches different conclusions and while admitting that most women writers do write like men, she suggests that this *mimétisme* can in fact be deliberately assumed and that in this way intentional mimicking of male writers can be a means of showing that the woman writer is not duped into submission by masculine logic:

Jouer de la mimésis est pour une femme, tenter de retrouver le lieu de son exploitation par le discours, sans s'y laisser simplement réduire . . . . C'est aussi "dévoiler" le fait que, si les femmes miment si bien, c'est qu'elles ne se résorbent pas simplement dans cette fonction. *Elles restent aussi ailleurs.* . . . Si les femmes peuvent jouer de la mimésis, c'est qu'elles peuvent en réalimenter le fonctionnement . . . . Gardiennes de la "nature," les femmes ne sont-elles pas celles qui entretiennent, qui permettent donc, la ressource de la mimésis pour les hommes? Pour le logos?[10]

To a male critic like myself who is doubtless unknowingly envelopped in the phallogocentric phallacy (to use Shoshana Felman's term), Irigaray's position does seem to be more logical (but then logic is a form of phallogocentrism according to some), as do the cautious attempts of many American feminist critics to discern signs of female difference in female-produced texts. Of course, such investigations must be conducted with prudence if we are to avoid the danger of repeating hackneyed stereotypes. We must also remember that "blind" readings of texts written by male and female authors have not successfully identified the sex of the author involved. If as Nancy Miller has stated (and correctly stated, I believe) there are "no infallible signs, no fail-safe technique by which to determine the gender of an author," there are however differences, sometimes slight but always important, in the way women writers deal with the material they borrow from male writers, as well as (and I quote Miller again) "in the insistence of a certain thematic structuration, in the form of content." I believe that we can postulate that *l'écriture féminine*, at least prior to the 19th century, consists above all in *ré-écriture*, a rewriting of traditionally male discourse in a way which, while apparently mimetic, challenges the idiom and insists quietly but firmly upon female difference. This difference usually manifests itself in the form of an ironic distance indicating that the *mimétisme* is, partially at least, a game, something of which the female writer is not the complete dupe.

When a poetess like Pernette du Guillet ventures into the arena of love poetry in 16th-century France, she finds herself in an unusual and somewhat unique position, given the predominant neo-Petrarchan mode of expression. According to this tradition, the Lady is, ostensibly at least, the dominant, if silent partner, a semi-divine, unearthly creature formed of fire and ice, capable of inflicting terrible punishment and occasional fleeting happiness upon the long-suffering Lover, that curiously passive participant whose main activity is to give voice to his suffering and the Lady's capricious cruelty. The Lady is portrayed in what we might call a stereotypical masculine role: she is cruel, merciless, aggressive, bellicose. Her literally piercing glances wound the hapless male and leave him in a love swoon in what, again according to traditional stereotypes, is a female role. The historical antecedents of courtly love and the *service d'amour*, while they help to explain the origins of this role reversal, do not alter the fact that, in the neo-Petrarchan tradition, we do have an active, aggressive Lady, inflicting suffering and pain upon a hapless, passive male. His situation is like a remake of the movie *King Kong* in which Fay Wray plays King Kong.

A woman writing in this tradition will, of course, reverse the roles again, so that instead of portraying a *Belle cruelle* in her poetry, she will present her Beloved as a *Beau cruel* who behaves like a real-life phallocrat rather than a meek, swooning, "effete intellectual" as the male neo-Petrarchan poet projects himself to be. Labé in her elegies tells how she played the role of the typical Petrarchan Lady, before succumbing to *le mal pétrarquiste*:

> Qui m'ust vu lors en armes, fiere, aller,
> Porter la lance et bois faire voler,
> Le devoir faire en l'estour furieus,
> Piquer, volter le cheval glorieus,
> Pour Bradamante, ou la haute Marphise,
> Seur de Roger, il m'ust, possible, prise.
>
> (*Elégie* III, vv. 37-42)

How Labé wrote both within but at the same time against neo-Petrarchan discourse has been intelligently, if only partially, analyzed by Ann Rosalind Jones.[12] In her discussion of Pernette du Guillet in the same article, Jones points out that Pernette was writing within a different, if equally male-dominated tradition, that of neo-Platonism, which makes her case somewhat different, even unique in the love poetry of the 16th century. Jones overstates the case when she places Pernette du Guillet entirely within the neo-Platonic mold, for the poetess does make considerable use of neo-Petrarchan imagery as Gillian Jondorff has shown.[13] However, in spite of this cross-gemination at the stylistic level and sometimes at the thematic level, her basic rhetorical and emotional situation is certainly closer to the neo-Platonic than to the neo-Petrarchan. Her poetry emphasizes the notion of intellectual and spiritual growth through love and there is, if not a total absence of jealousy, at least an unusually benign and tranquil treatment of this pervasive theme in neo-Petrarchan poetry. The emotion of love as described by Du Guillet is not a purgatorial, soul-searing experience, but instead is suffused with a glow of happiness and satisfaction.

Du Guillet's choice of a neo-Platonic rather than a neo-Petrarchan stance is already a sign that she does not intend to be assimilated by her poet-lover. Since her biography (what we know of it) and her literary production are, for better or for worse, inextricably linked with those of Scève who is presented both as her Beloved and Master (in all senses of the Latin *magister*), it is surprising indeed that she did not adopt a poetic style more closely in tune with his, which, in spite of numerous neo-Platonic elements is predominantly neo-Petrarchan. Much has been made of the *Rymes* and the *Délie* as constituting a poetic dialogue, but in fact the number of poems which can be read in this light is relatively small and such a point of view ignores or downplays the other intertextualities pertinent to Du Guillet's poetry.[14] Ann Jones is correct when she states that "it is misleading to speak . . . of a dialog between Scève and du Guillet. They circle rather in separate orbits defined by the fact that the mode in which they write has developed in an androcentric literary universe."[15] It also becomes quite clear when one passes from the terrible, all-powerful, cruel Lady who is the object of Scève's verse to the calm intellectual and reasoned persona of the *Rymes* that the notion of poetic dialogue is of little use in a consideration of their poetry. For all her apparent submission, Du Guillet is remarkably independent and what may at first sight appear to be a tamed and subjugated Délie is more than capable of preserving her own poetic autonomy and of expressing it in a way which is deliberately feminine.

The opening epigrammes of her *Rymes*[16] are on one level at least ironic rewritings of the opening dizains of Scève's *Délie*. In the first poem, we have a presentation of the *innamoramento* which stresses the divine origin

of her love ("Le hault pouvoir des Astres a permis . . ."), but which stands
by its serenity in notable contrast to the antithetical and paradoxical state
Scève describes. Whereas at the end of his sixth dizain Scève is vacillating
between life and death ("Et des ce jour continuellement / En sa beaulté
gist ma mort, et ma vie"), Du Guillet proceeds easily from a state of non-
being, of intellectual and spiritual unconsciousness to an unproblematic
contemplation of the divine and beneficent Beloved. *Vie*, which is the final
rhyme word of both dizains 1 and 6 of the *Délie* (rhyming with *desvie* in
dizain 1 and *asservie* in 6) is found at the end of line 4 in Du Guillet's first
epigramme in an expression which signifies the contrary of life: "sans sen-
timent de vie" and it is associated with the rhyme words *convie* and *servie*
which are positive counterparts to the pessimistic *desvie* and *asservie* of the
Délie. However, Du Guillet is not so naive as to suggest that virtuous love
is without complications and in lines 5 and 6 of the same poem she speaks
of "le sentir du mal, qui me convie / A regraver ma dure impression /
D'amour cruelle, et doulce passion . . . ." This brief nod to the suffering
endured by the neo-Petrarchan lover evokes in addition the act of writing
about her sufferings and textualizing them, thus giving them permanence
("regraver ma *dure impression*"—emphasis mine), as well as recalling the
durs Epigrammes of which Scève speaks in the *huitain liminaire* of the
Délie. Here the femininity of the persona is stressed on several levels,
firstly by the doubling of the feminine adjectives *heureuse* et *servie*, showing gender not simply by their endings but by the situation they describe.
A male author writing love poetry at this time in history is almost never
heureux. In the same way a poet is never *servi* but can only be *asservi*, so
that the playful echo of Scève's text that we find in the *servie* of Du Guillet's poem underlines the uniquely female situation of the poetic voice.
The fact that Du Guillet's first epigramme expresses the ideal and abstract
nature of her love[17] and contains none of the latent sensuality and ambiguity one can discern in the opening dizains of the *Délie* (indeed throughout the work) also establishes her distance from her Master and Beloved.
That Scève the teacher, whose love has an important sensual component,
should need to be so often reminded by his dependent disciple of the *hault
pouvoir* and the *haulte qualité* which should elevate love, is further irony.

   Both poets use images of light and darkness to describe the love state
and their respective Beloveds but in quite different ways. In her second
epigramme Du Guillet uses a common enough image in the neo-Petrarchan
lexicon: the coming of dawn as a symbol of the arrival of the Beloved, but
develops it in a way which is foreign to the tradition. In dizain 304 ("Ap-
paroissant l'Aulbe de mon beau jour"), Scève uses the image within the
limits of the convention by associating the beauty of the Dawn with the

beauty of the Beloved. For Du Guillet, however, night signifies not simply the absence of the Beloved but above all the night of ignorance, the night of the silence which preceded her capacity to analyze and give voice to her emotional and intellectual experience. The coming of dawn is associated not with physical light but above all with enlightenment, which dispels the darkness of ignorance (which according to Antoine Héroët was "le plus grief mal qui advienne à personne").[18]

It is noteworthy that throughout the *Rymes* Du Guillet never praises the Beloved for his physical beauty, nor even attempts to describe him, even though in both neo-Platonic and neo-Petrarchan discourse beauty is an important component of love. Ann Jones has suggested that this lack of description in both Du Guillet and Labé is due to the "absence of a standard for masculine beauty."[19] As *descriptio* is not limited to the Petrarchan mode and as descriptions of male beauty can be found at least as far back as Ovid, this argument is not particularly convincing. However, when Jones goes on to postulate that the silence concerning male beauty is perhaps a deliberate one, a further way of establishing their difference within the *mimétisme* of the male tradition they have been forced to use as their only possible means of expression, she is much closer to the mark. In the case of Du Guillet, the continual insistence upon the Beloved's intellectual and literary qualities stresses the cerebral nature of her love, underscores the weakness of the male poet who constantly has to battle his own sensuality, and serves as a discrete but definite "no" to the physical favors Scève's fictional Lover is surreptitiously asking from Délie. The only *jouyssance* he can hope for in Du Guillet's verse is the "pleine jouyssance" of "tous dons des Cieulx" (epigramme 3). However, we must beware of overstressing the poetess' autonomy and independence, for, in the same dizain, she denigrates herself for her lack of knowledge and for her inadequate gifts of literary expression, while once more praising the divinely inspired talents of her Beloved:

> Peu de sçavoir que tu fais grand nuysance
> A mon esprit qui n'a la promptitude
> De mercier les Cieulx pour l'habitude
> De celuy là, où les trois Graces prinses
> Contentes sont de telle servitude
> Par les vertus, qui en luy sont comprinses.

The virtue and eloquence of the Beloved cause the poetess to compare him to Apollo, a comparison which some have seen as part of the alleged dialogue between the *Rymes* and the *Délie*. However, closer examination reveals that this is not necessarily the case. In Scève's poem, Délie is pre-

sented as Apollo's sister according to mythological tradition, and is associated with the ambiguous Luna-Diana-Hecate triple goddess of Greek and
Roman antiquity. In the *Rymes*, Du Guillet deliberately shortcircuits any
real dialogue between her and Scève by her refusal to portray her persona
as in any way associated with either the Moon-Goddess or Hecate. In view
of her characterization of Scève as Apollo ("A Apollo peulx este con-
formé," épigramme 4) and his use of lunar imagery to describe Délie, this
would appear to be almost obligatory if we were in the presence of a real
dialogue. Yet only once, in a poem I will discuss later, does Du Guillet
make reference to the Diana of mythology and then only indirectly. If
in the pre-amatory state she is in darkness, once enlightened she refuses
to be simply a moon to her Beloved's sun. Rather she is the *journée* to his
jour and while the ending *-née* does suggest passivity and reflected light,
it is the constant and bright light associated with the day, not the ghostly
half-light of the moon. She is the complement of her *jour* rather than its
female antithesis, so that she is not only going against the grain of neo-
Petrarchan discourse but is breaking down traditional phallogocentric
oppositions: male/female, light/darkness, day/night.

One of the most interesting rewritings of neo-Petrarchan material is to
be found in chanson VI (which is also, partially at least, a rewriting of
Scève's first and sixth dizains):

> Sans congnoissance aucune en mon Printemps, j'estois:
> Alors aucun souspir encor point ne gectois
> Libre sans liberté: car rien ne regrectois
> En ma vague pensée
> De molz et vains desirs follement dispensée.

The pre-amatory state described here is neither a time of erotic desires (as
in Scève's first dizain), nor of happiness as in his sixth dizain, but represents instead an emotional and intellectual *néant*. *Amour*, here Cupid god
of sensual love, who attempts to fill this vacuum, is totally unsuccessful
and in desperation he is forced to turn to the *Archiers de vertu* who suc-
ceed in subjugating the person at whom the arrows of virtuous love are
fired. However, here, the persona is not the usual pitiable victim, since
Vertu only allows her heart to be *chastement blessé*. Thanks to the purity
of her love, she is superior to Cupid, can actually console him and even
thank him for awakening her to chaste love as personified by the fictional
Scève:

> Et tu me mis es mains, où heureuse devins
> D'un qui est haultement en ses escriptz divins
> Comme de nom, severe,
> Et chaste tellement que chascun l'en revere.

The pun on Scève's Latin name *Seva* (saevus/sévère/cruel) and the insistence upon his chastity are an example of what we might call learned levity (to use Jerry Nash's felicitous term) and her treatment of the jealousy motif which she takes up in chanson IV is both a way of signaling the fact that she has noticed Scève's attention to other women, and an affirmation of her own self-control:

> Si mainte Dame veult son amytié avoir,
> Voulant participer de son heureux sçavoir,
> Et par tout il tasche acquicter son debvoir,
>   Ses vertus j'en accuse
> Plus puissantes que luy, et tant que je l'excuse.

Even though the theme of the rival is treated with somewhat less equanimity in other poems of the *Rymes* (for example épigrammes XXXIV, XL and XLI), nowhere in Du Guillet do we find even a suggestion of the paroxysm of Scève's famous jealousy dizain ("Seul avec moy, elle avec sa partie . . . ," CLXI) and compared with the treatment of the theme by other contemporary poets, Du Guillet's utilization of it is a model of moderation.

That the poetess is not immune to the temptations of sensuality but that she is capable of mastering such tendencies in a way that most male poets are not, is clearly shown in her second elegy. Here Du Guillet describes a day dream in which she imagines herself alone with her Beloved. While he is philosophizing, she slips away, undresses and jumps naked into a nearby stream, from which she attempts to lure him to her by the sweetness of her singing, like a mythological siren or a female Orpheus. If he were to approach, she would, however, permit him no liberties, for should he attempt to touch her, she would throw a handful of cold water into his face. We are more than a little surprised at seeing the chaste persona of the *Rymes* play the role of *allumeuse* here, and it is presumably to quench any fire she may have kindled that she splashes him with water.

If the cool water dampens the ardor of the Poet-Beloved and diverts the erotic direction taken in the first part of the elegy, the poetess has not yet finished with her Beloved. She pursues the theme of the naked temptress, now placing it within a mythological framework, while at the same time subverting this framework, which is, incidentally, central to the mythology of the *Délie*. The nude bather approached by a man evokes of course the story of Actaeon and Diana, but with the important difference that the mythical Diana did nothing to attract the young hunter. When the poetess finally does refer directly to the Diana-Actaeon myth, she takes care to underline the important differences between her dream and the traditional version of the myth. When she splashes her Beloved with water, she does wish for a metamorphosis to take place. However, she neither wants her Beloved to be devoured by his dogs, nor to become a stag (*un cerf*), but her desire is that he should become her slave, her *serf*. The pun on *cerf*/*serf* is completely in keeping with the playful and slightly mocking tone adopted by the speaker of the poem. However, this is not simply another case of learned levity but above all a protest—albeit a good-natured one—against the submissive stance Du Guillet has, *de force ou de gré*, adopted elsewhere in her poetry and a desire for a reversal of the Master/Slave relationship in which she has been involved. Her treatment of the myth also expresses her desire to distance herself from the female object of Scève's poetry. In her reference to the Diana-Actaeon myth, she explicitly refuses to identify herself with Diana (and hence with Délie) but presents herself instead as a rival capable of arousing Diana's jealousy:

> Mais que de moy se sentist estre serf,
> Et serviteur transformé tellement
> Qu'ainsi cuydast en son entendement
> Tant que Dyane en eust sur moy envie,
> De luy avoir sa puissance ravie.

The feeling of superiority this metamorphosis would give her, both because she has subjugated Scève and taken him from Diana, is sufficient to bring about yet another metamorphosis, the transformation of the speaker into a divinity in her own right: "Combien heureuse et grande me dirois! / Certes Deesse estre me cuyderois." However, after this extended wish fulfillment daydream is developed, the poetess retreats to her submissive pose in the name of poetry and out of devotion to Apollo and the Muses, not wanting to deprive them of one of their most eloquent spokesmen. In deference to the god and goddesses of poetry, she undoes the spell she wished to cast over Scève with a typical denigration of her own worth:

> Laissez le aller les neuf Muses servir,
> Sans se vouloir dessoubz moy asservir,
> Soubz moy, qui suis sans grace, et sans merite.

However, beneath this self-depreciation, Du Guillet is also, paradoxically, proclaiming her power, both as woman and poetess, for it is not simply because she *cannot* subjugate Scève that she renounces doing so, but because she *will not* out of respect for his poetic gifts. As a final gesture, she even allows herself to be associated with Scève's writing and while she will in no way permit herself to be identified with that "Objet de haulte vertu" (and not because of any lack of her own virtue), she acknowledges

Scève's wish to reach contentment and happiness with her through his poetry:

> Laissez le aller, qu'Apollo je ne irrite,
> Le remplissant de Deité profonde,
> Pour contre moy susciter tout le Monde,
> Lequel un jour par ses escriptz s'attend
> D'estre avec moy et heureux, et content.

The taming of the muse is more apparent than real and Du Guillet is much less a slave to Scève than she appears to be. Her submission to him is partial and voluntary and is accepted in the name of a higher purpose: the continuance of his poetic creativity.

While imitating male-produced poetry, Pernette du Guillet has managed to maintain her essential difference as a woman writer and to indicate her specificity as a woman writing within a male-dominated tradition. Although reproducing certain elements of the neo-Petrarchan, neo-Platonizing style of Scève's verse, she is in many instances able to outdo her mentor in her use of abstractions and in her insistence upon virtuous and chaste love, largely free from the terrors (however *agréables*) which are part of his sentimental landscape. Scève, for all his nods to neo-Platonism, is in fact much more neo-Petrarchan than neo-Platonic and Délie never does become *l'Idée* in the true Platonic sense of the term. Du Guillet, although her Platonism is not always completely orthodox,[20] is nonetheless much closer to the concept of pure and chaste love than is her teacher Scève, and her poetic stance serves as a constant challenge to his philosophical and stylistic strategies, while at the same time affirming her autonomy as a woman and a poetess. Of course, all writers stand in an ambivalent relationship with their literary mentors, past and present, yet Du Guillet's establishment of her poetic individuality is much more than simply a case of the "anxiety of influence" (to use Harold Bloom's terminology). Through the medium of male discourse, the female poetic voice makes itself heard, sometimes as a complement, sometimes as a challenge to the male voice which attempts to subordinate it, but always calmly, always purposefully, proclaiming its difference.

NOTES

1. Montaigne, *Essais*, III, ix.

2. Sidney Abbott and Barbara Love, *Sappho Was a Right on Woman: A Liberated View of Lesbianism* (New York, 1973).

3. The poetry of the female troubadours is virtually indistinguishable from that of the male troubadours if one substitutes feminine pronouns for masculine.

4. See Joan Kelly-Gadol, "Did Women Have a Renaissance?," in *Becoming Visible: Women in European History*, eds. Renate Bridenthal and Claudia Koons (Boston, 1977).

5. See Verdun-L. Saulnier, "Etude sur Pernette du Guillet," *BHR*, 4 (1944), 7-119.

6. Natalie Davis, *Society and Culture in Early Modern France* (Stanford, 1965), p. 73.

7. Louise Labé, *Euvres* (Lyons, 1824), pp. 1-4. Emphasis mine.

8. Marguerite de Navarre was an exception to this tendency on account of her rank in society—women of the upper aristocracy had always enjoyed more freedom than women of other social classes—and because of the spiritual nature of her poetry.

9. Simone de Beauvoir, *Le Deuxième Sexe* (Paris, 1949), p. 235.

10. Luce Irigaray, *Ce Sexe qui n'en est pas un* (Paris, 1977), p. 74.

11. Nancy Miller, "Emphasis Added: Plots and Plausibilities in Women's Fiction," *PMLA*, 96 (1981), 37.

12. Ann Rosalin Jones, "Assimilation with a Difference: Renaissance Women Poets and Literary influence." *Yale French Studies*, 62 (1981), 135-53.

13. Gillian Jondorf, "Petrarchan Variations in Pernette du Guillet and Louise Labé," *MLR*, 71 (1976), 766-78.

14. See Joyce Miller, *Convention and Form in the* Rymes *of Pernette du Guillet*, Univ. of Pennsylvania Diss. 1977, pp. 52-54.

15. Jones, pp. 144-45.

16. We cannot be sure that they were in fact the first poems of her collection, but in view of their thematic material this would seem likely. All quotations from the *Rymes* come from the 1968 edition, ed. Victor E. Graham (Geneva).

17. Robert Griffin, "Pernette du Guillet's Response to Scève: A Case for Abstract Love," *L'Esprit Créateur*, 5 (1965), 110-16 and Robert D. Cottrell, "Pernette du Guillet's *Rymes*: An Adventure in Ideal Love," *BHR*, 31 (1969), 553-71, seem to me to be much closer to the mark than T. Anthony Perry, "Pernette du Guillet's Poetry of Love and Desire," *BHR*, 35 (1973), 260-71, in their assessment of the chaste nature of Du Guillet's love.

18. Antoine Héroët, *La Parfaycte Amye*, 2e livre, v. 1259.

19. Jones, p. 148.

20. See Joyce Miller, p. 14.

Le Sonnet et l'épigramme, ou:
l'enjeu de la "superscription"

François Rigolot

> "Le Sonnet suit l'épigramme de bien près."
> Thomas Sebillet

Tout au long du Moyen Age le mot "sonnet," dans des orthographes variées, a été d'usage courant pour désigner le chant lyrique au sens large. Diminutif de "son," le "sonnet" retenait la connotation diminutive d'une forme lyrique médiocre, à la fois par le style moyen (ni "altiloque" ni "pédestre") et par la modeste dimension. Du *Roman de Thèbes* à *Renaud de Montauban* et de Jean Molinet à Jean Bouchet, les exemples ne manquent pas qui traduisent en "sonnets" le chant d'amour ("De leur amor *sones* faisant") ou la déploration funèbre ("Sons et *sonnetz*, sonnés sans soneries").[1]

Il ne semble même pas qu'avec Clément Marot, reconnu généralement aujourd'hui comme l'"inventeur" du sonnet français,[2] l'importation et la francisation du "sonetto" italien ait profondément modifié la structure du champ sémantique d'un mot qui plongeait ses racines dans un lointain passé linguistique. En fait, les deux versants principaux du sens, général et restreint, français et italien, paraissent avoir subsisté côte à côte au cours du XVIe siècle comme l'atteste, par exemple, ce passage du *Triomphe de l'Agneau*, publié dans les *Marguerites de la Marguerite des Princesses* en 1547: "Fille Zion, chante la parabole, / Chante treshault le *sonnet* et le rolle [du Christ qui a vaincu la Mort]" (vv. 541-42).[3]

Cependant ce flottement a dû nécessairement se résorber, du moins en partie, sous la pression des poéticiens et des politiciens au moment où s'élaborait en France, vers 1547-48, une théorie du nouveau genre à forme fixe. Dans son *Art Poëtique françois*, qui date de 1548, Thomas Sebillet nous dit que le sonnet se rattache à l'épigramme par la "matiére" et la "mesure" mais qu'il est "emprunté par nous de l'Italien" et (sous-entendu: en conséquence) que sa "forme" est "autre que (celle de) nos epigrammes."[4] Autrement dit, seule la "forme" ne serait pas indigène. Ces trois mots, "matiére," "mesure" et "forme" sont explicités dans trois paragraphes distincts du second chapitre de l'ouvrage, intitulé *Du Sonnet* et qui fait suite au chapitre initial consacré à l'épigramme. Reprenons rapidement ces trois chefs d'intérêt pour analyser ce qui, selon Sebillet, distingue le sonnet de l'épigramme:

1) *Matière* (titre du paragraphe: "*Matiére de Sonnet*"): "La matiére de l'épigramme et la matiére du Sonnet sont toutes unes" (p. 116). Cependant Sebillet insiste sur la *gravité* du ton qui doit caractériser le sonnet: la "matiére facécieuse" doit être laissée à l'épigramme.

2) *Forme* (titre du paragraphe: "*Qu'est uniformité en Ryme*"): Sebillet s'en tient à la définition du sonnet régulier dit *lyonnais*, c'est-à-dire du quatorzain à quatrains embrassés selon le schéma abba, abba, cc, deed, avec une certaine liberté dans l'arrangement des rimes des tercets (pp. 116-18).

3) *Mesure* (titre du paragraphe: "*Quelz vers requiert le Sonnet*"): Ici le poéticien se montre très légaliste. Seul le décassylabe est admis dans le sonnet ce qui, comme on l'a fait remarqué, est paradoxal, l'année même où paraissent les premiers sonnets en alexandrins dans la *Laure d'Avignon* de Vasquin Philieul (p. 118). Cependant cette propriété exclusive du mètre de dix pieds se comprend par rapport au chapitre sur l'épigramme dans lequel Sebillet faisait remarquer que le décasyllabe convient le mieux aux matières "plus graves et sententieuses" (p. 113).

De ce court résumé il ressort bien que "matiére" et "mesure" ont partie liée, comme dans le dizain balladique dont Maurice Scève avait consacré la "gravité" quatre ans plus tôt dans sa *Délie*. On comprend alors pourquoi Sebillet a voulu ouvrir son chapitre sur le sonnet en disant: "Sonnet n'est autre chose que le parfait epigramme de l'Italien, comme le dizain du François" (p. 115). Comme nous l'avons montré ailleurs, il y a même dans le huitain initial (ou final, selon les éditions) du *canzoniere* scévien une notation qui semble indiquer clairement la novation formelle de l'épigramme commune: les "si *durs* Epygrammes" sont le signe de la fixité isométrique et isostrophique qui s'instaure dans le nouveau recueil.[5]

Cependant, dans la *Délie*, l'épigramme avait perdu son statut originel d'*inscription*. Scève avait tressé une couronne, une plénitude circulaire offerte à l'*Object de Plus Haulte Vertu* et avait laissé au huitain la fonction de poème-préface, inscrit en exergue, jouant le rôle étymologique de l'épigramme-épigraphe. Ailleurs, ce sera le sonnet qui tiendra cette place épigraphique: dans les *Marguerites* de la Reine de Navarre et dans son propre *Microcosme* où le sonnet joue le rôle de "poème d'escorte." La raison à cela est simple, si l'on en juge d'après les déclarations explicites

de Sebillet et ce que nous pouvons glaner des intentions de Scève: la "gravité" du dizain décasyllabique n'était pas propre à en faire un *poème d'inscription.* Sebillet insiste en effet sur la plénitude du chiffre dix ("nombre
plein et consommé") dans son éloge du dizain qu'il définit comme "l'épigramme aujourd'huy estimé premier" (p. 110). Il accorde "plus grande
perfection" et "plus parfaite modulation" à cette forme savante et déclare:
"c'est le plus communément usurpé dés savans" (ibid.). Enfin il est significatif que notre théoricien cite une "épigramme" de la *Délie* dans son inté-
gralité à la suite de ses remarques flatteuses.[6]
      Ainsi la fonction paradigmatique du dizain scévien n'a pas échappé à
Sebillet. D'ailleurs, s'il rapproche le sonnet de l'épigramme ce n'est pas de
n'importe quelle forme strophique mais bien de la "parfaite epigramme,"
autrement dit du dizain balladique en décasyllabe, du "dur Epygramme"
de la *Délie.* C'est en ce sens qu'il faut lire la définition, déjà citée, qu'il
nous donne du sonnet dans son *Art Poëtique françois.* La récurrence de
certaines expressions servant à qualifier les deux formes, italienne et française, concourt à affirmer le parallélisme, l'"equipollence" comme on
disait alors, entre les deux genres rivaux. Il en est ainsi de la tonalité ("gravité") et du travail artistique ("science"). Le sonnet, "fait par les *savans*
Poëtes,*"* émule le dizain qui "est le plus communément usurpé des *savans*"
(p. 110). Ce préjugé élitiste, valorisant le savoir comme critère de distinction générique, permet en fait d'opérer un clivage entre deux types radica-
lement opposés d'épigrammes: une épigramme imparfaite à forme libre qui
s'allonge "tant que le requiert la matiére prise" (p. 104); et une épigramme
parfaite et savante à forme fixe, dizain ou sonnet.
      La première est conforme à l'étymologie: elle est une inscription (Sebil-
let dit: "superscription"). Elle n'a pas d'autonomie; elle s'ajoute simplement à une autre œuvre, "*dessus* un portail *dedans* la frise enfoncée *entre*
l'architrave et la corniche prominentes *par dessus* lés chapiteauz dés Co-
lomnes" (p. 104). L'abondance des prépositions de lieu dans cette description est en elle-même le signe de son existence spatiale et de sa relativité:
elle n'existe que *sur, dans* ou *entre* une autre "nature," jugée, elle, essentielle. A cette écriture subsidiaire (Montaigne dirait: cet "emblème super-
numéraire") s'oppose l'épigramme autarcique, œuvre de poésie à part
entière et qui se suffit à elle-même, ayant atteint l'apogée de l'art et du
savoir: c'est le dizain; et le sonnet n'en est en fait qu'un avatar, une transposition à marque étrangère caractérisée par une "structure . . . un peu
facheuse," c'est-à-dire, sans connotation péjorative, ardue, difficile (p. 116).
      Si l'on revient maintenant à la théorie du sonnet, il semble que Sebillet
soit resté insensible à une différence considérable qui existait *de facto*
entre la nouvelle forme et l'épigramme: différence qui ne tient ni à la

matière, ni à la *mesure*, ni même à la *forme*, mais à l'*usage* qu'en faisaient les contemporains. Il ne se rend pas compte du fait que les sonnets de Marot, de Mellin de Saint-Gelais ou de Jacques Peletier du Mans sont des pièces encomiastiques ou préfacielles, quand elles ne sont pas des traductions de Pétrarque.[7] Encore plus curieusement, il reste aveugle au fait qu'il publie lui-même un sonnet, après l'Avis au lecteur, en tête de son édition de l'*Art Poëtique françois*:

A L'ENVIEUS

Qu'ay-je espéré de ce tant peu d'ouvrage,
Que ma plume a labouré *cy dedans?*
Honneur? nenny: je suis trop jeune d'ans
Pour le gaigner, de savoir d'avantage.

Profit? non plus: de tout tel labourage
Aujourd'huy sont lés fruis peu evidens.
T'enseigner? moins: je say tés yeux ardens
Ne s'éclercir de tant umbreux nuage.

Quoy donc? te plaire, entreprenant montrer
Quel vouloir j'ay de voir garder lés Muses
Entre François leur naïve douceur.

Et le montrant si j'ay peu rencontrer
Chemin pour y venir, que tu en uses:
Si non, que tu en montres un plus seur. (p. 5)

Ce sonnet est tout à fait typique des pièces préfacielles qui se publiaient alors. Qu'on pense au dizain dédicatoire composé par Hugues Salel, poète cadurcien de l'école de Marot, qui accompagne la troisième édition du *Pantagruel* de 1534; ou encore à l'avis au lecteur écrit de la main de Rabelais sur lequel s'ouvre la deuxième édition du *Gargantua* de 1535. On y trouve le même jeu rhétorique, aux variantes près, sur le précepte horatien du "miscendo utile dulci." La feinte de Sebillet consiste à repousser "honneur," "profit" et "enseignement" pour mettre en relief son intention de "plaire." Mais tout le projet de ce discours trouve sa fin hors de lui-même: le "*cy dedans*" du premier quatrain ne se réfère pas au sonnet mais au livre qu'il annonce; et l'on retrouve l'indication de lieu qui caractérisait précisément l'épigramme imparfaite et ancillaire.

Qu'est-ce à dire, dès lors, de la distinction subtile que l'on croyait pouvoir faire entre les deux types d'épigrammes? Aux mains des "bons Poëtes François" (p. 104)—et il n'y a pas de raison de douter, malgré la fausse modestie à l'adresse de l'"ENVIEUS," que Sebillet ne se soit placé parmi eux—le sonnet est-il vraiment l'égal du poème parfait, du dizain délien, ou n'est-il qu'un discours marginal, préfaciel, simple "superscription" (p. 103)?

Si l'on prend à la lettre ce qu'il nous dit dans les tercets de son sonnet "A L'ENVIEUS," on est frappé par l'aspect conservateur de sa poétique. Il s'agit de *plaire* aux lecteurs, c'est-à-dire aux poètes ou apprentis-poètes de son temps, en montrant le désir qu'il a ("entreprenant montrer / Quel vouloir j'ay") de perpétuer les règles d'une poésie essentiellement française ("de voir *garder* lés Muses / Entre François leur naïve douceur").

Sebillet nous tient d'ailleurs un langage semblable dans l'avis "AU LECTEUR" en prose sur lequel s'ouvre son livre et qui précède le sonnet "A L'ENVIEUS":

Ce que tu liras icy, lecteur, escrit en ta faveur touchant la bonne part de ce qui appartient a l'art de la *Pöésie Françoise*, n'est autre chose qu'un tesmoignage de ma bonne volunté. Volunté dy-je que j'ai grande long temps a de voir, ou moins d'escrivains en ryme, ou plus de *Pöétes François*. (p. 3)

Certes l'opposition entre "rymeurs" et "Pöétes" est en elle-même une condamnation des arts de seconde rhétorique, opposition qui sera reprise telle quelle par les poètes de la Pléiade. Mais Sebillet s'intéresse plus à multiplier le nombre des poètes ("plus de Pöétes François") qu'à les encourager à innover dans l'ordre poétique. Sa "bonne volunté" consiste à prodiguer une "congnoissance de l'art" (p. 3): c'est à cela, nous dit-il, que doit se limiter son "labeur" (p. 4). Il y aurait donc une tension entre, d'une part, la définition novatrice du sonnet comme forme parfaite à importer d'Italie et d'autre part, la position conservatrice qui consiste, en pratique (avec "L'ENVIEUS") et en théorie (avec l'avis "AU LECTEUR"), à maintenir des usages et à reproduire essentiellement "ce qui appartient a l'art de la Pöésie Françoise."

Cette vision de l'art comme reproduction d'un savoir acquis se trouve d'ailleurs inscrite à la première ligne du chapitre sur le sonnet. On y lit en effet: "CHAPITRE II. *Du Sonnet. Qu'est Sonnet.*—Le Sonnet suit l'épigramme de bien prés" (p. 115). Autrement dit, la théorie du nouveau genre reçoit une formulation purement métonymique. Elle suit celle de l'épigramme spatialement (le "CHAPITRE I" s'intitulait: "*De l'Epigramme, et de sés usages et differences,*" p. 103); et elle la suit thématiquement (en "matiére"), métriquement (en "mesure") et, comme nous l'avons vu, sémantiquement. Le sonnet ne serait donc qu'une extension à physionomie étrangère d'un genre typiquement français, emblématique même de "l'art de la Pöésie Françoise." La différence se réduirait à des questions formelles: nombre de vers et schéma de rimes embrassées. On comprend dans ces conditions que Sebillet ait voulu conserver à son propre sonnet un statut épigraphique, perpétuant ainsi l'usage scévien du poème d'escorte, mettant en exergue sa formule de "superscription" et finalement, comme il dit, exhibant sa volonté de "voir garder les Muses / Entre François leur naïve douceur."[8]

Or c'est précisément à ces limbes liminales du discours préfaciel (ou postfaciel) que Joachim Du Bellay va vouloir arracher le sonnet. Dans la *Deffence et Illustration de la Langue Françoise*, un an à peine après la publication de l'*Art Poëtique françois* de Sebillet, il va tenter d'effacer du nouveau genre les marques évidentes de la "superscription." C'est du moins dans cette vue, nous semble-t-il, qu'il va lancer aux futurs poètes la fameuse injonction: "*Sonne* moy ces beaux *sonnetz*, non moins docte que plaisante invention Italienne."[9] La figure paronomastique ("*Sonne*"/"*sonnetz*") a une fonction remotivante indéniable: c'est l'équivalent de la *figura etimologica* dans la rhétorique médiévale. Ce faisant, Du Bellay poursuit deux objectifs. D'une part, il affirme l'origine étrangère du genre, sa "nouvelleté": c'est une "invention Italienne"; et il ne manquera pas de le répéter ici et ailleurs.[10] Mais, d'autre part, cette trouvaille appartient, par sa structure linguistique, au patrimoine immémorial de la culture française. Si *chanson* a donné *chansonnette*, et *rondeau*, *rondelet*, alors le vieux *son*, au sens de *chant*, peut aisément donner *sonnet*. Bien mieux, la langue vulgaire retient encore ce mot comme vivant, en dehors de toute influence italienne, puisqu'il figure en bonne place dans le grand recueil lyrique de la sœur du feu roi, les *Marguerites de la Marguerite des Princesses*.

En outre, l'expression allitérée qu'emploie l'auteur de la *Deffence* a ses lettres d'antiquité. Le syntagme "sonner un sonnet" est calqué sur son modèle latin "*carmen canere*." Il y a l'illustre précédent des *Géorgiques* où Virgile nous dit chanter à la manière du poète d'Ascra, Hésiode, en faisant retentir ses vers à travers les bourgades romaines: "Ascraeumque cano Romana per oppida carmen."[11] Et l'expression se trouve encore dans un ouvrage assez proche d'esprit de la *Deffence* puisqu'il est aussi un manifeste et un traité de rhétorique: le *De oratore* de Cicéron.[12] Si elle joue un rôle d'*auctoritas* dans l'injonction française, cette référence structurelle au modèle ancien ne s'oppose pas au retour à la langue maternelle. Au contraire, elle permet à cette langue de se hausser naturellement au niveau de son illustre devancière, ce qui fait bien partie du programme de Du Bellay. Autrement dit, "sonner des sonnets," du strict point de vue formel et par le biais de l'intertexte latin, est une façon d'affirmer, c'est-à-dire de *défendre* et d'*illustrer* la langue française.

Il y a donc une double opération de prélèvement et d'enracinement dans le geste de Du Bellay vis-à-vis du sonnet renaissant. Il n'existe pas de "default de nature" (I, 3, p. 24)—"non per difetto della natura," avait dit

Speroni (p. 25, note 1)—puisque le mot faisait déjà partie de la langue, et
le syntagme de la littérature. Il y a simplement eu faute d'usage ou, comme
le dit Du Bellay, "coulpe de ceux qui l'ont euë en garde & ne l'ont cultivée
à suffisance" ("per colpa di loro che l'hebbero in guardia, che non la colti-
vorno a bastanza," I, 3, pp. 24 et 25, note 1). Et de même que les Romains
ont imité les Grecs pour enrichir leur culture, de même les Français doivent
emprunter cette nouvelle forme poétique aux Italiens: à condition toutefois que l'emprunt ne soit pas plaqué artificiellement sur la langue, qu'il ne
reste pas extérieur, pure "superscription," mais qu'il soit "transformé,"
"digéré," "converti en sang et nourriture" (I, 7, p. 42).

Il n'est pas surprenant que cette théorie de la "grephe" (pp. 42-43) ait
trouvé son application pratique dans la *défense* du sonnet puisque le manifeste s'accompagnait d'un recueil exclusivement composé de "parfaits epigrammes Italiens." Il faut pourtant remarquer que si la première édition de
l'*Olive* (1549) s'ouvrait par un huitain dédicatoire, la seconde édition
(1550) place en exergue un sonnet encomiastique tout à fait dans la tradition de la "superscription":

A TRESILLUSTRE
PRINCESSE MADAME MARGUERITE
SEUR UNIQUE DU ROY
LUY PRESENTANT CE LIVRE

sonnet

Par un sentier inconneu à mes yeux
Vostre grandeur sur ses ailes me porte
Où de Phebus la main sçavante et forte
Guide le frein du chariot des cieulx.

Là elevé au cercle radieux
Par un Demon heureux, qui me conforte,
Celle fureur tant doulce j'en rapporte,
Dont vostre nom j'egalle aux plus haulx Dieux.

O vierge donc, sous qui la Vierge Astrée
A faict encor' en nostre siecle entrée!
Prenez en gré *ces poëtiques fleurs.*

Ce sont mes vers, que les chastes Carites
Ont emaillez de plus de cent couleurs
Pour aler voir la fleur des MARGUERITES.

COELO MUSA BEAT[13]

Comment interpréter cette apparente palinodie du genre? Comment accepter à la fois le plaidoyer théorique du "Sonne moy ces beaux sonnetz" et
l'écriture épigraphique du discours préfaciel? Les "poëtiques fleurs" promises dans les tercets renverraient donc à d'autres tercets, après l'avis "AU

LECTEUR" en prose, après le titre même qui introduit les 115 sonnets véritables de l'édition définitive. Quand Du Bellay écrit: "Ce sont mes vers" au début du second tercet, il ne se réfère pas aux vers mêmes où il s'exprime mais à ceux qu'il promet au-delà de ce sonnet initial qui, paradoxalement, devrait se faire oublier en annonçant la nature d'une "autre" poésie.

L'exemple de Maurice Scève a dû compter pour beaucoup dans le choix du sonnet comme poème-dédicace. La "fleur des MARGUERITES" du quatorzième et dernier vers se réfère, comme on le sait, à la sœur du roi Henri II, Marguerite de France, à laquelle il dédiera encore les derniers sonnets de ses *Regrets*. Or une autre Marguerite, décédée l'année même de la *Deffence* et de la première *Olive*, avait fait publier à Lyon, chez Jean de Tournes en 1547, son fameux recueil de poésies, les *Marguerites de la Marguerite des Princesses*. Et la reine de Navarre avait eu pour laudateur le plus grand poète de l'époque, un Lyonnais comme cela s'imposait, l'auteur de la *Délie*. Placé en tête de l'œuvre en deux tomes, immédiatement après l'Epître de Jean de La Haye, le sonnet de Maurice Scève avait un chapeau assez voisin de celui qu'allait choisir Du Bellay dans sa seconde *Olive*: "AUX DAMES DES VERTUS DE LA TRESILLUSTRE & TRESVERTUEUSE PRINCESSE MARGUERITE DE FRANCE, ROYNE DE NAVARRE DEVOTEMENT AFFECTIONEES. M. Sc." Il n'est pas douteux que le précédent scévien ait pesé en faveur de l'adoption du sonnet pour remplacer le huitain de la première *Olive*, surtout avec la réédition des *Marguerites* en un volume par Pierre de Tours en 1549.[14]

Il semble donc qu'on retrouve chez Du Bellay la tension que nous avions déjà notée chez Sebillet; à savoir entre une attitude novatrice tournée vers la "plaisante invention Italienne" du *canzoniere* et une position traditionnelle qui considère encore le sonnet comme un poème d'escorte, une épigramme commune, une "superscription." Cependant Du Bellay cherchera toujours à affirmer le caractère essentiellement lyrique du sonnet: en l'opposant à l'épigramme et en le rattachant à l'ode. C'est la raison pour laquelle il écrit dans la *Deffence*:

> Sonne moy ces beaux sonnetz, non moins docte que plaisante invention Italienne, *conforme de nom à l'ode*, & differente d'elle seulement pource que le sonnet a certains vers reiglez & limitez, & l'ode peut courir par toutes manieres de vers librement, voyre en inventer à plaisir . . . (II, 4, pp. 120-22)

Le *Quintil Horatian* et, à sa suite, la plupart des critiques vont s'étonner de cette prétendue ressemblance entre le sonnet et l'ode ou se demander ce qui a bien pu motiver Du Bellay à établir une telle analogie.[15]

La lecture que nous proposons ici permet pourtant de lever en grande partie les objections. Tout d'abord, il y a le fait, déjà suggéré par Chamard, que le verbe grec *adô*, d'où vient le substantif *ôdê*, *ode*, s'emploie à l'égal du latin *sonare* pour désigner le chant vocal tout aussi bien que la musique instrumentale. Il n'y a donc pas lieu de distinguer entre la "voix naturelle" de l'ode et "l'organe artificiel" du sonnet (p. 121, note 1). Ensuite, il est assez évident que Du Bellay veut rattacher les nouvelles formes lyriques qu'il propose à un passé glorieux: la "lyre Greque & Romaine" (p. 113) pour les odes; les *canzonieri* de Pétrarque et des pétrarquistes italiens pour les sonnets (pp. 120-22). Cependant, obéissant toujours à la double postulation qui caractérise sa démarche, il ne peut accueillir cette altérité du lyrisme sans lui postuler une origine, même inculte, dans le patrimoine ancestral. Il s'agit, comme il le dit lui-même, de trouver la "plante sauvaige" d'origine, que le jardinier-poéticien pourra faire "fructifier" en la cultivant de façon adéquate (pp. 24-25).

De là le besoin de se référer à la sémantique du chant, là où elle se trouve le plus naturellement: dans la bouche lexicale du bon vieux vernaculaire. Le sonnet retrouve son nom propre puisqu'il appartient de tout temps à la "Langue Françoyse" et que, tout comme elle, il "ne doit estre nommé barbare" (c'est le titre du chapitre II du premier Livre de la *Deffence*, p. 15). Autrement dit, en rapprochant le sonnet de l'ode, Du Bellay opère une double *naturalisation* des nouvelles formes lyriques qu'il propose: par le biais de ce qu'on pourrait appeler l'*isotopie du chant*. La structure même de son texte en porte d'ailleurs les stigmates. Au chapitre IV du Livre II, le parallélisme des injonctions du poéticien ne laisse aucun doute sur l'effet recherché. C'est à un "Chante moy ces odes" (p. 112) que répond le fameux "Sonne moy ces . . . sonnetz" (p. 120). Les deux expressions, formées sur le modèle ancien du *carmen canere*, comme nous l'avons déjà vu, mettent en évidence une double tautologie du second degré puisque toutes deux reviennent finalement à signifier, si on laisse de côté les détails techniques, la simple proposition suivante: "chante-moi ces chants-là!"

Cette volonté de faire triompher l'isotopie du chant dans son enracinement linguistique et culturel peut s'interpréter *a contrario* comme un désir de refouler une écriture antagoniste, c'est-à-dire ce non-chant de la "superscription" qui servait, pour Sebillet, de définition à l'épigramme (*Art Poëtique françois*, p. 103). Pour Du Bellay, en effet, deux exigences se disputent le champ de la conscience de tout vrai poète. Il lui faut à la fois rejeter la conception épigrammatique du sonnet, illustrée par Marot et Saint-Gelais, et codifiée par Sebillet; et abandonner la conception strophique d'une épigramme qui serait l'équivalent parfait du sonnet italien, et qui était celle à laquelle Scève avait donné cinq ans plus tôt ses lettres de noblesse.

La difficulté de réaliser ce double programme se trouve, sans nul doute, reflétée dans les hésitations, les troubles, les incohérences du texte de la *Deffence*. Du Bellay accueille certes l'épigramme; mais c'est une épigramme "autre," différente, à l'en croire, de celle des praticiens de son temps. Il écrit à l'adresse du futur écrivain:

> Jéte toy à ces plaisans epigrammes, *non point comme font au jourd'huy un tas de faiseurs de contes nouveaux, qui en un dizain sont contens n'avoir rien dict qui vaille aux IX. premiers vers, pourveu qu'au dixiesme il y ait le petit mot pour rire.*
>
> (pp. 109-10)

La négation de la proposition comparative s'oppose par sa longueur au laconisme de l'impératif. La brusquerie du "Jéte toy" n'échappera pas au *Quintil* qui relèvera ironiquement: "Tu veux que l'on se *jette* (comme tu parles) à ces plaisans epigrammes"! Elle est pour ainsi dire mimétique de la brièveté du genre: inscription qui doit donner l'impression d'être vive et "enlevée." En cela elle est conforme à la recommandation de Sebillet qui voulait que "les deux vers derniers soient agus en conclusion: car en cés deuz consiste la louenge de l'epigramme" (*Art Poëtique françois*, p. 114).

En outre, le "Jéte toy" de l'épigramme s'oppose nettement au "Chante moy" de l'ode et au "Sonne moy" du sonnet. La qualité lyrique du *chant* ou du *son* est passée sous silence dans le cas de l'épigramme. Qu'on *jette* des mots plaisants sur la page (l'anglais "jot down" pourrait bien convenir ici si les dictionnaires ne nous disaient que ce verbe vient de la lettre grecque *iota*...); mais qu'on ne prétende pas chanter un poème nommé "épigramme" (sous-entendu: même "dur Epygramme," au sens scévien). De plus, le changement de personne et de fonction du pronom personnel indique une autre modification profonde dans l'attitude du poéticien. Sans entrer dans les détails, disons que le datif d'attribution du "chante moy" et du "sonne moy" trahit un investissement affectif profond chez le législateur qui fait appel à la sollicitude personnelle de son interlocuteur (fais entendre ton chant *pour moi, pour mon plus grand plaisir*). En revanche, le *moy* du locuteur reste absent du propos sur l'épigramme. Au datif d'attribution s'est substitué l'objet direct du pronom réfléchi ("Jéte toy") comme si l'écriture, si plaisante qu'elle fût, n'était plus qu'une affaire de métier pour l'écrivain et laissait le locuteur indifférent. En somme, l'alternative équivaudrait à peu près à la formule suivante: "Si tu es graveur, occupe-toi de ta gravure; mais si tu es chanteur, alors chante pour mon plaisir . . ."

Il est remarquable que, parmi toutes les épigrammes possibles, ce soit justement le dizain que Du Bellay ait pris pour cible: ce "parfait epigramme . . . du François" comme disait Sebillet dans son chapitre sur le sonnet

(*Art Poëtique françois*, p. 115). La condamnation d'une forme fixe qu'on avait pu croire un moment (c'était en tout cas l'opinion de Scève et de Sebillet) destinée à devenir l'équivalent du sonnet italien pour les lettres françaises, s'inscrit donc fort opportunément dans le programme de réhabilitation du sonnet comme chant lyrique privilégié: cette "ancienne renouvelée Poësie" dont parle la seconde Préface de l'*Olive*.[16]

On peut se demander d'ailleurs si Du Bellay ne s'empresse pas de conseiller d'écrire les épigrammes "à l'immitation de Martial" (p. 110) pour laisser entendre, *a contrario*, qu'il ne s'agit pas de confondre cette forme avec le sonnet, "parfait epigramme de l'Italien" (*Art Poëtique françois*, p. 115). Le bruit courait à Lyon que Maurice Scève avait composé et traduit de nombreux "sonnets" d'amour.[17] S'il y a pu y avoir confusion, comme cela semble être le cas, avec les dizains de la *Délie*, alors cette confusion est elle-même significative de l'assimilation qu'on faisait alors couramment entre le sonnet et l'épigramme. Du Bellay a donc pu avoir intérêt à mettre fin à cette regrettable confusion; et il l'a fait sans ambiguïté. Qu'on se tourne, nous dit-il en somme (et c'est une concession à Clément Marot), du côté de Martial pour l'épigramme; mais que l'on rassemble de véritable sonnets, et non des dizains balladiques, dans les futurs *canzonieri* de la poésie française! On peut se demander pourtant si l'auteur de la *Deffence* n'a pas conservé quelque nostalgie pour le vieux genre français qu'avait si brillamment illustré le poète de la *Délie*. Dans la seconde Préface de l'*Olive*, en 1550, n'allait-il pas jusqu'à confier à son lecteur, à propos des œuvres de l'Italien Luigi Cassola: "Je finissoy' ou m'efforçoy de finir mes *sonnetz* par ceste grace qu'entre les aultres langues s'est faict propre l'*epigramme* françois."[18] L'illustrateur du sonnet ne pouvait oublier, au-delà de toutes les polémiques d'écoles, qu'il était avant tout le défenseur de la langue française.

Ainsi donc, dans la *Deffence et Illustration de la Langue Françoyse*, la campagne pour le sonnet nous est présentée comme une campagne à la fois contre l'aliénation de la "superscription," pour une naturalisation de la forme étrangère et pour une remotivation du vieux sens ancestral du chant lyrique. Ce retour en force de la *phonè*, c'est-à-dire de la voix du corps, s'accorde fort bien avec les vues, alors en vogue, du néoplatonisme ficinien et hébréen. Habité par la fureur, par l'*afflatio* poétique, l'auteur de sonnets inspirés se promène désormais dans la plaine angevine où souffle le Vent de l'Esprit. Or la hardiesse d'une telle conception ne va pas susciter que de l'admiration. On va même s'ingénier à en montrer tout le ridicule; et on le fera justement en jouant sur le sens de ce "sonnet" qui avait tant fait parlé de lui. Les esprits malins ne manqueront pas d'aller repêcher une signification oubliée du mot, cette fois comme vent du corps et non plus Vent de l'Esprit.

Puisqu'il faut toujours en revenir aux rhétoriqueurs lorsqu'on considère l'évolution poétique au XVIᵉ siècle, c'est à Jean Molinet que nous nous arrêterons un instant, lui qui savait bien que le mot "sonnet," avant l'importation italienne, pouvait aussi s'employer par euphémisme pour "pet." Dans une lettre en vers bilingue d'allure fatrasique, il décrit un déjeuner de moines gourmands en faisant alterner des formules gnomiques françaises et latines:

> Desjunés vous de pain tosté,
> *Fratres, sobrii estote*;
>
> L'Homme qui boit bien est bénit:
> *Primum vinum bonum ponit*;
>
> Ne faites jamès nul *sonet*
> *Ne litis horror insonet.* (vv. 31-36)[19]

On reconnaît ici l'antimonachisme plaisant des manières de table: "vous mangez du pain? sobriété; vous buvez du vin? ébriété; pour qu'on vous laisse en paix, abstenez-vous de pets!" Or c'est ce même Molinet qui employait le mot "sonnet" avec le sens le plus grave dans le *Trosne d'Honneur*, composé peu après la mort de Philippe le Bon (1467). Dame Noblesse y faisait entendre une "tres-doloreuse complainte" et invitait tous les oiseaux à se joindre, en un concert funèbre, à sa cruelle lamentation: "Plaisans montans [verdiers], rossignols, cardonnés [chardonnerets], / Nets sansonnés, sonans sus buissonnés / *Sons et sonnetz*, sonés sans soneries / Dœul angoisseux en vos sansonneries."[20] On n'hésitait donc pas à employer le mot "sonnet" dans des registres fort différents à la fin du XVᵉ siècle, quelque soixante-dix ans avant que Clément Marot ne se mît à composer un sonnet.

Cette leçon ne sera pas perdue pour la littérature comique du XVIᵉ siècle. Les rustres appellent un chat "un chat" et un pet "un pet"; mais les "affettées" dit Du Fail, les "sanctimoniales" dit Rabelais, préfèrent nommer ce dernier "un sonnet."[21] Ce sens n'échappera pas non plus à Barthélemy Aneau, le critique le plus acerbe de la *Deffence*. Dans le *Quintil Horatian*, il montrera qu'il a fort bien compris la démarche de Du Bellay en prouvant, si l'on peut dire, par l'absurde le caractère "naturalisateur" du manifeste. C'est en effet à la sémantique exclusivement française du "sonnet" que renvoie la remarque du censeur à propos de la fameuse formule: "*Sonne moy ces beaux sonnetz.*" Il y a certes parti-pris; mais ce parti-pris nous éclaire sur les connotations diverses que pouvait avoir le mot vers le milieu du XVIᵉ siècle. L'idée du *Quintil* est que Du Bellay aurait dû "laisser" sinon la forme du moins le nom de la forme "aux Italiens": "pour ce que un sonnet en François sonne vilainement, pour l'acte du verbe que Alexandre Villedieu declare honnestement sans le nommer, disant: *Quod turpe sonat fit in edi*" (p. 121, note 1). La référence au *Doctrinale Puerorum* d'Alexandre de Villedieu (XIIIe siècle) ne manque pas d'humour: le verbe *pedo* (je pète) fait *pepedi* au parfait; et le grammairien emploie une périphrase (*Quod turpe sonat*) pour désigner la règle qui gouverne ce verbe au *son* malencontreux. Ainsi, nous dit Aneau, traduisant la périphrase de Villedieu et reprenant paradoxalement l'allitération de Du Bellay: "un *sonnet* en François *sonne* vilainement." Il n'est pas de pastiche qui soit une meilleure parodie.

Des deux sens "naturels" possibles du mot français "sonnet" (*chant* et *pet*) le *Quintil* a donc retenu le moins avouable, le plus osé; et l'on voit bien pourquoi. De même que Rabelais prenait un malin plaisir à faire se conchier son écolier limousin, de même Aneau entend ramener au plus bas niveau de la physiologie le discours jugé élevé et prétentieux de la *Deffence*. Les "beaux sonnetz" sont devenus de vulgaires pétarades parce que leur auteur n'a pas su se méfier des "motz espaves."

Cependant, dans l'ordre symbolique, ce qui nous intéresse ici c'est que le *Quintil*, en tant que lecteur de la *Deffence*, ait justement retenu ce sens-ci et l'ait enregistré comme tel dans sa critique. Ce retour à une sémantique des fonctions organiques élémentaires est significatif d'un réflexe de *défense* contre l'*estrangement* que représente la "grephe" d'un nouveau sens. En soulignant l'aspect *vulgaire* (au sens esthétique) de la langue *vulgaire* (au sens linguistique), le censeur cherche à se prémunir contre toute "invention Italienne" intempestive. Le *Quintil* avait déjà reproché à Du Bellay son ingratitude vis-à-vis de la culture française du passé ("Tu accuses à grand tort & tresingratement l'ignorance de noz majeurs," p. 23, note 1) et son impatience à emprunter aux étrangers des ornements qui dénaturent la langue naturelle ("Tu veux nous induire à greciser & latiniser en Françoys, vituperant tousjours nostre forme de poësie, comme *vile & populaire*," p. 28, note 1). "*Vile et populaire*," voilà bien ce que va redevenir le "sonnet," de gré ou de force, parce que son altérité, contrairement à celle de l'épigramme, est devenue insupportable.

Il est bien certain, en effet, que l'épigramme, malgré sa physionomie grecque (ou à cause d'elle, puisque la franche altérité met à l'abri de la polysémie), n'aurait jamais pu connaître ce curieux sort: d'être devenu au moment de son apogée à la fois le signe du Vent de l'Esprit (chez Marguerite de Navarre et Du Bellay) et du vent du corps (chez Aneau, Du Fail et Rabelais). Preuve, s'il en est, qu'on ne manie pas impunément les formes et qu'on n'efface pas aisément les "superscriptions."

NOTES

1. *Roman de Thèbes*, éd. Richel, v. 375, cité d'après le *Dictionnaire de l'ancienne langue française* de Godefroy (Paris: E. Bouillon, 1892), tome 7. Jean Molinet, *Les Faictz et dictz*, éd. N. Dupire (Paris: SATF, 1936), I, 39.

2. Sur l'origine du sonnet en France voir en particulier les articles de P. Villey, "Marot et le premier sonnet français," *RHLF*, 20 (1920), 538-47 et de John McClelland, "Sonnet ou quatorzain? Marot et le choix d'une forme poétique," *RHLF*, 73 (1973), 591-607.

3. (Lyon: Jean de Tournes, 1547), I, 401-02.

4. *Art Poëtique françoys*, éd. F. Gaiffe (Paris: Cornély, 1910), p. 115. Désormais le numéro des pages sera donné entre parenthèses dans le texte.

5. Voir à ce sujet "L'Intertexte du dizain scévien," *CAIEF*, 32 (1980), 91-106. Nous avons aussi montré que dans la *Délie* les dizains atypiques découpaient par leur distribution et signalaient par leur emploi du quatrain embrassé une forme suggestive de celle du sonnet. Voir "Prosodie et sémantique: une hypothèse sur le sens des quatrains atypiques de la *Délie*," dans *The Equilibrium of Wit*, éd. P. Bayley et D.G. Coleman, French Forum Monographs, 36 (Lexington: French Forum, 1982), pp. 28-40.

6. C'est le dizain 302, "Amour plouroit, voire si tendrement."

7. Cf. Max Jasinski, *Histoire du sonnet en France* (Douai: H. Brugère, 1903), pp. 32-46.

8. L'autre sonnet que nous avons gardé de Sebillet a également un statut préfaciel. Paradoxalement il est placé, en compagnie de deux distiques latins, en tête du IVe livre de l'*Enéide* dans la tradution de Joachim Du Bellay (Paris: V. Certenas [sic], 1552).

9. Ed. H. Chamard (Paris: Didier, 1948), Livre II, ch. IV, p. 120. Le numéro de la page sera désormais donné entre parenthèses dans le texte.

10. Cf. *Deffence*, p. 122; *L'Olive*, éd. E. Caldarini (Genève: Droz, 1974), seconde Préface de 1550, p. 44; "Contre les envieux poëtes," *Oeuvres de J. Du Bellay*, éd. Ch. Marty-Laveaux (Paris: A. Lemerre [La Pléiade Françoise], 1866), I, 164.

11. *Géorgiques*, Livre II, v. 176.

12. *De oratore*, II, 352: "Cecinissetque id carmen quod . . . scripsisset."

13. Ed. E. Caldarini, p. 41. Sur ce sonnet et sa fonction emblématique dans le recueil, voir notre *Poétique et onomastique* (Genève: Droz, 1977), pp. 132-33.

14. Un second sonnet-dédicace de Maurice Scève était dédié "A TRESILLUSTRE & TRESVERTUEUSE PRINCESSE MADAME IANE INFANTE DE NAVARRE M. Sc.," autrement dit à Jeanne d'Albret, fille de Marguerite. Il avait pour incipit: "La Marguerite, ou la celeste Aurore:" En outre, un sonnet anonyme à la louange de la Reine de Navarre se trouvait placé après le mot FIN dans l'édition de 1547, et après l'épître de Jean de La Haye dans celle de 1549.

15. Dans son article important sur le sonnet et le quatorzain, John McClelland écrivait encore: "Nous nous étonnons même que Du Bellay ait eu l'idée de rapprocher le sonnet de l'ode," p. 598.

16. Ed. citée, p. 44.

17. Sur le témoignage de Ridolfi à ce sujet, voir V.-L. Saulnier, *Maurice Scève* (Paris: Klincksieck, 1948), II, 290.

18. Ed. citée, p. 50.

19. *Faictz et dictz*, II [1937], 813.
20. *Faictz et dictz*, I, 39.
21. Du Fail, *Eutrapel*, I, 246; Rabelais, *Quart Livre*, ch. 43. Le *Dictionnaire* de Huguet les cite sous l'entrée "sonnet."

Scève's Délie: Correcting Petrarch's Errors

Terence Cave

Everyone knows that the *Délie* begins and ends with an allusion to Petrarch in the form of a borrowed phrase which is sufficiently marked for a reader who knows the *Canzoniere* and *Trionfi* reasonably well to be able to recognize it. In both cases, too, as Coleman, Rigolot, Minta and others have pointed out, the borrowing is accompanied by a change of context and hence of meaning. Indeed, Minta argues that this change reduces the pertinence of the borrowing: it shows, in his view, that Scève's knowledge and understanding of Petrarch were only superficial.[1]

The first part of my essay will attempt to determine as precisely as possible the implications of the two quotations as allusions. I shall then deal with a general problem arising from this analysis, namely the status of poetry as a thematic preoccupation of the *Délie*. Throughout, a further issue will be kept in play: the relationship between the use of allusive quotation as a poetic device and the tradition of moral commentary which still flourished in the earlier 16th century. I shall here make the presupposition that allusiveness and glossing are variants of the same activity, but significantly different variants. Glossing, whatever its force in constituting the meaning of a consecrated work, has by definition a secondary status: the commentator places himself in a position of humility and subservience, and thus renounces any bid for personal fame. Quotation may also have this status, insofar as the quoted text is presented as an "authority"; but when the quotation is assimilated into a context that changes its meaning (that is to say, when it becomes a part of a *new* text), a transfer of power and authority may occur. Allusiveness in a literary work is the mark of such a transfer: the writer who alludes to a venerated text exploits the power of that text for his own ends, and for his own eventual renown.[2]

The allusive phrase in dizain 1—"mes jeunes erreurs"—is by far the less precise of the two. It appears to echo Petrarch's "mio . . . giovenile errore" from the opening sonnet of the *Canzoniere*; but it substitutes plural for singular, and one can find other instances of the formula in neo-Petrarchan *epigoni* whom Scève may also have read.[3] One may thus suspend one's judgment for the moment as to whether it *is* a specific quotation, still less an allusion: it may be regarded as a Petrarchan topos, similar in kind to phrases which occur elsewhere in the *Délie*.[4] Even at this level, however, it must be conceded that the topos has been finely readjusted to a new context. The phrase is normally used in the Italian tradition to denote the youthful error of being in love; that is to say, it implies a negative evaluation of love as an experience, the lover recognizing that he is, or was, in a state of error. Scève, by contrast, applies it to a time of desire and inconstancy *preceding* his love for Délie: the *innamoramento* which is the principal theme of the dizain marks the end, not the beginning, of his *jeunes erreurs*. The use of the plural sharpens the point by suggesting a multiplicity of youthful, superficial loves: these have been superseded by the single love which henceforward will dominate the poet's life (cf. line 10: "Constituée Idole de ma vie").

Such a measured inversion of the sense of the phrase at the very threshold of Scève's cycle of poems makes it highly probable that "mes jeunes erreurs" is, in fact, an allusion to its counterpart in the first sonnet of the *Canzoniere* rather than a poetic reflex conditioned by a common fund of Petrarchan themes. For Petrarch uses the opening poem of his cycle to denounce the moral vanity of love in terms that color the whole spiritual odyssey charted by the *Canzoniere*. Scève's opening move is the exact reverse of Petrarch's; and if the reader is to take the point fully, he must recognize the allusion and the crucial inversion of the context.[5] The thematic function of the allusion would then be to permit Scève with great economy to open the *Délie* with a resounding and provocative affirmation of love against all the moral odds.

The point is confirmed by even a cursory glance at the 16th-century editions of the *Canzoniere* which Scève is likely to have known. They are all accompanied by commentaries, the most popular being those of Filelfo and Vellutello: the 1528 edition of the version with Vellutello's commentary contains not only, like most other editions, a *vita* of Petrarch, but also half-a-dozen pages entitled "Origine di Madonna Laura con la descrittione di Valclusa e del luogo ove il poeta a principio di lei s'innamoro," and even a map of the Vaucluse[6]—it might have been an edition such as this that encouraged Scève to set out in 1533 on his celebrated quest for Laura's tomb. Both Filelfo and Vellutello begin their gloss on the opening sonnet ("Voi ch'ascoltate . . .") by saying that it is really not the first but the last poem in the sequence: it carries a retrospective judgment on the "error" and vanity of the poet's love, and thus provides the key to a moral reading of the *Canzoniere*:

Quantunque il presente sonetto fusse da Misser Francesco Petrarcha . . . in loco di prefatione collocato non fu perho il primo che lui facesse: ma lultimo di tutti come per la sententia desso chiaramente comprendere si puote. Il che principalmente mi par lui havere fatto per potere inqualche parte remediare alla infamia . . .[7]

Utilissimo e notabilissimo documento è veramente quello, chel nostro Poe[ta] nel presente (perquanto la sua sententia ne dimostra) non primo, ma ultimo Son[etto] scritto da lui, & in escusatione del suo amoroso errore . . . di se stesso ne porge, che quantunque l'huomo, ne suoi giovenili anni si lassi . . . in qualche lascivo errore incorrere, almeno giunto poi negli anni discreti, si debba da quelli del tutto rimanere . . .[8]

The two commentators thus read "Voi ch'ascoltate" as if it were itself a gloss, so that for future Petrarchan readers and writers it provides a perfect springboard for the production of new glosses. It will be noted that Vellutello insists on the word "errore": in a prefatory note on the cycle as a whole, he uses it three times to characterize the poems written "in vita di Madonna Laura" (fol. 1 r°). Filelfo, for his part, suggests that in providing a retrospective moral preface for the sequence, Petrarch was concerned to protect his reputation: the triumph (or defeat) of fame is a theme to which I shall return later.

If the phrase "mes jeunes erreurs" is a version of a topos, then, it is one which is inserted with great precision into the spectrum of possible senses defined by the tradition of commentary. Dizain 1 appears in this light as a new gloss, a commentary that gives rise to a re-reading; yet it produces this effect by means of allusion, arrogating to itself the prestige of rivalry with no less a work than the *Canzoniere*. Hence it is also an instance of *imitatio* in the full 16th-century sense of the term, that is to say the appropriation and transformation of a consecrated text.

The last line of the *Délie* indisputably alludes to lines 74-75 of the *Trionfo del Tempo*: "Nostre Geneure ainsi doncques viura / Non offensé d'aulcun mortel Letharge";[9] "Ma io v'annunzio che voi sete offesi / da un grave e mortifero letargo . . ."[10] The transposition of the three key words —"offensé," "mortel," "Letharge"—from Italian into French, together with the strikingly dense character of the metaphor, make the identification as positive as anyone could wish. But here again, it is possible to demonstrate that Scève has transformed the sense in a quite precise way.

In the *Trionfo del Tempo*, the aging poet (see lines 58-60) warns man of the passage of time and the vanity of life: more particularly, he addres-

ses the young ("gioveni"), reminding them of the error ("fallo") they are
making:

> Or vi riconfortate in vostre fole,
> gioveni, e misurate il tempo largo!
> Ma piaga antiveduta assai men dole.
> Forse che 'ndarno mie parole spargo,
> ma io v'annunzio che voi sete offesi
> da un grave e mortifero letargo,
> ché volan l'ore, e' giorni e gli anni e' mesi:
> insieme, con brevissimo intervallo,
> tutti avemo a cercar altri paesi.
> Non fate contra 'l vero al core un callo,
> come sete usi, anzi volgete gli occhi
> mentre emendar si pòte il vostro fallo.
>
> (II. 70-81)

The similarity of this passage to the first sonnet of the *Canzoniere* may be
accidental, in the sense that both develop a standard topos of the brevity
and vanity of life; besides, this section of the *Trionfo* takes the form of a
second-person moral exhortation, while "Voi ch'ascoltate" is a penitential
soliloquy. Yet the sermon is preceded by a first-person meditation, so that
the voice of the preacher is fused with that of the repentant poet, con-
demning youthful error and "scaterring" his words for the moral benefit
of his readers as well as himself ("Voi ch'ascoltate in rime *sparse* il suono
. . ."; "Forse che 'ndarno mie parole *spargo*"). Furthermore, Vellutello's
gloss on the formula borrowed by Scève from the *Trionfo* introduces quite
explicitly the notion of "error": "egli gli annuntia, che sono da un grieve e
mortifero lethargo offesi, cio è da un cieco e dannoso errore oppressi, Le-
thargia è una infirmita, che rende l'huomo immemore de le cose passate"
(op. cit., fol. [miii] v°). One may also note in passing that the commentator brings out the theme of memory implicit in "letargo": it is as if the
memory of his past errors, recorded in the *Canzoniere*, allowed the poet
of the *Trionfi* to achieve true understanding of their moral vanity. Memory,
from the vantage point of the *Trionfo del Tempo*, triumphs over the
youthful folly of love.

It seems to me likely that Scève saw the connection between the two
texts he refers to at the beginning and end of the *Délie* and exploited it
for his own purposes. Both of them, in their original context, adopt a
perspective which goes beyond love, seeing it as an episode whose moral
emptiness has been revealed by memory and the passage of time. Having
reversed this order in dizain 1, thus presenting the poet's love for Délie as
a value transcending the ephemerality and errors of youth, Scève closes his
cycle with exactly the same inversion of Petrarch's theme. His "Flamme si

saincte" will endure eternally and cosmically; embodied in the figure of an evergreen *"non* offensé d'aulcun mortel Letharge," it will be remembered without a trace of penitential doubt. The *Délie* flamboyantly corrects Petrarch's errors by celebrating the triumph of love over time.

Unlike Du Bellay and Ronsard, Scève did not pillage the *Canzoniere* for themes, figures of speech and turns of phrase at the rhetorical level. But this does not mean that he did not understand Petrarch, or read him superficially: only that he read him differently, and for a different purpose. Whereas for the Pléiade Petrarch will join the classical authors as a source of *copia,* Scève's reading still belongs, in part at least, to a tradition of moral commentary characteristic of late medieval France, one which moreover gave priority to the *Trionfi* over the *Canzoniere:* of the nineteen putative borrowings from Petrarch's works listed by McFarlane, five are from the *Trionfi,* including of course the crucial one discussed above. The tradition has been admirably traced by Simone, who also shows how the significance of, for example, the *Triumphus Cupidinis* could be orientated towards a politico-moral theme apparently quite alien to the text itself.[11] Scève's interpretation of Petrarch was no doubt more imaginative, but was no less an attempt to grasp and reshape the significance, distilled in certain key lines, of the *œuvre* as a whole, rather than to wander like the commonplace bee through the flowers of Petrarch's rhetoric. And so, when he rewrites his model, he does so in terms of a synthetic view, placing thematic signposts with utmost care at either end of his sequence. Of course, it is true that between the signposts the rhetoric of epigrammatic love-poetry will often divert the reader from the prescribed path; I would not wish to argue that there is some hidden but necessary order lurking just beneath the surface. Nevertheless, the tone and themes are relatively consistent, and for anyone prepared to read Scève as Scève seems to have read Petrarch, the structure will appear as a coherent whole rendering a coherent meaning.

One might, indeed, argue that what Scève was trying to do was just this: to naturalize the *canzoniere* form not as a collection of diverse poems but as a single unified structure. Thus he adopted not only the mirage of teleology provided by an end consonant with the beginning, but also the device of the name-motif, which allows many poetic variations to be subsumed under one apparently significant category. I say "apparently" significant because the device could be considered as an expanded form of paronomasia, drawing into its orbit other figures of speech such as metonymy and periphrasis. But there is no doubt that, in the *Délie* as in the

Canzoniere, significance *can* be produced by this means; the name and its concomitant allusions can provide a meeting point for any number of thematic threads, a single sense for a multiple collection.

The figure of "Délie" as moon-goddess, huntress, Hecate and so forth has been amply explored by other critics, and will be familiar enough to readers of, for example, Ian McFarlane's edition. I would simply indicate a single aspect of the device, one which is particularly relevant to my argument. The point may be summarized by saying that Petrarch's image of fame (Laura = the laurel wreath) is suppressed, while at the same time the name of Délie and the renown it carries with it are generously advertized. There are many dizains in which this configuration is apparent, but 449 is no doubt the clearest illustration. Here, it is the fame of the poet's *love* (of his "flamme si saincte") which will endure "en publique apparence," becoming precisely that evergreen "Geneure" which will surmount time and oblivion. At this most visible point in the sequence, the juniper outdoes the laurel. For in the *Trionfi*, time triumphs not only over love, but also over fame. Love is at the very bottom of the triumphal ladder: it succumbs to Chastity, which is overcome by Death, which is outreached by Fame, which in its turn falls victim to Time. Thus Scève has again glossed Petrarch in a contrary sense: love and fame are identified in the *Délie*, particularly in the last dizain, and both triumph over time.

But whose fame, what kind of fame? In the *Canzoniere*, Laura by her very name confers *poetic* fame on Petrarch, since it is Apollo, god of music and poetry, who gains the laurel crown. He gains it, moreover, precisely at the expense of love, since he gets the laurel, as it were, only by losing his Daphne. Petrarch lives on in the memory of men as a *poeta*: his love, being unrequited and in the end dismissed as vanity, finally serves to promote his greatness as a creator of unrivalled verses. Filelfo's commentary on "Voi ch'ascoltate" (quoted above) endorses this reading by presenting Petrarch's renunciation of love as a gesture designed to protect him against "infamia." And within the *Canzoniere* itself, the figure of the lover is also, visibly and insistently, the figure of a poet, as if the erring youth were always accompanied by his elder, wiser, and above all more famous double. Ronsard will give poetry even greater priority;[12] but in the *Délie* things are very different. Scève rarely advertizes the role of poetry or the mastery of the poet; Apollo, Orpheus and the Muses appear incidentally, in scattered dizains, but they could hardly be said to provide the keynote of the sequence.

Such, at least, is the impression which most readers of the *Délie* are likely to come away with. But some distinctions need to be made here, and some counter-arguments allowed for. To begin with, I exclude from

the category of "poems about poetry" some twenty dizains which refer to
the (mainly oral) language of the lover's complaints, or to his inability to
speak, although I will return briefly to these a little later: in such poems,
the poet is represented as a lover, not a poet. I also exclude most of the
poems which Jerry Nash discusses in his excellent article "The Notion and
Meaning of Art in the *Délie*." Nash claims that "[Scève's] critical ideas,
abstractly developed through poetic display rather than expository presentation of theory, emerge obliquely . . . from the dense framework of his
love experience . . . for him art and life were hardly conceived of as separate entities."[13] He then goes on to argue that Scève's analysis of the
contemplative activity engendered by love may be read as a reflection on
the nature of art, and more particularly, of course, of poetry. I would
agree that, within the neo-Platonist language Scève often adopts, the assimilation of contemplative to poetic or musical activity is a standard presupposition: dizain 445 and its source in Speroni's *Dialogo d'Amore*
provide a perfect example, to which I will return shortly. Yet it still seems
to me to be useful to distinguish dizains which represent activity (mental
or otherwise) in the realm of love from those which explicitly refer to the
means of representation: that is to say, those where the poet or poetry
figure unmistakably as themes in their own right. On a first reading of the
cycle I found some twelve poems of this latter type: the introductory
huitain and dizains 23, 59, 149, 188, 192, 227, 239, 388, 394, 417 and
445. Jerry Nash mentions only one of these (239); but I would agree that
perhaps three of the dizains he discusses (90, 119, 329) should be added
to my list since they clearly imply a consciousness of the poet's role.

Of these fifteen poems, one (149) includes a passing reference to the
Muses, unconnected with Scève's own status as a poet. Two refer to Petrarch. Dizain 388 measures its distance (like dizain 1) from the master:
autumn, not springtime, is the figure of the poet's love for Délie. Dizain
417 celebrates Vaucluse as the site of Petrarch's love and thus gives prominence to the "Thuscan Apollo" and his fame; although Scève, in the last
two lines, sets his own love next to Petrarch's, he makes no reference to
his *poetic* powers, and I do not believe any is implied: indeed, his rejection
of such an obvious opportunity should, I think, be taken as significant.
Two further dizains (59, 394) allude in their own way to the Petrarchan
model in that they defend the poet's choice of a pseudonym for his lady
(its connection with the notoriously fickle moon being open to misunder-
standing).[14]

In dizain 188, "ce papier de tous costez noircy / Du mortel dueil de
mes iustes querelles" and its margins form a graphic image of Scève's
poetic lamentations; and 192, in a complex conceit drawing on the rhe-

torical terminology of praise and blame, ends with the image of his poems as "tristes Archives" in the dark enclosure of which his suffering lives on. If these two poems celebrate the powers of poetry, it is in a distinctly minor key.

There has been little indication, up to this point, of the poet's relative status *as* a poet, or of his belief in his art. I now come to a group of dizains which do provide some such indication, but which point towards a sense of inadequacy rather than mastery.

Dizain 239 develops the familiar enough theme of the poet's inability to move his mistress to compassion: the first six lines celebrate in general terms the persuasive force of prayer, rhetoric, preaching, song and verse, but only in order to emphasize the futility of the poet's "ryme pitoyable."[15] In 329, Scève uses the topos according to which poetry, while incapable of persuading the lady, provides some relief from the suffering of love; the conceit which closes the poem suggests that even this relief is fugitive.

A more ample development of the theme of poetic inadequacy in dizain 227 strikes the note which seems to me to characterize the sequence as a whole:

> Pour m'efforcer a degluer les yeulx
> De ma pensée enracinez en elle,
> Ie m'en veulx taire, & lors i'y pense mieulx,
> Qui iuge en moy ma peine estre eternelle.
>   Parquoy ma plume au bas vol de son aele
> Se demettra de plus en raisonner,
> Aussi pour plus haultement resonner,
> Vueille le Temps, vueille la Fame, ou non,
> Sa grace asses, sans moy, luy peult donner
> Corps a ses faictz, & Ame a son hault nom.

Lines 5-6 are a gesture of renunciation; his "plume" cannot fly high enough, so he will desist, leaving her "grace" and her name (her renown) to speak for themselves, triumphing over Time and over Fame itself.[16] This reading, it must be admitted, takes line 7 as an adjunct of the following lines, a part of the activity of "sa grace"; to take it with the preceding lines, while grammatically plausible, would create a contradiction, since the "sans moy" of line 9 excludes the poet from any connection with Délie's triumph. Dizain 23 confirms this reading:

> . . . en vain trauailleroit ma plume
> Pour t'entailler a perpetuité:
> Mais ton sainct feu, qui a tout bien m'allume,
> Resplendira a la posterité.

It is the light of Délie's divine nature which ensures its own immortality: the poet's inscription is at best a secondary activity (and note that there is no suggestion that he is inspired *as a poet* by Délie, only that she illuminates him morally as a lover). Similarly, in 90, the double fame of the lovers is a consequence of her *vertu* operating on his *espritz*: if there is a reference to poetry itself here, as Nash claims, it remains implicit, so that pre-eminence is given to a power external to the poet.[17]

I now come to the complex and exceptional case of dizain 445:

> Ainsi qu'Amour en la face au plus beau,
> Propice obiect a noz yeulx agreable,
> Hault colloqua le reluysant flambeau
> Qui nous esclaire a tout bien desirable,
> Affin qu'a tous son feu soit admirable,
> Sans a l'honneur faire aulcun preiudice[:]
> Ainsi veult il par plus louable indice,
> Que mon Orphée haultement anobly,
> Maulgré la Mort, tire son Euridice
> Hors des Enfers de l'eternel obly.

A first reading would suggest that in this instance the poet does glorify his own activity by identifying himself with Orpheus rescuing his beloved from death and oblivion: Scève has even, characteristically enough, "corrected" the myth by omitting any reference to the loss of Eurydice—the metonymy "*mon* Orphée" seems to affirm yet another triumphant reversal of the Petrarchan hierarchy, but one in which poetry now clearly has its part to play.[18] Yet nobility is still conferred on poetry by "Amour," who is primarily responsible for publicizing ("illuminating") the lover and his lady. And then, the metonymy cannot simply be read as "ma poésie." It is well known that in the later part of the *Délie* Scève draws regularly on Speroni, elaborating the theory that love is perfected by the separation of the lovers, and hence by the contemplative activity of memory. In the *Dialogo d'Amore*, Orpheus is a figure of poetry as a medium analogous to memory: poetry is itself, in fact, a form of memory, refining love and at the same time rendering it immortal ("immemorial"). Scève is using a neo-Platonist myth of which the connotations are moral and spiritual rather than esthetic: poetry is subsumed into a higher order. It is no doubt because poetry is subordinated in this way that the final dizain, while celebrating a love which will be remembered eternally by posterity, refrains from glorifying—or even mentioning—the poet *qua* poet. Just as the laurel is displaced by the juniper, so too "*mon* Orphée" gives way to "*nostre* Geneure."[19]

It is at this point that I should like to return briefly to the way in which the lover's utterances—words, cries, lamentations—are represented in the *Délie*. In virtually all of the dizains which allude thus to fragments of the lover's discourse, the discourse is, precisely, fragmented, or even negated: silence is a recurrent theme.[20] The lover suffers from aphasia; and if in other Petrarchan poets this theme is turned—by means of a kind of *praeteritio*—into a source of eloquent conceits, in the *Délie* it coincides with the image of a writer who constantly acknowledges his inadequacy, or at least his subservience to a higher source of values.

Inadequacy and subservience already provide the keynote of the introductory huitain. Scève acknowledges that the reader will find in his epigrams "mainte erreur," but goes on to claim that Love has purified them in his flames. The poem, by its very position, echoes "Voi ch'ascoltate" no less than does dizain 1. It is a retrospective prelude, written for the most part in the past tense; it establishes a moral distinction between frivolous and serious forms of love, or rather of love-poetry; and it is in this context that the word *erreur* appears for the first time, on the very threshold of the sequence. But here error is neither condemned as a moral failing external to poetry, as in Petrarch, nor excluded from the sacred sphere of authentic love, as in dizain 1. It is a property of the poems themselves, an inadequacy written into the sequence; the value of love as a transcendant force is constituted, as it were, by the imperfection of the mere vehicle. In a gesture which will be repeated time and again throughout the sequence, Scève consigns to the refining fire the errors not of youthful love but of writing.

Scève's stance in relation to the status of poetry is consonant with the marked suspicion of eloquence which characterizes Marguerite de Navarre and her circle.[21] As I suggested earlier, it may also be seen as a particular instance of the persistence in earlier 16th-century French writing of the moralizing habits of which the preference for the *Trionfi* over the *Canzoniere* is such a pertinent example: the *Délie* is in this sense still a corrective gloss, restoring that supremacy of moral values over poetry which the *Canzoniere*, despite its opening sonnet, appears at times so openly to threaten. Scève will take great care not to pose in the foreground of his emblematic landscape, graciously accepting from his lady's hand the final accolade for his poetic prowess.

One could—and perhaps ought to—leave it there. But I think it would be naïve to take such a many-sided work solely at face value, as it were—to assume that it means exclusively what its own built-in glosses tell us it means. It is true that once one goes past that point many possibilities open

up, perhaps too many. So I will restrict myself to a kind of deliberate dislocation of the themes and emphases I have already brought out.

The first move is simply to recall what any reader of Renaissance texts
knows: that a gesture of renunciation or self-abasement may perfectly well
accompany an assertive movement. The name of Délie, the fame conferred
by love, are in fact, regardless of all claims to the contrary, the name and
fame of the *Délie* and its poet. The memory that abstracts the moral
essence of love, purifies it and advertizes it permanently to the world
is a textual memory, and even one that aggressively destroys and displaces
the name and fame of the famous text it claims humbly to gloss. Scève's
resounding achievement—the naturalization into French of the *canzoniere*
form—institutes the possibility of Petrarchan poetic fame in France, a
possibility which many poets less inhibited in the demonstration of their
eloquence will soon take up. The erasing of Petrarch's errors, the triumph
of love and fame over time and poetry, is a triumph, in the end, of successful imitation and assimilation: it brings about the *translatio studii* that
French culture, and specifically French poetry, need for their glory.

Yet simply to reverse the perspective in this way, changing the minus
sign into a plus, is to fall again into the error of removing the tension and
the complexity from a work that thrives on these very qualities. The two
sides of the coin—repression and assertion—are both equally essential to its
themes, its language and its position in relation to other poetry. It is as if
Scève, by means of his transcendental frame of reference, his dissatisfac-
tion with the merely contingent, were attempting to put the greatest possible pressure on poetry, and through poetry on language itself. The triumph
of the *Délie* is not a facile triumph, a display of unrestrained *copia*: reduced
virtually to silence, to a constant acknowledgement of its errors and limits,
Scève's verse nevertheless articulates—by default, as it were—the possibility
of some future renown.

And so, poised between moral austerity and a bid for power, the *Délie*
dramatically illustrates one of the central problems of writing in the French
Renaissance. With his aphasia and his aposiopesis, Scève is both within the
tradition of moral commentary and trying to break out of it. Zealously
quoting from and glossing an "authority," a major work from another
culture, he deprecates his own activity; deprived of his *bien*, which is
always elsewhere and above, he is obliged to suffer the "mal clos . . . en
l'obscur de [s]es tristes Archives." But, by a kind of sleight of hand, the
Délie also proclaims itself as self-sufficient. Quotation, while masquerading
as a recourse to moral authority, may also begin to play the game of allusion and thus act as a *table tournante*, opening the way to new poetic
possibilities. This, I believe, is why it is so important to notice the collusion

between the opening and closing lines of the sequence: it perfectly demonstrates the versatility with which a text may escape even from the most obscure of archives.[22]

NOTES

1. Stephen Minta, *Love Poetry in Sixteenth-Century France* (Manchester Univ. Press, 1977), pp. 95-96, and chapter 3 in general. See also Dorothy Gabe Coleman, *Maurice Scève: Poet of Love. Tradition and Originality* (Cambridge Univ. Press, 1975), pp. 24-25; François Rigolot, "L'Intertexte du dizain scévien: Pétrarque et Marot," *CAIEF*, 32 (1980), 91-106; Doranne Fenoaltea, in her article "The Poet in Nature: Sources of Scève's *Délie* in Petrarch's *Rime*," *French Studies*, 27 (1973), 257-70, argues that Scève's selective borrowings from Petrarch indicate a precise understanding of their context, and stresses "the remarkable counterpoint often present between the two works" (p. 269), but does not refer to the opening and closing dizains.

2. On the relationship between glossing and quotation, see in particular Antoine Compagnon, *La Seconde Main ou le travail de la citation* (Paris, 1979), pp. 235-327. Compagnon advances the hypothesis that, in the course of the Renaissance, "creative" quotation gradually displaces the gloss in certain areas of literary activity: Montaigne is his principal example. The shift is no doubt more apparent in prose than in poetry, but I believe that it is valuable to reassess the role of allusiveness in Renaissance poetry in a similar perspective.

3. See Coleman, p. 24.

4. In the Introduction to his edition of the *Délie* (Cambridge Univ. Press, 1966), Ian McFarlane lists a number of apparently direct borrowings from Petrarch and his successors (pp. 26-27). The notes of Eugène Parturier's edition (Paris, 1916) give a less cautious view of Scève's debt to the Petrarchan tradition.

5. The Petrarchism of the Lyons poets, and of Scève in particular, is discussed by Jacqueline Risset in *L'Anagramme du désir. Essai sur la Délie de Maurice Scève* (Rome, 1971), especially pp. 21-38. Risset draws particular attention to the theme of error (e.g. in the introductory huitain and dizain 1) and speaks of a "pétrarquisme citationnel"; her analysis is thus closer to mine on these points than that of any other critic I have read.

6. *Il Petrarca con l'espositione d'Alessandro Vellutello e con molte altre ultilissime cose in diversi luoghi di quella nuovamente da lui aggiunte* (Vinegia: Bernardino de Vidali, 1528).

7. *Petrarcha con doi commenti sopra li sonetti e canzone . . .* (Venice: Bernardinus Stagninus, 1522), fol. iii r°.

8. *Il Petrarcha* (see above, note 6), fol. 1 v°.

9. I quote here and elsewhere from Ian McFarlane's edition (see above, note 4). Page references will not be given, since the dizain number is specified in each case.

10. Francesco Petrarca, *Opere*, ed. Giovanni Ponte (Milan, 1968), p. 311 (II. 74-75).

11. Franco Simone, *Il Rinascimento francese* (Turin, 1961), Part I, ch. 5. See also Minta, p. 74.

12. See my article "Ronsard as Apollo: Myth, Poetry and Experience in a Renaissance Sonnet-Cycle," *Yale French Studies*, 47 (1972), 76-89.

13. Jerry C. Nash, "The Notion and Meaning of Art in the *Délie*," *Romanic Review*, 71 (1980), 28-46 (quotation p. 29).

14. I omit, of course, poems which simply use or play on the name itself or refer to its transcendance over time. But reference should be made in this context to those dizains where the mythological resonances of Délie's name evoke the figure of Apollo (e.g. 102, 310 and, by implication, 407) (see also below, notes 19 and 20).

15. Dizain 166 contains an analogous topos, the inexpressibility of the beloved's perfections. There is no reference to poetry here, but it is surely implied both by the theme and by the way in which the language visibly strains towards adequate expression.

16. See also dizain 284.

17. This theme should be distinguished from the neo-Platonist topos of the divine fury as used by the Pléiade, where the supernatural power explicitly consecrates the poet's own status. In 119, the poet vows to rival both Time and Fame in speaking of his love; but the notion of "speaking" is introduced by means of a negative phrasing ("me taisant de toy") and is inserted into an expression of the moral value of love and its spiritual impact on him.

18. Scève distinguishes *his* Orpheus from the traditional Orpheus, whose error led to the loss of Eurydice. See Speroni, *Dialogo d'Amore* (quoted in McFarlane's edition, p. 489), where the full story is glossed in a neo-Platonist sense, Orpheus' lapse being interpreted as the distraction of the soul from its spiritual goal by "disordinato appetito."

19. None of the dizains in which the story of Apollo, Daphne and the laurel appear (102, 310, 407) exploit the image of the laurel as the poet's crown: at best, as in 407, immortality is conferred by the virtue of Daphne.

20. See, for example, dizains 8, 76, 112, 197, 227, 228, 244, 291, 364, 376, 381. Another rather striking example occurs in 102, where the Apollo-Daphne myth is presented as an instance of broken or failed *dialogue*. The theme of silence (or of the difficulty of utterance) is discussed, for example, by Pascal Quignard, *La Parole de la Délie* (n.p., 1974), especially sections II and III.

21. See Gérard Defaux's remarks on this topic in his contribution to the present volume; and cf. François Rigolot's contribution on the ambivalent status of the epigram (its role as an epigraph or *marginal* text).

22. JoAnn DellaNeva's study, *Song and Counter-Song: Scève's* Délie *and Petrarch's* Rime, French Forum Monographs, 49 (Lexington: French Forum, Publishers, 1983), appeared after this paper had gone to press, so that I was unable to take account of it. In general, it would seem that my conclusions concur with hers.

The Poetic Sensibility of Scève

Dorothy Gabe Coleman

The intellectual difficulty of Scève ever challenges literary critics. Trying to interpret *Délie* has been a constant with me from the time I studied him as an undergraduate twenty eight years ago until today. It has been and still is a tremendous intellectual and esthetic experience: the fascination of a poet who refuses to give himself to us immediately. As Eliot has it "our first reading of a work of literature which we do not understand is itself the beginning of understanding for understanding begins in the sensibility." For me, at first, there were moments of bliss in a single line like "En la clarté de mes desirs funebres" or "Plongé au Stix de la melancolie." Or there was the sudden imaginative intuition of what true love is: every thing is altered when we are in love—the shape of being, the values that we have, the sense of time, the perception of space; the whole world is seen through love:

> De toute Mer tout long, & large espace,
> De terre aussi tout tournoyant circuit
> Des Montz tout terme en forme haulte, & basse,
> Tout lieu distant, du iour et de la nuict,
> Tout interualle, ô qui par trop me nuyt,
> Seront rempliz de ta doulce rigueur.
> (dizain 259)[1]

Scève's best dizains are not very many; they are the product of a Gallo-Roman culture as is the best poetry of Sponde. The reorientation of criticism and taste in France and in the Anglo-Saxon world has established Scève as an Old Master and given him a prominent place in anthologies of poetry.

There are two main ways of "tackling" Scève: editing the text and evaluating the text. Every serious reader of *Délie* knows that there is not yet a standard edition. The reader has to have the Parturier, the Guégan and the McFarlane text on his desk to cross-check, cross-refer and cross-examine punctuation and spelling, words and lines. The lovely line 7 of dizain 372, "Celle doulceur celestement humaine," has turned into "Celle douleur celestement humaine" in the McFarlane text and, unfortunately, Nash's Concordance and some critics have followed it; as a result we have to play with some extra paradoxical effects! Alas! Saulnier's promise in 1948 of an edition of all Scève's work remains unfulfilled. Perhaps Giudici's pledge will, in course of time, bear fruit. Perhaps, one day, someone will do a full-scale bibliography of Scève. The reputation which he had among emblem and device writers in the 16th and 17th centuries gives the lie to the frequent assertion that he was completely forgotten for three centuries. His fate was not that of Sponde. Desportes owned and annotated a copy of *Microcosme*—now in the Bibliothèque Nationale. We have the manuscript of an Album made in 1575-76 for the wife of Albert de Gondi, Claude-Catherine de Clermont, where Scève is the most often-quoted poet. He was remembered not as a writer perhaps of serious poetry but as the author of *Délie*, which was remarkable for the inclusion of *imprese amorose* and dizains around them. Of course he was known to people like Pasquier, Adrian d'Amboise, Colletet, Menestrier and Lemoyne in the 17th century and to the Abbé Goujet and Rigoley de Juvigny in the 18th century. Between 1821 and 1824 Rev. H.F. Cary published in the *London Magazine* a series of articles which includes one on Scève and remarked on "some fine things" which are "somewhat in the way of our own Donne." And there was a *réimpression* of *Délie* in Lyons, chez N. Scheuring in 1862. But these tasks come under the first way of "tackling" him. It is in the second way—that of evaluation—that I wish to see him today. And, in particular, to attempt to distinguish his emotional consciousness, the quickness and acuteness of his feelings and his power of sensation or perception. The poetic value lies in the individual dizain, each one offering a moment or aspect of experience, and the best dizains exploring the full significance of this *en profondeur*. What is the quality of Scève in his best dizains? That firm grasp of human experience, that hold on human values, that deep psychology around love, that sensitivity to acute feeling, that quick reaction to stimulus and that sensibility which expresses so well emotional consciousness—all controlled by the intensiveness, density, allusiveness and the fiery vision that is his poetic imagination. It is Scève's introspective attitude which tries to control his inner world.

There is nothing, I think, more blatantly dishonest in critics wearing the "sincerity" jacket than a refusal to say that one can *never* tell whether a poet is sincere or insincere. What one hopes to be able to tell is whether Scève's dizains are good or bad and why. Similarly, it is dishonest to talk about the macrotextual structure, the numerical patterning, the sequential

linking device, or to try and prove anything by "breakdown of structure"
rules or by making the number 6 the controlling point of the text. Dishonest in that the writers have not engrained themselves in the text, have
not remembered that poetry is made of words and have forgotten that
"the business of the critic is to perceive for himself and to make the finest
and sharpest relevant discriminations" (F.R. Leavis).
    Poetry is largely myth and symbol. It is almost impossible to make up
your own symbols and still be understood. Blake used original symbols but
it was at the price of not being understood. Eliot displayed erudite signs
but had to write annotations for the reader to understand *The Waste
Land*. The communication/intelligibility depends on heritage, the assumptions shared by poet and reader. We shall not be able to assess the sensibility of Scève if we see him in a void. And so, let us start with the year
1536, the year when Marot and Scève met in Lyons; the former writes an
epigram to the latter:

> En m'oyant chanter quelcque foys
> Tu te plainds qu'estre je ne daigne
> Musicien, et que ma voix
> Merite bien que l'on m'enseigne,
> Voyre que la peine je preigne
> D'apprendre ut, re, my, fa, sol, la.
> Que Diable veulx tu que j'appreigne?
> Je ne boy que trop sans cela.[2]

A light-hearted romp. Marot is at the height of his powers (he will die in
1544, the year of the publication of *Délie*); Scève is known to us at this
time only by minor works. Scève took from Marot the form of his *Epigrammes*; the huitain with which *Délie* opens is a compliment, perhaps,
to Marot's huitain addressed to him. Perhaps François Rigolot is right in
seeing Scève using a rondeau form for the fifteen exceptions to the schema
of ABAB BC CDCD.[3] The rondeau form, *clos en soy*, this circularity and
hardness fit in well to the *durs* poems of Scève and, maybe, put him in a
literary, historical, Marotian perspective. But this tells us nothing of their
sensibility.
    We all know Marot the ribald, the *grivois*, the gaulois, the jovial; we are
not surprised by his *blason Du beau Tetin* and his anti-*blason Du laid
Tetin*. This *prince des poètes* organizes a competition in which every French
poet indulges in a praise of one part of a woman's body: her hair, fore-
head, ear, hearing, eyebrows, eye, look; her tear, nose, cheek, tongue,
teeth, voice, sigh; her laugh, hand, nails, embrace, bosom, nipples, heart;
her belly, navel, bum, thigh, knee, leg, and her whole body—all are played
with, on an ambiguous level halfway between lubricity and preciosity.

These *blasons du corps féminin* reveal something of the sensibility of the 1530s in France: a crudeness of thought and feeling, a certain rawness of expression, a brutal lack of *finesse* and a blunt treatment of erotic and sexual excitement. Titles like *Le . . .* , lines like "Si sont tetins, nez, joues, et menton, / Gorge, estomach, ventre, cuysses, et . . . ," details like "Cuisse qui faitz Tetin mouvoir," or the absurdity of the analogy "Connin vestu de ton poil folaston, / Plus riche que la toison de Colcos," show up the limitations of the poets. We are surprised to find Scève submitting a *Blason de la gorge*: Cotgrave gives the meaning of *gorge* as "in a woman, the outward, and upper part of the breast, between the neck and pappes." But our curiosity over the subject is dashed with just two lines on the shape, the color, the ivory-like delicacy of the breast, "Par une gorge, yvoirine et tresblanche, / Ronde et unie, en forme d'une branche . . ." and the poem continues on a chaste level. *Tetin* is not in the vocabulary of Scève, whereas it is constantly present in poetry from the 1530s, through the Pléiade to Marc de Papillon with his Late Renaissance priapic poetry. Ronsard[4] not only has thousands of *tetins* in his amorous poetry but is often *tatonnant*, *baisant*, *mordant* them, or "la main sous ta cotte, ou la levre dessus / Ton tetin" savoring the feel of them, the perfume of them, the look of them:

> Vous avés les tetins comme deus mons de lait,
> Caillé bien blanchement sus du jonc nouvelet
> Qu'une jeune pucelle au mois de Juin façonne.
> (*Continuation des Amours*, p. 178)

Absent from Scève's vocabulary are too the *ammorciller*, *lecher*, *mamelle*, *mamelette*, *mignoter*, *œillader*, *rebaisoter*, *accoller*, *fretillard*, *mignarder*, *s'entrembrasser*, *s'entrebaiser* so beloved by the Pléiade poets; there is no *gorge* in *Délie* neither is there a *cuisse*.[5] Marot can give us the five points of carnal love (épigramme 52), can tell us of the moment "Qu'entre mes bras vous tenoys nue à nu" (épigramme 7), speak of "O dur baiser, rude & mal gracieux" (épigramme 56), of a "Bouche de coral precieux" (épigramme 102) which invites a flurry of kisses and in rondeau 55,

> En la baisant m'a dit: Amy sans blasme,
> Ce seul baiser qui deux bouches embasme
> Les arres sont du bien tant esperé.[6]

All this is done with a light-hearted touch, sometimes with a certain delicacy. He can delight his reader with these "trivial" matters which concern man and woman—touching, feeling softly, fondling, caressing, kissing and embracing. Frere Thibault's exploits with women—*Passez le Cul, ou vous retirez donc!* (épigramme 47) are rather more coarse. Ronsard can show a luxurious intensity of voluptuous and carnal delight in the famous,

> Quand en songeant ma follastre j'acolle,
> Laissant mes flancz sus les siens s'allonger,
> Et que d'un bransle habillement leger,
> En sa moytié ma moytié je recolle:
>
> (*Les Amours*, p. 80)

Now as serious readers of poetry we are not going to say that Marot and Ronsard are erotic poets and Scève is not, for we have the superb artistic creation of a Rodin-like embrace which even outshines Marot and Ronsard in terms of sensuality and delicacy:

> Car en mon corps: mon Ame, tu reuins,
> Sentant ses mains, mains celestement blanches,
> Auec leurs bras mortellement diuins
> L'vn coronner mon col, l'aultre mes hanches.
>
> (dizain 367)

For Marot love is a kind of game and so is poetry. I shall just take one poem to demonstrate this—the epigram *A la bouche de Dyane*, No. 102:

> Bouche de coral precieux,
> Qui à baiser semblez semondre;
> Bouche qui d'ung cueur gracieux
> Savez tant bien dire & respondre;
> Respondez moy: doibt mon cueur fondre
> Devant vous comme au feu la cire?
> Voulez vous bien celluy occire
> Qui craint vous estre deplaisant?
> Ha, bouche que tant je desire,
> Dictes nenny en me baisant.

Marot, although not expressing the complexities of his personality or the subtleties of his loves or the layers of change and uncertainty in his existence, succeeds in weaving within the framework of court poetry threads of his witty and amusing turn of mind on a limited number of topics. The epigram is typical of Marot's style, taking up the Petrarchist game lightheartedly and then reverting in the last line to his native tradition. He seems to believe in the serious treatment of the kiss for nine lines but then dismisses it in a careless "uncommitted" attitude in the last line. The final flippant casualness throws an amusing light on the whole mock-serious poem. He has transformed the concrete, physical world into a framework of light witty verse. With Marot there is never any idea that love is being taken seriously and this is one of the things that separates him from Scève. Scève, although he tries in many of his précieux poems to associate himself with the same reality often fails to do so. Marot hardly ever fails.

Ronsard is not really a serious poet of love. There is in him no fatal passion which can be seen to reveal some of the deeper, unconscious levels of mind. Intellectually, Ronsard is simple and uncomplicated. He is not deepening our experience of love; there is no metaphysical doubt or analysis of his own emotions. This is not to say he is not a great poet; I am stating simply that he is not a great love poet. But he is a sensual man and the transience, fragility of man and life and the beauty of a woman are transmuted by his artistic genius. For example, in this final version of the famous sonnet,

> Douce, belle, amoureuse et bien-fleurente Rose,
> Que tu es à bon droit aux amours consacrée,
> Ta delicate odeur hommes & Dieus recrée,
> Et bref, Rose, tu es belle sur toute chose.
>
> Marie pour son chef un beau bouquet compose
> De ta fueille, & tousjours sa teste en est parée:
> Tousjours ceste Angevine, unique Cytherée,
> Du parfum de ton eau sa jeune face arrose.
>
> Hé Dieu, que je suis aise alors que je te voi
> Esclorre au point du jour sur l'espine à requoy
> Aux jardins de Bourgueil pres d'une eau solitaire.
>
> De toi les Nymphes ont les coudes & le sein:
> De toi l'Aurore emprunte & sa joue, & sa main,
> Et son teint la beauté qu'on adore en Cythere.
>   (*Continuation des Amours*, pp. 211-12)

there is a wealth of quiet mixtures. The sonnet is a perfect circle: it starts with *Rose*, emblem of Venus and ends with Cythera, the favored residence of Aphrodite (Vergil, *Aeneid* 1. 680). A rose is more than a beautiful object: it is almost the quintessence of beauty and grace and love. The emotion in the poem is that of a mature artist. Ronsard's rare sensitivity to verbal music is shown immediately for in the first hemistich he has knocked out *gentille* and brought in *amoureuse* which repeats the *ou* resonance of *Douce*. The precise intonations, the tone-values are there: *Douce*—an infinitely tender, delicate and soft being; *belle*—in ancient art perhaps a beautiful Aphrodite with always an oval face, languishing eyes and laughing mouth; in the Renaissance, Botticelli's Venus on a shell being driven to the shore by flying gods amid a shower of roses; a certain dreamy remoteness and yet the appeal to the senses. *Amoureuse*-Venus, Aphrodite, love-making, sensual love, charm and beauty. The second hemistich brings in the perfume, an attar of roses, impregnated with sweet odors, the natural scent of a blossom and of a young woman. The grace and freshness of this first line are superb. In the whole sonnet Ronsard can change tone colors, add harmonics gradually, use the *jugement de l'oreille* and mould his *Angevine* in the gardens of Bourgueil into a *unique Cytherée* who dominates the architecture of this perfect sonnet. But Scève is far more complex, intellectually. To Scève the important things are Délie and himself. There is only one theme, constantly renewed and contradictory and made up of approximations—love: the continual presence of Délie within the poet and more particularly in his memory (which is a leitmotif of the whole cycle), the permanence of the torment assured by her occupation of his whole being. Within this psychology of love there are contradictions which the poet tackles and his tone is often puzzled, tense and strained—very different from Ronsard who is out to aggrandize the mistress and himself. Scève's feeling that he knows nothing, his whole world seen through his love, the importance of sounds, shocks to nerves (see the poem which ends with the petrified hare, 129), the sense of panic (159 and 164), the way love distrubs his thought and makes him taste the plant aloe as if it were manna (dizain 10), the torturing power of time from infinitesimal seconds to the longest possible lapse of time imagined by scientists of the age (367, 114, 216), the profound introspection of himself, the mechanism of overlapping memory—these are some of the themes Scève introduces with psychological depth and subtlety and with acutely involved complexity. Valéry wrote that "Le mot *sensibilité* est ambigu. Il signifie tantôt—faculté de sentir, production de sensations; et tantôt mode de réaction, réactivité, mode de transmission. Et il signifie aussi liaison irrationnelle" (italics in text).[7] The *liaison irrationnelle* is present always in love poetry but an intellectual love poet is, according to Eliot, always "trying to find the verbal equivalents for states of mind or feeling." Scève is always inspecting and criticizing his experience. For instance dizain 156 is unengaged in a metaphysical shudder but is concerned with the poet's physical, nervous and panic-struck reaction to the voice of Délie:

> Estre ne peult le bien de mon malheur
> Plus esleué sur sa triste Montioye,
> Que celuy là, qui estaint la douleur
> Lors que ie deusse augmenter en ma ioye.
>   Car a toute heure il m'est aduis, que i'oye
> Celle parler a son heureux Consort:
> Et le doulx son, qui de sa bouche sort,
> Me fait fremir en si ardente doubte,
> Que desdaingnant & la loy, & le sort,
> Tout hors de moy du droit ie me deboute.

This is a typical instance of the dizains that Valéry Larbaud thus described: lines 1-6 do not at first seduce you, then you have a wonderful four lines which forces you to read the poem again in the gaze of new sight. The experience in this dizain is very reminiscent of a Sappho poem where she is sitting beside a maiden and her husband.[8] Her own emotions are given strongly; her love for the girl is very evident; and the seeing of her and hearing her talk are shattering. It does not matter whether Scève could have known of this poem; we never know how much a poet has read; we have simply the text and this we read, trying to make sense of it in terms of our own reading and sensibility. The underlying passion in the Scève dizain is jealousy and the whole situation is the fact that *son heureux Consort* enjoys her company and attention while the poet is outside the picture. Lines 5-10 gives us the concrete experience in physical and intense terms: *a toute heure . . . que i'oye*—at every hour of the day or night, every split second I hear her speak; is this the poet imagining the experience or is he really present? It could be either; the present tense is kept throughout. The sweetness of the sound makes him react in a very violent way: the verb *fremir* means "to quake, tremble, shiver, shake; be exceedingly moved" (Cotgrave). It evokes the convulsive shake, the febrile sensation and the subcutaneous shiver of pleasure and desire. The adjective *ardente* is one of Scève's key words: in the cycle as a whole it comes five times as *ardemment*, thirteen times as *ardent*, nine as *ardente*, twice as *ardentes*, three times as *ardentz*, thirty as *ardeur*, twice as *ardeurs*, once as *ardit*, five times as *ardoir*, once as *ardois* and once as *ardz*. Here it is qualifying *doubte*: this word is stronger than it is in modern times; it can mean "a reverent awe, or dread of" (Cotgrave); juxtaposed with *ardente* the phrase means a burning and fervent dread or awe. This powerful eighth line gives way to the final turn—he thrusts himself, drives himself from his SELF, *Tout hors de moy*. It reminds us of the fine dizain where he is wandering like a dead body in open sea, and then the name of Délie sounds in his ears, "Et a ce son me cornantz les oreilles, / Tout estourdy point ne me congnoissoys" (dizain 164). Is this not true of any love? As Alain Bosquet said, "L'amour, c'est méconnaître, perdre le sens des proportions et, en fin de compte, accéder à une sorte de non-connaissance." Scève's intelligence makes him try and transform these private feelings into language which he moulds and sculpts as if he were not dashed into fragments, disrupted into parts by his experience of love.

The intense emotivity that is present in these two poems relies on the sound of her name. More intense is touching her or she touching him. There are many entries in the Concordance on *touchant/touche/touché*, *toucher* and *touchoit* but look at one in dizain 159. If and when she touches me with her hand *vn rien*, ever so slightly,

> ma pensée endormye
> Plus, que le mort soubz sa pesante lame,
> Tressaulte en moy, comme si d'ardent flamme
> Lon me touchoit dormant profondement.

It is only once that Scève uses the word *Tressaulte* and it is not in Cotgrave. It is a neologism and Robert gives the verb *tressauter* rightly as 1544 Scève: *sursauter (en particulier sous l'effet de la surprise)*. Whereas the near synonym *tressaillir* has a psychological value, *tressauter* is chiefly tied to the physical domain. Furthermore, Scève compares it with a man who is profoundly sleeping being touched by burning flame. The acute physical effect pushes the mind *poulsant hors roidement* (only twice does Scève use *roidement*); the splinters of his mind are near death.

Thanks to the Concordance we can now check up neologisms: words like *gruer, girouetter, degluer, ahontir, apourir, illusif, encombreux, apollinées, fulminatoire, neronnerie* and *vacilamment* occur once only. They occur not in his précieux poems but in poems where Scève expresses some things that he had experienced or imagined. Take dizain 99 with the use in line 5 of *gruer*, "to waste away our time in fruitless waiting." The argument of the poem centers around hope: lines 1-4—if uncertainty were the least of his troubles, at least in a paradoxical way he would "soit en vain" have "limité / Le bout sans fin de ma vaine esperance." We feel Scève moulding and rhythmically structuring this line so that the word *esperance* is thrust to the end and seems even more remote. But lines 5-8 explain how he wears himself out with the vain assurance that he will be cured eventually. Note that he exploits vocabulary with a physical, erotic nuance: for example, *la grand prurison*: hope is like an itching, or tickling of a lustful desire, it may even mean an itching of the skin, in a lascivious inclination (Cotgrave). And this is immediately followed by *Qui nous chatouille*: "to tickle, to touch gently." Every time Scève uses the verb it brings into the picture acute sensation (dizain 258, l. 2, "Souffroit asses la chatouillant poincture" or dizain 289, l. 5, "Nouveau plaisir alors me chatouilloit"). The time element is stressed also—*tous les iours*. And his passion is a *fiebure*. We may compare this dizain to No. 155 where the physical is uppermost: *froit tremblant, glacées frisons, les mouelles consume, / Cuysant le Corps, chaleur par ardentes cuysons / Le demourant violemment escume* to end with the stupendous last line, "Ma fiebure r'entre en plus grand parocisme," with the use of *parocisme* (once only in the whole of *Délie*) suggesting "The returne, or fit, of an ague" (Cotgrave), which was a medical term. The last two lines of dizain 99 show the effect of this

illusion which is brought about by hope. The analogy is based on the likeness between two pairs of things: *printemps* and *noz ans*, which is summed
up in the proverbial expression "the flower of my age," and *la maigre
Caresme* and the "prison" of hope. The phrase *la maigre Caresme* suggests
the period of fasting and abstinence, a lean and gloomy time for the flesh.
Caresme was used in a number of phrases to suggest the passing of time
and youth: for example, "bien et beau s'en va caresme," meaning time
passes quickly while we waste out youth.[9] The image is effective in that it
brings together the season of Spring and that of Lent, the youth of the
poet and the frustrating captivity of hope which has been the main point
of the dizain.

My last example of Scève's poetic and artistic sensibility shall be dizain
165 which combines a major motive of *Délie*—that is, memory—with the
allusiveness which I have written about elsewhere. The allusions in the last
two lines are richly emotive: "le m'apperçoy la memoyre abismée / Auec
Dathan au centre d'Abiron." After startling the reader with the first line
of the poem, "Mes pleurs clouantz au front ses tristes yeulx," the poet
announces the familiar theme of how his memory tries to recapture the
essence of Délie. He states in line 5 that "Sa haultesse . . . ne peult estre
estimée" by such a lowly subject as himself. Line 7 means that he has out-
stretched himself thinking that he could express the quintessence of Délie.
He realizes how false this is and sees his memory as linked with Dathan.
The force of the allusion lies firstly in the evocation of a physical punishment—the opening of the earth and the engulfing of the victims in a bot-
tomless pit. Secondly, there has to be brought in the associations around
this episode in the Bible: "They, and all that appertained to them, went
down alive into the pit, and the earth closed upon them: and they per-
ished from among the congregation" (*Numbers*, 16. 33). This refers to the
rebellion of Dathan and Abiram against Moses, and for their presumption
the two are swallowed up by the earth which opened beneath their feet.
In the glosses of the *Biblia Pauperum* this punishment is a prefiguration of
punishments in Hell. Dathan is of the race of perjurers; the allusion to him
in Racine's *Athalie* links him with Athalie and others of this race: "Dieu
s'apprête à te joindre à la race parjure, / Abiron et Dathan, Doëg, Achi-
tophel . . ." The feeling that the poet's memory is cast down as into a pit
is brought about by the *parjure* he has done to Délie in imagining that his
memory can attain a realization of her greatness. This is a supreme form of
an exacting artistic conscience with tremendous emotivity channelled and
controlled by Scève's own intellect.

How can I conclude on Scève? He composed one of the masterpieces of
16th-century love poetry. His *Délie* reflects the depths of his intuitive

contact with the world and his introspective contact with the self. An assessment of his value rests heavily on careful reading of his poetry. He was the first French poet to be moulding a new literary language, a language that was rich in texture and form. He was the first French poet who was difficult to understand and evaluate. Scève remains for me an authentic original poet who has nowhere any disciples.

NOTES

1. See the superb commentary on this dizain by Odette de Mourgues in "Deux Triomphes de l'hyperbole," in *De Shakespeare à T.S. Eliot. Mélanges offerts à Henri Fluchère* (Paris, 1976), pp. 73-79.

2. The edition used is by C.A. Mayer (London: The Athlone Press, 1958-1973). This reference is to *Les Epigrammes*, p. 201.

3. "Prosodie et sémantique: une hypothèse sur le sens des quatrains atypiques dans la *Délie* de Maurice Scève," in *The Equilibrium of Wit. Essays for Odette de Mourgues*, eds. Peter Bayley and Dorothy Gabe Coleman, French Forum Monographs, 36 (Lexington: French Forum, 1982), pp. 28-41.

4. The edition used is *Les Amours*, eds. H. and C. Weber (Paris, 1963).

5. The furthest down that Scève can go is *hanches* (dizain 367).

6. *Oeuvres diverses*, ed. C.A. Mayer, pp. 123-24.

7. *Cahiers*, ed. Judith Robinson, 2 vols. (Paris: Gallimard, 1973-74), I, 1206.

8. *Lyra Graeca*, ed. J.M. Edmonds, 3 vols. (Harvard Univ. Press, 1952), I, 186-87.

9. Huguet gives an example from Ph. de Marnix of the use of this phrase: "Nous ne ferons que battre l'air et perdre l'escrime et le beau printemps de nostre jeunesse: et cependant bien et beau s'en va quaresme," where Spring, youth and Lent are close to the meaning of the line in *Délie*.

Scève's Délie and Marot: A Study of Intertextualities

Doranne Fenoaltea

Recent and growing interest in literary intertextuality has given rise to a number of theories which have aimed to define the nature and function of the relation between texts; they range from the narrow focus of Bloom's "anxiety of influence" to Barthes's more encompassing notion of intertextuality as the *éclats* of what has been "déjà lu, vu, fait, vécu."[1] Theoretical and practical studies have greatly sharpened critical awareness of the complexity of a topic which earlier scholars tended to lump somewhat indiscriminately under the heading "sources et influences." Despite the variety of theoretical positions and the sometimes imperfect fit between theory and practice in studies of intertextuality, we now recognize with far greater clarity that texts are related to other texts—however defined— in various and complex ways. With such concepts in mind, it should be possible to map with more assurance the discursive space of specific texts in order to gain insight into their constitution, into their historical and ideological bases, and finally, into the process of reading and interpreting them.[2]

While theoretical discussions of intertextuality have largely focused on the 19th and 20th centuries, students of French Renaissance poetry are well aware that literary intertextualities play an important, indeed decisive, role in the formulation of poetic texts of the period. The establishment of texts with respect to other texts was one of the poet's conscious goals,[3] and a wide variety of practices ensured referentiality. Some, such as translation, imitation, and citation, are primarily textual in nature, while others, such as form, versification, choice of themes and rhetorical motifs, as well as some types of allusion, are principally metatextual.[4] It thus appears important to consider how a broad range of intertextual relations participate in the creation of a literary context and define the discursive space of a work.[5]

This essay seeks to make a contribution to a mapping of the (historical) discursive space of Scève's *Délie* by examining its intertextual relations to the poetry of Clément Marot. Despite Marot's clear position as the most important French poet of the 1530s, his poetry has not appeared to have furnished a strong model for the poet of the *Délie*.[6] Parturier's edition of the *Délie* indicates a number of poems of Marot as models for Scève's treatment of certain themes,[7] gives two instances of verses whose formulation closely parallels verses of Marot, and links the expression "un doulx Nenny" in D133 to Marot's epigram, "De Ouy, & de Nenny."[8] Marot is also mentioned in connection with the allusion to Scève's "blason du Sourcil" in D270.

Parturier's "sources" here are of two very different types.[9] One category, by far the larger, is metatextual rather than textual in nature. The thematic *rapprochements* show that both poets draw on or share a certain conventional intertextual space. The reference in D270 to Scève's rivalry with other poets in the blason genre may also be viewed as alluding to a shared metatextual space, defined by the writing of a certain type of poem and, perhaps, the notion of poetic emulation. Such relations help define the discursive space which both poets share; they give little or no information about a direct (i.e., textual) link between the works of the two poets nor about possibilities of meaning generated by contact between the works. D67, D130, and perhaps D133, have, instead, textual reminiscences which create specific intertextual ties between poetic texts; these poems also have related themes.

With respect to the metatextual space shared by the two poets, Parturier's notes thus suggest an area of overlap, which may be due largely to the fact that the poets are contemporaries, working to some extent at least in the same field of poetic activity. At most, Marot's prestige might appear to serve—in a domain where innovation went hand in hand with authority and tradition—as a precedent for incorporating certain motifs from the discursive space of Italian and neo-Latin love poetry into French poetry.

In the case of textual reminiscences, the situation is rather different. Where metatextual intertextualities are concerned, only the *déja lu*—the recognition that the text belongs to a known type—is activated. Textual reminiscences evoke instead a specific text. Thus, the echo in the final verse of D67 of the final verse of Marot's "Dizain de l'image de Venus armée R.F." which begins "Vous chevalier de la basse bataille" and the allusive value of the "doulx Nenny" in D133 would undoubtedly have recalled, to the contemporary 16th-century reader, these witty epigrams, with their clearly sexual implications.

The effects of recalling another specific text are complex—difficult to define and to some extent variable from reader to reader. But in any case, one result of recognizing such an allusion is the disturbance of the linearity (the strict self-referentiality) of the text[10] and the creation of a dialogic relationship between two texts, both of which are, because of the nature of the later formulation, present in the reader's mind. In the case of the textual reminiscences of D67 and D130, the resonances of Marot's poem will affect in some fashion the serious tenor of Scève's text. Recollection of the earlier text may work to undermine the linear meaning or it may suggest an ironic deflation: the reader brings another interpretation to words whose apparent contextual implications are rather different. The literariness of the utterance is reinforced, and the poet and the reader may appear to share a vantage point at some distance from the lover's experience. Is the poet showing the double nature of the lover's desire or even his duplicity? On the other hand, the view of love taken by Marot may appear negated by the appropriation and reinsertion of his language into a very different context. Some readers may feel that Scève is challenging—and attempting to dominate—his predecessor's text and perhaps by extension the attitude towards love it expresses. However the reader is affected, the textual echo clearly opens the text to the reverberations of another text, calls attention to the essential literariness of the poet's enterprise, and complicates the meaning which the reader attributes to the lover's expressed experience. The complexity of the work is to some extent a function of its intertextualities.

As attention to these instances indicates, the intertextual relation between the *Délie* and the poetic corpus of Marot is not a simple one, but on Parturier's evidence, there is little more than the sharing of a common ground. A more careful comparison of the works of the two poets reveals, however, many more textual allusions than Parturier's notes suggest and a shared metatextual domain more than simply thematic in scope. Taking as the basis of analysis Marot's *Oeuvres* of 1538, the important collection published in Lyons in that year and Marot's first major publication after the *Adolescence clementine* of 1532, one finds some twenty-five additional textual echoes, verse-length or longer, which recall formulations of Marot's. Like the two noted by Parturier (and like the mottoes of the *emblesmes* which establish an intratextual intertextuality of a similar type), they show minor variations of formulation. This relatively high number of textual ties will tend to affect the view taken of the shared metatext as well, since they suggest that instead of resulting simply from a common referential ground, the shared metatextual space may also be determined in part by the later poet's reading of his predecessor.

The textual links are presented in the Table below, and several general remarks may be made about them. Many are from Marot's early, particularly lyric, works: elegies, chansons, and the *Temple de Cupidon* and the

Deploration de Florimond Robertet. Many of the cited fragments from
Marot's works occur at the beginning or end of a poem or, in the case of
long poems, of a section; these are obviously moments which tend to
remain more clearly fixed in a reader's (or hearer's) mind.[11] In Scève's
text, the related expression falls often, but less consistently, at the beginning or end of dizains. The echoes are close but far from slavish replicas;
they often suggest an assimilated recollection of the earlier text, a pattern
freely manipulated by the later poet. Scève's reformulations generally
show a decided tendency to redirect Marot's expression to create a more
personal situation (e.g., D70, D224) and to condense and heighten the
intensity of the earlier poet's expression (e.g., D9, D17, D185, D224).

In some instances, these poems share thematic elements as well. D52
and Elegie 3 share related but differently weighted concerns: Marot
develops the theme of steadfastness and alludes indirectly to mourning
and the color black; Scève is less concerned with steadfastness (vv. 3-4)
and focuses on the theme of death by developing the implications of
"embrunir." D224 uses the repetitive structure of Marot's chanson "Si
de nouveau j'ay nouvelles couleurs" similarly but then moves in a very
different direction. Both D264 and the "Epitre au Dauphin," despite the
difference of focus, are concerned with the sustaining of life through
representation, in a situation of absence. In all these cases, the textual echo
serves both to create a link and to call attention to a fundamental difference of point of view; in this respect Scève's procedure vis-à-vis Marot is
rather like his procedure vis-à-vis Petrarch.[12]

We may note that textual fragments recalling Marot's work often occur
in poems which also establish ties to a Petrarchan text, particularly from
the *Rime*; the reminiscences from Marot are often used to formulate
succinctly one element of Scève's transformation of a Petrarchan development. D9, which incorporates and transforms a passage from Petrarch's
Trionfo d'Amore, makes extremely effective use of a Marotic fragment in
the final line.[13] Similarly, D227 and D423 use brief Marotic formulations
in texts which also reflect Petrarchan texts.[14] One may wonder if D352,
which develops the Petrarchan image of the fleeing stag in a discussion of
the effects of presence and absence, may not also contain an echo and an
implicit ironic judgment of an extended and somewhat pedestrian exposi-
tion from one of Marot's elegies. Marot's text reads:

> . . . J'ay tousjours ouy dire:
> Qui plus est pres plus ardemment desire;
> Parquoy, pour moins ardemment desirer,
> Raison me dit qu'il me fault retirer,
> En m'asseurant (si je croy son propos)

Que mon esprit par temps aura repos.
Et si promect rendre à ma triste vie
La liberté que luy avez ravie.
Et vostre amour (helas) ne me promect
Fors desespoir qui au Tombeau me mect.
                    Elegie 13, vv. 25-34 (OL, p. 238)

If one recalls Marot's text, Scève's *raccourci* in vv. 5-6 contains a rather sharp-edged judgment of both the poetic formulation and Marot's status as a lover:

Non moins ardoir ie me sens en l'absence
Du tout de moy pour elle me priuant,
Que congeler en la doulce presence,
Qui par ses yeulx me rend mort, & viuant.
    Or si ie suis le vulgaire suyuant,
Pour en guerir, fuyr la me fauldroit.
    Le Cerf blessé par l'archier bien adroit
Plus fuyt la mort, & plus sa fin approche.
Donc ce remede a mon mal ne vauldroit
Sinon, moy mort, desesperé reproche.[15]

At the midpoint of the *Délie*, D224 balances textual allusion to both poets: Marot's chanson is recalled in the first section, with a similar use of anaphora in both texts, while a Petrarchan sonnet concerned with the *piaga* of love is recalled in the second.[16] In this poem, Scève's reformulation of the texts of his predecessors makes very clear the distinctive nature of his art and his vision of the love experience. At the same time, the placing of the poem at the center of the work suggests Scève's desire to recognize two major predecessors.

D6, the first *emblesme* poem of the *Délie*, contains in v. 1 a brief echo from Petrarch's "Tacer non posso" ("Libre viuois en l'Auril de mon aage" / "Ch'era de l'anno e di mi'etate aprile," *Rime* 325, v. 13). More generally, it follows a chanson of Marot's in which he links his own work to that of his poetic predecessors. Marot's chanson "Quand j'ay pensé en vous, ma bien aymée" (*OL*, p. 182) expresses the beauty and virtue of the lady, the loss of the lover's heart to her, and his potential death if in her cruelty she should refuse him mercy.[17] In three successive verses (vv. 15-17), the chanson cites earlier works on the same theme: the *Arrest de la louange de la dame sans si* of F. Robertet, G. Cretin, and O. de Saint-Gelais; *La belle dame sans mercy* of A. Chartier; and an anonymous song, "Vostre pitié vœult doncques que je meure." The echoes of these texts tie Marot's chanson firmly to earlier texts on the theme of the cruel lady and serve both textual and metatextual ends. By echoing in "Ou l'œil . . . Se veit surpris de la doulce presence . . . Ma *liberté* luy a *toute* asseruie" Marot's "Des que mon *œil* apperceut vostre face, / Ma *liberté* du *tout* m'abandonna," Scève's text becomes part of the same intertextual space. In addition, the word "adolescence" in v. 2 of the dizain ("De cure exempt soubz celle adolescence") may recall the *Adolescence clementine*, in which the chanson was included, and serve to link the *Délie* to Marot's first collection. The first *emblesme* poem of Scève's work thus appears to invite the reader to consider Scève's dizain as an example of a traditional theme which had been treated by Scève's notable predecessors—Petrarch, but also Marot, and through Marot, Robertet, Cretin, Saint-Gelais, Chartier, and the anonymous lyric tradition. In comparison to the earlier elaborations, the greater conceptual complexity of Scève's dizain is immediately evident, and the allusions thus serve to draw attention to the originality of Scève's formulation and the particular contribution his work will make to the lyric tradition in French poetry. As the first *emblesme* poem, the dizain is structurally important and one in which the recollection of poetic predecessors is thus more strongly emphasized.

In general, the intertextuality established by means of textual echoes between the *Délie* and Marot's work appears more closely tied to verbalization than to conceptualization or attitude. Marot's voice echoes in the *Délie* perhaps most tellingly as a specifically French poetic voice, a model and a precursor in a domain undergoing rapid transformation. In forging his own, very different voice, Scève recalls the texture of a linguistic idiom which he is transforming into an instrument for expressing a more complex experience than that contained in the works of his French predecessors.

As an authoritative contemporary French voice, Marot may also furnish a starting point for other, largely metatextual, aspects of Scève's poetic expression, elements common to the works of both poets but which do not constitute the kind of verbal echo of specific texts previously discussed. They include lexicon and mythical and geographic allusion. An examination of Scève's lexicon with respect to its apparently innovative elements shows that among the words labeled neologisms or new or unusual words in McFarlane's notes to the *Délie*, many are also present in Marot's work, notably in the *Temple de Cupidon* and the *Deploration de Florimond Robertet*. Thus, *desuie* (D1) occurs in the *Deploration*, v. 298 (*OL*, p. 153), *escondire* (D8) in chanson 20, v. 7 (*OL*, p. 192); *habitude* (also rhymed with *servitude*, as in D12) occurs in the same sense and tied to the theme of seeing in Epitre 20, vv. 9-10: "mais la grande servitude / De ceste Court, où est nostre habitude, / M'oste souvent par force le plaisir" (*Epit.*, p. 156). *Montioye* (D58, D156) occurs in several places in Marot, once in the *Tem-*

ple, v. 103 (*OL*, p. 92); *impropere* (D83) is also employed several times, including the *Deploration*, v. 345 (*OL*, p. 154); the old French *Bracquemart* (D110) occurs in the *Temple*, v. 288, where it is also associated with Mars (*OL*, p. 102), *apourir* (D166) occurs in the *Deploration*, vv. 216-17: "...d'apovrir ce bas monde, / Pour enrichir de noz biens les haultz cieulx" (*OL*, p. 149; cf. also D53, v. 3); *idoyne* (D308) occurs in the *Temple*, v. 374, although the sense appears rather different (*OL*, p. 105), the old form *poursuyuir* (D322) occurs in the *Temple*, vv. 90, 140, 496 (*OL*, pp. 92, 94, 111). Other striking words employed by Scève can be found in the work of Marot as well. Thus, while Scève certainly sometimes innovates in his lexicon, particularly perhaps in the coinage of Latinisms, he is far more conservative in this respect than either the rhétoriqueurs or Ronsard.

Similarly, a comparison of natural and legendary geographic allusions and references to historical and legendary figures in both poets shows that Scève's field of reference, far from being recondite, shows a considerable overlap with Marot's, with the notable and logical exception of some of the ramifications of the Delian myth. Since Marot's allusions, like his lexicon and syntax, can probably be considered as accessible to a cultivated but not learned contemporary audience, this suggests once again a largely conservative position.[18] With respect to his own text, Scève's allusions to less well-known figures of the Delian myth, because they are more obscure and therefore more opaque, draw attention to this central figure who appears as a result more mysterious, requiring a greater effort of explicitation, or a vaster or deeper knowledge of myth. This difference of transparency appears poetically appropriate. At the same time, these allusions will increase the range of the intertext of available mythical figures to include a multiform Delian figure; just as Scève puts Lyons on the map of lyric geography, so too he inserts the Delian figure into a known body of reference on which subsequent poets can draw, as he did on the previously available body of allusions.

Other, more technical aspects of Scève's poetic voice also tend to tie his work to Marot's and to the French tradition. One of them, difficult to document particularly because Scève's syntax is generally far more complex than Marot's, lies in the adoption and adaptation of Marot's considerable rhythmic skills. One example is to be found in the use of repetition, as in D224 and D264, both of which recall specific texts (see Table). D264, like the *Epitre au Dauphin*, uses a repetitive technique to build to a resonant climax. Marot's more extended repetition is appropriate to the longer poem; Scève's adaptation in the briefer scope of the dizain achieves a similar effect with greater economy of means. Similarly, the balanced and rhythmical structure of "Plustost escripte, & plustost effacée, / Soubdain fermée, & tout soubdain declose" (Elegie 1, vv. 4-5, OL, p. 211) is often echoed by Scève: "Qui tost estaincte, & soubdain rallumée" (D48, v. 7), "le veulx soubdain, & plus soubdain ie n'ose" (D184, v. 2), "Soubdain m'estainct, & plus soubdain m'enflamme" (D196, v. 10), "Plus tost vaincu, plus tost victorieux" (D222, v. 1).

Another device employed by both poets, often to similarly effective ends, is the use of parentheses, whose effects are both rhetorical and subtly rhythmical. For example, the parenthetical "(toy seule)" of D378, "Mais toy, qui as (toy seule) le possible," has a parallel in Rondeau 50, v. 8: "C'est que tu as (toy seulle) double grace" (OD, p. 118). The final lines of Elegie 4 furnish several examples of parenthetical interpolation of a type to be found, for example, in D90, D116, D161, D162, D235, among many others:

> Seroit à vous (trop plus qu'à moy) aperte,
> D'aultant qu'il est (& vous le sçavez bien)
> Beaucoup plus vostre (en effect) qu'il n'est mien.
> Elegie 4, vv. 88-90 (OL, p. 225)

Other rhetorical devices link Scève's practice to Marot and beyond Marot to the rhétoriqueur tradition. These include, for example, alliteration (e.g., D7), rime équivoque (e.g., D28), and the insistent and varied repetition of forms of a word. A particularly striking example of this technique occurs in D421:

> Voulant ie veulx, que mon si hault vouloir
> De son bas vol s'estende a la vollée,
> Ou ce mien vueil ne peult en rien valoir,
> Ne la pensée, ainsi comme auolée,
> Craingnant qu'en fin Fortune l'esuolée
> Auec Amour pareillement volage
> Vueillent voler le sens, & le fol aage,
> Qui s'enuolantz auec ma destinée,
> Ne soubstrairont l'espoir, qui me soulage
> Ma volenté sainctement obstinée.

By taking advantage of the phonetic similarities of *voler* and *vouloir*, Scève creates a tour de force in which the sense is strained by the insistent pressure of the sound.[19] It is also a *réplique* to Marot. The expression "Fortune, l'esuolée" is a reminiscence from the rondeau "De la mal mariée" which begins, "Contre raison, Fortune, l'esvollée, / Trop lourdement devers moy est vollée" (OD, p. 131). This pointer to Marot is integrated in a poem which as a whole recalls developments in the *Deploration de Florimond Robertet*, concentrating and intensifying them:

> Jadis ma plume on vid son vol estendre
> Au gré d'amours, et d'un bas stille et tendre
> Distiller dictz que soulois mettre en chant
>   (vv. 1-3, *OL*, p. 140)
> Ainsi le fault, et quant ne le fauldroit,
> Mon cueur (helas) encores le vouldroit;
> Et quant mon cueur ne le vouldroit encores,
> Oultre son vueil contrainct y seroit ores
>   (vv. 7-10, *OL*, p. 141)
> Dieu immortel, diz ie lors, voicy l'esle
> Qui a vollé ainsi que voller fault
> Entre deux aers, ne trop bas ne trop hault.
> Voicy, pour vray, l'esle dont la vollée,
> Par sa vertu, a la France extollée,
> Circonvolant ce monde spacieux
> Et survolant maintenant les neuf cieulx.
> C'est l'esle noire en la bende dorée,
> L'esle en vollant jamais non essorée,
> Et dont sortye est la mieulx escripvant
> Plume qui fust de nostre aage vivant.
>   (vv. 128-38, *OL*, p. 146)

In addition, in the *Second livre des epigrammes dedié à Anne*, the epigram
"Au Poete Borbonius" (135) following the one addressed "A Maurice
Seve, Lyonnoys" (134), joins the two major terms in the final line, "Le
voller bas et le vouloir haultain" (*Epig.*, p. 202). In D421, Scève's text
implicitly challenges Marot's by its mastery of a technique employed with
extraordinary skill within the confines of the dizain; at the same time, the
dizain's formulation recalls a significant text, the role of an indigenous
poetic tradition for the *Délie*, and Marot's skill in continuing and preserving that tradition.[20]

Finally, an important intertextual (metatextual) relation between the
works of Marot and Scève is furnished, as Rigolot has convincingly argued,
by Scève's choice of the dizain, or epigram, as the form in which the poems
of the *Délie* are cast.[21] Rigolot shows that historical reasons suggest the
intertextual value to be accorded both the term and the form in Scève's
choice of the epigram. Scève's liminary huitain recalls the initial quintil
of Marot's "proto-canzoniere," the *Second livre des epigrammes*, thereby
suggesting at the very least an indication of his recognition of Marot's
collection of epigrams addressed, like his, to a "Dame." Thematically,
both poems constitute an invitation to the Lady to read the collection
dedicated to her. In the use of the rhyme epigramme(s)/flamme(s) and
perhaps in other echoes as well, Scève creates explicit textual ties to the
earlier work.

Structural relationships between Marot's *Second livre* and the *Délie* do not stop here. The final poem of Marot's collection has as its theme the eternal renown which the Lady will gain from the poet's attention; Scève's final poem, very different in tone and resonances, has its basis in the same theme. In addition, the notion of the renewal of the piaga of love which recurs in the quarterly clusters of the *Délie*[22] recalls the first poem after the liminary quintil addressed to Anne (and the seventh in sequence). The "Estreines à Anne" begins: "Ce *nouvel* an pour Estreines vous donne / Mon cueur blesse d'une *nouelle playe*." Marot's formulation of this Petrarchan theme is echoed in D112 ("Renouellant ce mien feu ancien. / Dont du grief mal l'Ame toute playeuse"), in D224 ("Nouelle amour, nouelle affection, / Nouelles fleurs parmy l'herbe nouelle: / Et, ia passée, encor se renouelle . . . Ce neantmoins la renouation / De mon vieulx mal, & vlcere ancienne . . . playe Egyptienne"), and in D333 ("Ce neantmoins tousiours se renouelle / Le mal, qui vient ma playe reunir"). The entire introductory section of the *Délie* shows a notable concentration of textual and formal links to Marot's work and thus helps establish the importance of Marot's work as an element of the Scevian intertext. The points of contact with Marot's *Second livre des epigrammes* at structurally important places in Scève's text suggest the desire to insure a formal link between the *Délie* and the only collection in Marot's *œuvre*—and the only major contemporary work of French poetry—which constitutes a precedent, in French, for a collection of poems addressed to a *Dame*.

At the same time, of course, Scève's text is also linked at all these points to the Petrarchan *œuvre*, and thus to the intertextual space of Italian love poetry, exemplified in the most illustrious (and for Scève, the first) among them. Thus, the midpoint, endpoint, and quarterly clusters of the *Délie* contain clear textual allusions to Petrarch's works.[24] At the beginning of the *Délie*, Scève's initial allusion to Petrarch comes in D1. As in the case of the allusion to Marot's initial epigram of the *Second livre des epigrammes* in the liminary huitain, D1 recalls the first poem of the *Rime* ("en mes ieunes erreurs"/"in su'l mio primo giovenile errore"). Since the liminary huitain is concerned with poetry and poetic form and D1 with the *innamoramento*, one is tempted to see a distinction made between a more formal and technical contribution from the work of Marot and a more thematic or experiential one from Petrarch. Textual and metatextual links created in the first words of the *Délie* strongly suggest that Scève deliberately placed his work in an intertextual space which the work of two major predecessors, and through them two poetic traditions, help define.

The means by which the *Délie* is tied to the poetic intertext largely reflects the practice of the Italian followers of Petrarch who effected ties to the Petrarchan text by textual means, using procedures of imitation and textual reminiscence. Marot, instead, includes in the *Second livre des epigrammes* a large number of poems addressed to other poets and discussing poetic activity; to some extent, he establishes links to the practitioners of the art of poetry rather than to their works, a metatextual rather than a textual intertextuality. Thus, following the initial quintil, there is a sizain "A Merlin de Sainct Gelais," a dizain "A soy mesmes" in which Petrarch's Laura is named and Marot considers his capacity as a love poet, a huitain "De la Royne de Navarre" which praises Marguerite's writing, and a huitain "A Françoys Daulphin de France" describing Marot's poetic activity. Later in the collection, there is a huitain addressed "A Maurice Seve, Lyonnoys" followed by a dizain "Au Poete Borbonius." Far more reticent, Scève names no poet, alluding only to Petrarch by periphrasis in two places; his recognition of his predecessors and contemporaries takes the form of textual reminiscence, as did Petrarch's.

In sum, Marot's work appears to stand as a corpus of French poetry as practiced in the 1530s, which furnishes a model and an accepted standard. Textual allusions to Marot's work appear to acknowledge both Scève's participation in a "style" and the value of a specific predecessor whose work is recognized as a significant element in the elaboration of Scève's poetic voice. In particular, certain major, especially lyric works of Marot appear to have left their mark on the poet and been used to serve rather different poetic ends. Some of Marot's linguistic practices, his lexicon and the body of allusions on which he draws suggest a basis for Scève's use and extension of the field of poetic expression, in a form for which Marot's *Second livre des epigrammes* represents an indigenous precedent. The importance accorded Marot at structurally important moments of the work and the choice of the dizain strongly indicate an intention to affirm the formal contribution of the French tradition and to recognize Marot's consummate skill in using it.

French poetic style, as exemplified by Marot, is of course only one of the idioms which constitute the voice of the poet of Délie. The work also draws on the tradition of serious Italian love poetry (for which Petrarch plays the role of dominant predecessor), that of neo-Latin verse (for which Angeriano, whom Scève translated in several poems, may serve as major predecessor), and perhaps the more brilliant epigrammatic style of the Italian *strambottisti* (for whom Serafino dell' Aquila, whose conceits are reflected in a number of dizains, may serve as a dominant figure).

The *Délie* contains many poems whose dominant characteristics reflect one or another of the poetic idioms available to a trilingual poet of the late

1530s and early 1540s, but as he does with the materials from Marot, Scève transforms them, personalizing, intensifying, concentrating. Scève's characteristic linguistic expression draws on but is different from that of all his predecessors: it has a complex rhythm, a telling use of consonants, and a verbal agility characteristic of French verse, a tightness of syntax which appears to reflect the poet's knowledge of Latin poetry, and the vocalic resonance, but not, generally speaking, the lyrical *dolcezza* of Italian love poetry. It is a unique voice, forged to express a complex experience, but it draws no small part of its authority from the diversity and vitality of pre-Pléiade poetic activity.

NOTES

1. The term is J. Kristeva's, in *La Révolution du langage poétique* (1969), pp. 337-58. See H. Bloom, *The Anxiety of Influence* (New York: Oxford Univ. Press, 1973) and R. Barthes, *S/Z* (Paris: Seuil, 1970), esp. pp. 27-28.

2. See notably the discussion of L. Jenny, "La Stratégie de la forme," *Poétique*, 27 (1974), 257-81; also the comments on his study by J. Culler in *The Pursuit of Signs* (Ithaca: Cornell Univ. Press, 1981), pp. 104-05.

3. T. Sebillet, *Art poétique françoys*, ed. F. Gaiffe (Paris: Droz, 1932), ch. XIV, "De la version," et passim; J. Du Bellay, *La Deffence et Illustration de la Langue Françoyse*, ed. H. Chamard (Paris: Didier, 1948), Book I, chs. 35-39 (pp. 32-48), and passim; and J. Peletier du Mans, *L'Art poëtique*, ed. A. Boulenger (Paris: Société des Belles Lettres, 1930), pp. 95-111 all treat in detail questions of imitation and translation, thereby suggesting the importance accorded these activities for poetic composition. For a recent discussion of the implications of these concepts, see T. Cave, *The Cornucopian Text* (Oxford: Clarendon Press, 1979), pp. 53-77.

4. The close attention to the codification of technical aspects of poetic composition has suggested to some modern scholars that 16th-century theory was unable to cope with poetry except as "second rhetoric," i.e., as versified prose, but it may perhaps be more usefully viewed in the light of an awareness of the importance of metatextual elements for establishing intertextuality and, as a result, participation in the poetic corpus.

5. Such analyses might help create a more sophisticated—because textually based—means of undertaking literary history.

6. Since Parturier, *Délie, obiect de plus haulte vertu* (Paris: Didier, 1916), first undertook to establish an intertextual framework for the *Délie* by an exhaustive but ill-defined search for sources, the problem of the constitution of the intertextual space of this particular text has continued to attract critical attention. It has, however, been defined in very different ways, largely, it would appear, because of differences arising from the views implicitly held by different scholars of what constitutes (meaningful) intertextual space. See D. Fenoaltea, "Lumière et obscurité: à la recherche de la *Délie* de Maurice Scève," *Oeuvres & Critiques*, 5 (1980), esp. pp. 29-33.

7. The Dizains are D36, D51, D81, D96, D109, D110, D125, D205, D214, and D374.

8. The textual reminiscences are: "Mais tout armé l'ay vaincu toute nue" (D67, v. 10)/"Vaincu vous ay tant de fois toute nue" (In P. Jannet, *Oeuvres complètes de Clément Marot*, 4 vols. [Paris: Flammarion, 1909], III, 119) and "Voulut respondre, vn seul mot ne rendit" (D130, v. 4) / "Voulant parler, un seul mot ne puis dire" (Jannet, III, 114). Texts from the *Délie* are taken from *The Délie of Maurice Scève*, ed. I.D. McFarlane (Cambridge Univ. Press, 1966), and those of Marot are cited from C.A. Mayer's edition of Marot's work: *Oeuvres lyriques* (abbreviated as *OL*), *Oeuvres diverses* (abbreviated as *OD*), *Epigrammes* (abbreviated as *Epig.*), *Epitres* (abbreviated as *Epit.*), unless otherwise indicated (London: The Athlone Press, 1959-70). The two texts indicated in Parturier's notes are not included in the Mayer edition.

9. V.-L. Saulnier categorized Parturier's sources into types. See *Maurice Scève* (Paris: Klincksieck, 1948), pp. 260-70.

10. Jenny, p. 266.

11. This is the case of the texts cited in conjunction with D6, D9, D17 (the elegy), D52, D124, D185, D221 (both), D224, D227, D264, D309, D322, D387, D389, D423, D427.

12. For a discussion of the relation between Scève's and Petrarch's texts see D. Fenoaltea, "Establishing Contrasts: An Aspect of Scève's Use of Petrarch's Poetry in the 'Délie,'" *Studi Francesi*, 27 (1975), 17-33.

13. Ibid., 31-33.

14. For D227, see "Establishing Contrasts," pp. 25-26; for D423, see D. Fenoaltea, "The Poet in Nature," *French Studies*, 27 (1973), 262-65.

15. For the Petrarchan aspect of D352, see D. Fenoaltea, "Three Animal Images in the *Délie*," *BHR*, 34 (1972), 414-18.

16. See "Establishing Contrasts," pp. 27-28 and D. Fenoaltea, "*Si haulte Architecture*": *The Design of Scève's Délie*, French Forum Monographs, 35 (Lexington: French Forum, Publishers, 1982), p. 71.

17. "Quand j'ay pensé en vous, ma bien aymée, / Trouver n'en puis de si grande beaulté. / Et de vertu seriez plus estimée / Qu'aultre qui soit, si n'estoit cruaulté. / Mais pour vous aymer loyaulment / J'ay recompense de tourment. / Toutefois quand il vous plaira, / Mon mal par mercy finera. / Des que mon œil apperceut vostre face, / Ma liberté du tout m'abandonna, / Car mon las cueur esperant vostre grace / De moy partit et à vous se donna. / Or s'est il voulu retirer / En lieu dont ne se peult tirer, / Et vous a trouvée sans sy, / Fors qu'estes Dame sans mercy. / Vostre rigueur veult doncques que je meure, / Puis que pitié vostre cueur ne remord; / Si n'aurez vous (de ce je vous asseure) / Loz ny honneur de si cruelle mort. / Car on ne doibt mettre en langueur / Celluy quy ayme de bon cueur. / Trop est rude à son Ennemy / Qui est cruel à son Amy." The Petrarchan reminiscence in v. 1 of D6 is indicated by both Parturier and McFarlane. In a number of instances, Scève follows one Petrarchan development and textually recalls another, but several of these poems suggest that Scève also combines a clear textual allusion to a text of Marot or Petrarch, while drawing on the general development on the other, significantly transforming it.

18. In Marot, one finds references, for example, to Apelles, Aquilon, Argus, Aurora, Babylon, Bourbon, Cain, Champs Elysées, Cytharea, Daphne, Diana, Dido, Ecosse (roy de), Endymion, Eurydice, François I, Helicon, Hydra, Mars, Minos, Orpheus, Parnassus, Petrarch, Phoebus, Provence, Pyramus, Savoye, Styx, Thessaly (cf. Hemonie), Troy, Vulcan. Marot also refers to Charles Quint as Aigle, to Fran-

çois I's Salamander, to the serpent of Moses (*Depl. Flor. Rob.*, vv. 397 ff.), and to a number of more or less contemporary events to which Scève also alludes.

19. P. Zumthor, *Le Masque et la lumière: la poétique des grands rhétoriqueurs* (Paris: Seuil, 1978), pp. 244-46.

20. For a contextual discussion of D421 which justifies this assertion, see "*Si haulte Architecture*," pp. 177-78, 212.

21. F. Rigolot, "Intertexte du dizain scévien: Pétrarque et Marot," *CAIEF*, 32 (1980), 96-106.

22. This point is reinforced by the evidence of the quarterly divisions of the text. See "*Si haulte Architecture*," ch. 4.

23. Italics added.

24. For D224, see "Establishing Contrasts," pp. 27-28; for D449, McFarlane, p. 481; and for the quarterly markers, "*Si haulte Architecture*," pp. 70-73.

TABLE OF TEXTUAL REMINISCENCES

Délie

Des neuf Cieulx à l'influence empirée
    D4, v. 3

Ou l'œil. . . .
Se veit surpris de la doulce presence,
. . . .
Ma liberté luy a toute asseruie:
    D6, vv. 3-4, 8

Beaulté logée en amere doulceur.
    D9, v. 10

Quoy que du *temps tout grand* oultrage face,
Les *seches fleurs* en leur odeur viuront:
Prœuue pour ceulz, qui le bien poursuyruront
De non *mourir*, mais de reuiure encore.
Tes *vertus* donc, qui ton corps ne suyuront,
Dès l'Indien s'estendront iusqu'au *More*.
    D11, vv. 5-10 (italics mine)

Plus tost seront Rhosne, & Saone disjoinctz,
Que d'auec toy mon cœur se desassemble:
Plus tost seront l'vn, & l'aultre Mont ioinctz,
. . . .
Le Rhosne aller contremont lentement.
    D17, vv. 1-3, 6

Works of Marot

Des neuf Cieulx a la haulteur excedée
Chant-Royal de la Conception nostre Dame, v. 35
    (*OD*, p. 187)

Des que mon œil apperceut vostre face,
Ma liberté du tout m'abandonna,
    Ch. 9, vv. 9-10 (*OL*, p. 182)

O Cruaulté logée en grand beaulté,
O grand beaulté qui loges cruaulté,
    Ch. 29, vv. 1-2 (*OL*, p. 197)

Je luy responds: toutes tes *fleurs* perissent
Incontinent que Yver les vient toucher;
Mais en *tout temps* de Madame *florissent*
Les *grands vertus* que *Mort* ne peult *secher*.
    Epig. 8, vv. 7-10 (*Epig.*, p. 101, italics mine)

Plustost sera Montaigne sans Vallée,
Plustost la Mer on voirra dessalée,
Et plustost Seine encontrement ira
Que mon amour de toy se partira.
    Elegie 15, vv. 35-38 (*OL*, p. 244)

Plus tost le Rosne encontremont courra,
Egl. 3, Au roy, v. 252 (*OL*, p. 353)[a]

. . . en douleur ilz mourront
Et noz plaisirs tousjours nous demourront.
Elegie 3, vv. 87-88 (*OL*, p. 223)

Ce clair souleil qui estoit tant duisant
A esclaircir de ce temps la bruyne.
Depl. Flor. Rob., vv. 208-09 (*OL*, p. 149)

Incontinent que je te vy venue,
Epig. 31, v. 1 (*Epig*, p. 121)

C'est luy qui veult que mon œil se recrée,
Comme souloye, en vostre doulx regart!
Cant. 3, Le Dieu Gard, vv. 12-13 (*OL*, p. 285)[b]

Que hors de moy cheurent plainctes & pleurs,
Comme en yver seiches fueilles et fleurs.
Templ. Cup., vv. 501-02 (*OL*, p. 112)

Mon Cueur se fend & mon pauvre Oeil lamoie,
Elegie 2, v. 76 (*OL*, p. 219)

Sur le Printemps que la belle Flora
Templ. Cup., v. 1 (*OL*, p. 87)

Car il la tire hors de sa prison vile
Depl. Flor. Rob., v. 339 (*OL*, p. 154)

Si de nouveau j'ay nouelles couleurs,
Il n'en fault jà prendre esbahissement,
Car de nouveau j'ay nouelles douleurs,
Nouvelle amour & nouveau pensement.
Ch. 8, vv. 1-4 (*OL*, p. 181)

Jadis ma plume on vid son vol estendre
. . . d'un bas stille et tendre
Depl. Flor. Rob., vv. 1-2 (*OL*, p. 140)

Me demeurantz seulement les couleurs
De mes plaisirs, qui, me naissantz, me meurent.
D52, vv. 9-10

Vysse ie au moins esclercir ma bruyne
Pour vn cler iour en desirs prosperer.
D70, vv. 7-8

Parquoy soubdain, qu'icy tu es venue,
D124, v. 5

Ie me recrée aux rayons de ses yeulx.
D141, v. 3

Dont a l'espoir de tes glassons hurté,
Tu verrois cheoir les fueilles vne a vne.
D185, vv. 3-4

L'œil en larmoye, & le cœur en lamente
D190, v. 5

Sur le Printemps, que les Aloses montent,
D221, v. 1

Car il est hors de prison vehemente,
D221, v. 9

Nouelle amour, nouelle affection,
Nouelles fleurs parmy l'herbe nouelle:
Et, ià passée, encor se renouelle
Ma Primeuere en sa verte action.
Ce neantmoins la renouation
D224, vv. 1-5

Parquoy ma plume au bas vol de son aele
D227, v. 5

Car tout ie sers, & vis en Dame telle,
Que le parfaict, dont sa beaulté abonde,
Enrichit tant ceste Machine ronde,
    D245, vv. 5-7

De la clere vnde yssant hors Cytharée,
    D255, v. 1

Qui, maulgré Mort, & maulgré toute absence,
Te represente a moy trop plus, que viue.
    D264, vv. 9-10

Soit que l'ardeur en deux cœurs attrempée
    D273, v. 3

Ie contentois mon obstiné vouloir;
    D309, v. 3

Mais congnoissant soubz tes celestes mains
Estre mon ame heureusement traictée,
l'ay beaucoup plus de tes actes humains,
Que liberté de tous tant souhaictée.
    D322, vv. 7-10

Pour me trouuer briefue expedition.
    D326, v. 6

Ce neantmoins tousiours se renouelle
Le mal, qui vient ma playe reunir.
    D333, vv. 7-8

Va depeuplant les champs delicieux,
    D351, v. 5

Mais tout ainsi qu'a son aduenement
Le cler Soleil les estoilles efface,
    D387, vv. 7-8

O moy, heureux d'avoir Maistresse au Monde,
En qui Vertu soubz grand beaulté abonde!
    Elegie 16, vv. 27-28 (OL, p. 248)

Jusqu'à les faire yssir de la clere unde
    Complaincte de J. Chauvain, v. 7 (OL, p. 164)

Qui maulgré temps, maulgré feu, maulgré flamme,
Et maulgré mort fera vivre sans fin
    Epit. au Daulphin, vv. 76-77 (Epit., p. 243)[c]

Brandon de Venus rigoreux,
Qui son ardeur jamais n'attrempe.
    Templ. Cup., v. 240 (OL, p. 99)

    J'ay contenté
    Ma voulenté
    Suffisamment,
        Ch. 16, vv. 1-3 (OL, p. 188)

Et trop plus ayme estre serf en tes mains
Qu'en liberté parmy tous les Humains
    Elegie 1, vv. 95-96 (OL, p. 214)

Ont tres bien quis, & tresbien sceu trouver,
Pour me fascher, briefve expedition.
    Epit. au Roy, vv. 78-79 (Epit., p. 200)[d]

Ce nouvel an pour Estreines vous donne
Mon cueur blessé d'une novelle playe.
    Epig. 85, vv. 1-2 (Epig., p. 167)[e]

Aller ne veult aux Champs delicieux,
    Chant-Royal 3, v. 49 (OD, p. 185)

Le cler Soleil par sa presence efface
Et faict fuyr les tenebreuses nuictz
    Epig. 209, vv. 1-2 (Epig., p. 268)[f]

Elle à le cœur en si hault lieu assis
    D389, v. 1

Ton gentil cœur si haultement assis,
    Elegie 15, v. 1 (*OL*, p. 243)

Qui de douleur a ioye me pourmeine:
Y frequentantz, comme en propre domeine,
· · · · · · ·
Tousiours le long de ses riues prochaines
    D423, vv. 4-5, 8

Dedans la Nef du triumphant dommaine,
Songeant, resvant, longuement me pourmaine,
    Templ. Cup., vv. 423-24 (*OL*, p. 108)

De m'enflamber de ce dueil meslé d'ire
    D427, v. 3g

Joye y est & dueil remply de ire,
    Templ. Cup., v. 413 (*OL*, p. 108)

---

a. The eclogue, composed shortly after July 1539, was published independently. It was not included in the *Oeuvres* of 1538, but it does appear in those of 1539 and 1541. See *OL*, p. 63.

b. Not included in *Oeuvres* 1538. Cf. also D266, vv. 9-10, "Repaissez donc, comme le Coeur souloit, / Vous loing priuez d'vne telle iour-née."

c. Not in *Oeuvres* 1538; published separately, probably before the death of the Dauphin. See *Epit.*, p. 243.

d. Not in *Oeuvres* 1538, but composed in 1535 and published in 1536. See *Epit.*, p. 194.

e. See also D112, vv. 8-9, and D224, vv. 1-5, 9; these poems are discussed on p. 145.

f. Not in *Oeuvres* 1538. Mayer indicates 1538-40 as probable date of composition. First published in *Epigrammes de Clement Marot*, 1547.

g. This poem, in the final section which is closely tied to Sperone Speroni's *Dialogo d'Amore*, contains an unusually long development (vv. 1-8) with no textual ties to the dialogue. See D. Fenoaltea, "The Final Dizains of Scève's *Délie* and the *Dialogo d'Amore* of Sperone Speroni," *Studi Francesi*, 20 (1976), 201-05.

NOTE: For the texts associated with D421, see pp. 143-44.

FRENCH FORUM MONOGRAPHS

1. Karolyn Waterson. *Molière et l'autorité: Structures sociales, structures comiques.* 1976.
2. Donna Kuizenga. *Narrative Strategies in* La Princesse de Clèves. 1976.
3. Ian J. Winter. *Montaigne's Self-Portrait and Its Influence in France, 1580-1630.* 1976.
4. Judith G. Miller. *Theater and Revolution in France since 1968.* 1977.
5. Raymond C. La Charité, ed. *O un amy! Essays on Montaigne in Honor of Donald M. Frame.* 1977.
6. Rupert T. Pickens. *The Welsh Knight: Paradoxicality in Chrétien's* Conte del Graal. 1977.
7. Carol Clark. *The Web of Metaphor: Studies in the Imagery of Montaigne's* Essais. 1978.
8. Donald Maddox. *Structure and Sacring: The Systematic Kingdom in Chrétien's* Erec et Enide. 1978.
9. Betty J. Davis. *The Storytellers in Marguerite de Navarre's* Heptaméron. 1978.
10. Laurence M. Porter. *The Renaissance of the Lyric in French Romanticism: Elegy, "Poëme" and Ode.* 1978.
11. Bruce R. Leslie. *Ronsard's Successful Epic Venture: The Epyllion.* 1979.
12. Michelle A. Freeman. *The Poetics of* Translatio Studii *and* Conjointure: Chrétien de Troyes's Cligés. 1979.
13. Robert T. Corum, Jr. *Other Worlds and Other Seas: Art and Vision in Saint-Amant's Nature Poetry.* 1979.
14. Marcel Muller. *Préfiguration et structure romanesque dans* A la recherche du temps perdu *(avec un inédit de Marcel Proust).* 1979.
15. Ross Chambers. *Meaning and Meaningfulness: Studies in the Analysis and Interpretation of Texts.* 1979.
16. Lois Oppenheim. *Intentionality and Intersubjectivity: A Phenomenological Study of Butor's* La Modification. 1980.
17. Matilda T. Bruckner. *Narrative Invention in Twelfth-Century French Romance: The Convention of Hospitality (1160-1200).* 1980.
18. Gérard Defaux. *Molière, ou les métamorphoses du comique: De la comédie morale au triomphe de la folie.* 1980.
19. Raymond C. La Charité. *Recreation, Reflection and Re-Creation: Perspectives on Rabelais's* Pantagruel. 1980.
20. Jules Brody. *Du style à la pensée: Trois études sur les* Caractères de La Bruyère. 1980.
21. Lawrence D. Kritzman. *Destruction/Découverte: Le Fonctionnement de la rhétorique dans les* Essais de Montaigne. 1980.
22. Minnette Grunmann-Gaudet and Robin F. Jones, eds. *The Nature of Medieval Narrative.* 1980.
23. J.A. Hiddleston. *Essai sur Laforgue et les* Derniers Vers *suivi de* Laforgue et Baudelaire. 1980.
24. Michael S. Koppisch. *The Dissolution of Character: Changing Perspectives in La Bruyère's* Caractères. 1981.
25. Hope H. Glidden. *The Storyteller as Humanist: The* Serées *of Guillaume Bouchet.* 1981.
26. Mary B. McKinley. *Words in a Corner: Studies in Montaigne's Latin Quotations.* 1981.

27. Donald M. Frame and Mary B. McKinley, eds. *Columbia Montaigne Conference Papers*. 1981.

28. Jean-Pierre Dens. *L'Honnête Homme et la critique du goût: Esthétique et société au XVIIe siècle*. 1981.

29. Vivian Kogan. *The Flowers of Fiction: Time and Space in Raymond Queneau's Les Fleurs bleues*. 1982.

30. Michael Issacharcff et Jean-Claude Vilquin, éds. *Sartre et la mise en signe*. 1982.

31. James W. Mileham. *The Conspiracy Novel: Structure and Metaphor in Balzac's Comédie humaine*. 1982.

32. Andrew G. Suozzo, Jr. *The Comic Novels of Charles Sorel: A Study of Structure, Characterization and Disguise*. 1982.

33. Margaret Whitford. *Merleau-Ponty's Critique of Sartre's Philosophy*. 1982.

34. Gérard Defaux. *Le Curieux, le glorieux et la sagesse du monde dans la première moitié du XVIe siècle: L'exemple de Panurge (Ulysse, Démosthène, Empédocle)*. 1982.

35. Doranne Fenoaltea. *"Si haulte Architecture." The Design of Scève's Délie*. 1982.

36. Peter Bayley and Dorothy Gabe Coleman, eds. *The Equilibrium of Wit: Essays for Odette de Mourgues*. 1982.

37. Carol J. Murphy. *Alienation and Absence in the Novels of Marguerite Duras*. 1982.

38. Mary Ellen Birkett. *Lamartine and the Poetics of Landscape*. 1982.

39. Jules Brody. *Lectures de Montaigne*. 1982.

40. John D. Lyons. *The Listening Voice: An Essay on the Rhetoric of Saint-Amant*. 1982.

41. Edward C. Knox. *Patterns of Person: Studies in Style and Form from Corneille to Laclos*. 1983.

42. Marshall C. Olds. *Desire Seeking Expression: Mallarmé's "Prose pour des Esseintes."* 1983.

43. Ceri Crossley. *Edgar Quinet (1803-1875): A Study in Romantic Thought*. 1983.

44. Rupert T. Pickens, ed. *The Sower and His Seed: Essays on Chrétien de Troyes*. 1983.

45. Barbara C. Bowen. *Words and the Man in French Renaissance Literature*. 1983.

46. Clifton Cherpack. *Logos in Mythos. Ideas and Early French Narrative*. 1983.

47. Donald Stone, Jr. *Mellin de Saint-Gelais and Literary History*. 1983.

48. Louisa E. Jones. *Sad Clowns and Pale Pierrots: Literature and the Popular Comic Arts in 19th-Century France*. 1984.

49. JoAnn DellaNeva. *Song and Counter-Song: Scève's Délie and Petrarch's Rime*. 1983.

50. John D. Lyons and Nancy J. Vickers, eds. *The Dialectic of Discovery: Essays on the Teaching and Interpretation of Literature Presented to Lawrence E. Harvey*. 1984.

51. Warren F. Motte, Jr. *The Poetics of Experiment: A Study of the Work of Georges Perec*. 1984.

52. Jean R. Joseph. *Crébillon fils. Economie érotique et narrative*. 1984.

53. Carol A. Mossman. *The Narrative Matrix: Stendhal's Le Rouge et le Noir*. 1984.

54. Ora Avni. *Tics, tics et tics. Figures, syllogismes, récit dans Les Chants de Maldoror*. 1984.

55. Robert J. Morrissey. *La Rêverie jusqu'à Rousseau. Recherches sur un topos littéraire*. 1984.

56. Pauline M. Smith and I. D. McFarlane, eds. *Literature and the Arts in the Reign of Francis I. Essays Presented to C.A. Mayer*. 1985.

57. Jerry C. Nash, ed. *Pre-Pléiade Poetry*. 1985.

French Forum, Publishers, Inc.
P.O. Box 5108, Lexington, Kentucky 40505

Publishers of *French Forum*, a journal of literary criticism